By Southern Playwrights

By Southern Playwrights

Plays from Actors Theatre of Louisville

Michael Bigelow Dixon and Michele Volansky
Editors

Foreword by Jon Jory

THE UNIVERSITY PRESS OF KENTUCKY

Copyright © 1996 by The University Press of Kentucky

Scholarly publisher for the Commonwealth, serving Bellarmine College, Berea College, Centre College of Kentucky, Eastern Kentucky University, The Filson Club, Georgetown College, Kentucky Historical Society, Kentucky State University, Morehead State University, Murray State University, Northern Kentucky University, Transylvania University, University of Kentucky, University of Louisville, and Western Kentucky University.

Editorial and Sales Offices: The University Press of Kentucky
663 South Limestone, Lexington, Kentucky 40508-4008

Library of Congress Cataloging-in-Publication Data

By Southern playwrights : plays from Actors Theatre of Louisville /
    Michael Bigelow Dixon and Michele Volansky, editors ; foreword by
    Jon Jory.
        p.   cm.
    ISBN 0-8131-1967-7 (cloth : alk. paper). — ISBN 0-8131-0877-2
(pbk. : alk. paper)
        1. American drama—Southern States.   2. American drama—20th
century.   3. Southern States—Drama.   I. Dixon, Michael Bigelow.
II. Volansky, Michele.   III. Actors Theatre of Louisville.
PS551.B9   1996
812'.54080975—dc20   95-42493

This book is printed on acid-free recycled paper meeting
the requirements of the American National Standard
for Permanence of Paper for Printed Library Materials.

Manufactured in the United States of America

Contents

Foreword

The good thing about Southern writing is that everybody knows its qualities. "What's Southern writing?" you say to your dry cleaners and, without missing a beat, they rattle off, "Great language, family, strong women, religion, the land, and the past." And, of course, they're right. Nobody, on the other hand, knows what Southwestern or Northeastern writing is. Try it. Southern writing wins out on definition every time.

The South has somehow managed to convey its folk wisdom and geographic metaphors to the rest of us. Maybe, with the legions of fine Southern writers, it's just a matter of the numbers; on the other hand, maybe it's great theatrical sense. Once we got to know Blanche Dubois and Willie Stark, they became "Southern writing," and that was that.

Southerners are continually called "characters," and that, of course, is nothing but good news in dramatic writing. The plays in this volume are character-driven, and they pull the plot along behind them at a good clip. They celebrate the strong opinions of their leading characters and give the overall impression of people infamous down in the gossip mart of the town square. Even when Romulus Linney writes of the monstrous Hermann Goering of the Third Reich, there is that quality of the charming monster that the South knows so well.

Exaggerated qualities are the stock-in-trade of gossip, and we could make a case that these plays are extensions of that universally enjoyed style of exchange that, below the Mason-Dixon line, has been raised to a veritable art form. If gossip creates "characters" and usually places those "characters" in conflicted situations, then if you write that gossip down, you have the makings of a pretty good play.

The other quality here is humor that draws blood. Humor as a corrective and social discipline. These aren't "relativist" plays. They each have a pretty strong idea about how things should be, and they'll get you laughing when it's time to make you agree with them.

And land. There are strong threads here spun out of an agrarian society, and they make feelings that are passionately held and deeply, deeply felt.

The odd thing is that these likenesses don't make the work predictable—they just give it its recognizable flavor, tone, and rhythm. That, plus one thing more: speakability. In the crush of new plays that are weeded the moment they are spoken aloud, the Southern play struts its stuff. Actors love these plays because you can say them, and that, as they say, makes all the difference.

Read them out loud to yourself. You'll see.

Jon Jory
Producing Director
Actors Theatre of Louisville

Actors Theatre of Louisville

Actors Theatre of Louisville is the state theater of Kentucky. Founded in 1964 and under the artistic direction of Jon Jory since 1969, Actors Theatre has emerged as one of America's most consistently innovative professional theatre companies. For twenty years it has been a major force in revitalizing American playwriting with more than two hundred ATL-premiered scripts in publication. The annual Humana Festival of New American Plays is recognized as the premiere event of its kind and draws producers, journalists, critics, playwrights, and theater lovers from around the world for a marathon of new works. The seasonal Classics in Context Festival/ Modern Masters is an internationally celebrated multidisciplinary event including plays, exhibits, lectures, and workshops. Flying Solo & Friends gives the Louisville area a rare presentation of acclaimed cutting-edge solo and ensemble performances. The biennial Bingham Signature Shakespeare series offers Louisville audiences Shakespeare's work on an uncompromised production level.

Actors Theatre of Louisville is distinguished as one of the few regional companies in the country which operates three diverse theaters under one roof: the 637-seat Pamela Brown Auditorium, the 318-seat Bingham Theatre, and the 159-seat Victor Jory Theatre. Its programming includes a broad range of classical and contemporary work presenting over five hundred performances of thirty or more plays in a July through June season. Actors Theatre performs annual to over 200,000 people and is the recipient of the most prestigious awards bestowed on a regional theater: a special Tony Award for Distinguished Achievement and Contribution to the Development of Professional Theatre, and the Margo Jones Award for the Encouragement of New Plays. Actors Theatre's international appearances include performances in twenty-nine cities and fifteen foreign countries.

Acknowledgments

The editors are indebted to the following persons for their contributions to this volume: Val Smith, Corby Tushla, Jeffrey Ullom, Jimmy Seacat, Alexander Speer, Wanda Snyder, Jeffrey Rogers, Linda Green, David Kuntz, and Sean Kaplan.

By Southern Playwrights

Plays from Actors Theatre of Louisville

The Cool of the Day

WENDELL BERRY

Photo by Dan Carroco

WENDELL BERRY is the author of more than thirty books, including, most recently, *Another Turn of the Crank, Watch With Me, Fidelity,* and *Sex, Economy, Freedom & Community.* He lives and farms with his wife, Tanya Berry, on 125 acres in Henry County, Kentucky. He is a recipient of the Orion Society's John Hay Award and of the 1994 T.S. Eliot Award for creative writing.

THE COOL OF THE DAY

was first presented by Actors Theatre of Louisville on October 31, 1984.

CAST

EDGAR ....Bob Burrus
ELLIE ....Susan Bruyn
BILLY ....Will Oldham
DOC ....Michael Kevin
PASCAL ....Vaughn McBride
BERTHA ....Kathleen Chalfant

Director ....Robert Spera
Set Design ....Paul Owen
Costume Design ....Marcia Dixcy
Light Design ....Jeff Hill
Sound Design ....James M. Bay
Properties Mistress ....Diann Fay
Fight Director ....Steve Rankin
Stage Manager ....Bob Hornung
Assistant Stage Manager ....Cynthia A. Hood

A farm in the bottom land along the Kentucky River near Port William, an evening of early June, about 1910. The foreground is the Steadums' front yard, bordering on a dirt road. Slightly to the left of center is their house, weather-boarded, one-story, with a roofed porch all the way along the front. To the right, set somewhat farther back than the house, is the side wall and eave of a feed barn. There is a cleared field behind the buildings; behind the field is a wall of trees; behind the trees rise the wooded slopes of the eastward side of the valley. The light of the low sun is clear even in the distances. It is as though this light is the element, like air or water, in which people and events will have their being.

The light has lengthened the shadows and thrown them back from the face of the house. The day's work in the fields is done, and all around is quiet. From various distances can be heard a cowbell, a bobwhite, a field sparrow, a cat. These sounds occur singly, spaced by intervals of silence.

In front of the house is a pair of tulip poplars. This is where the family comes to sit from supper to bedtime on warm evenings. There are three or four mismatched kitchen chairs, and a porch swing swung from a branch of one of the poplars. Otherwise, the yard is bare. So is the porch of the house.

Edgar Steadum is sitting alone in the swing. He is a tall man in his mid-fifties, his hair beginning to turn gray. He wears no hat. His clothes are soiled from the field, but are nevertheless neatly worn. His hands are large, work-stiffened, and yet as expressive as his face.

Edgar's elbows are on his knees. His hands are clasped together. His head is bent. He is looking a little off to the side, as though waiting to hear something. It is a posture of trouble, and it has in it little anticipation of relief. Sitting so, Edgar is quieter even than the surroundings.

The quiet lasts a long moment, and then a watcher who is not seen strikes the first notes of "How Firm a Foundation" on a mandolin. Like the cowbell and the bird songs, this old tune will be heard at intervals throughout the play—not exactly a commentary on what is happening, and yet clearly in relation to it. The tune is played, and heard, by someone only half thinking about it, while he ponders what he sees. Stress, tempo, even volume are varied to some extent in response to what happens, and yet the tune always remains faithful to itself, as do the other sounds.

The first line of the tune is played, the notes just rising above the quiet and then lapsing back into it. After a moment Ellie, wearing a soiled apron over a gingham dress comes out onto the porch. She sees Edgar, and steps across to the trees. She is carrying a handkerchief wadded in her left hand, as though some time ago she expected she might cry. She has not cried, and she is not crying now. Recognizing her, though he has not looked at her, Edgar turns his head and looks past her.

EDGAR: He's breathing?
ELLIE: Yes.
EDGAR: His mother's by him?

ELLIE: Yes.
EDGAR: They're different, I reckon,
            the worry of a mother
            and of a wife. She'll stay
            by him there and fret,
            though there's nothing she can do
            until the doctor comes.
ELLIE: It's not
            worry now. It's grief.
            The doctor'll be no help.
            You know as well as I do.
            He's breathing still, but only
            for a little while. And yes,
            her grief and mine are different.
            She has been his mother all
            his life. I've been his wife
            since the new year. She grieves
            for what she knew, and I
            for what I might have known.
            And yet they are the same,
            for both our wombs are cold.

Edgar looks directly at her now for the first time, and then looks away, as at first. Ellie has never looked at him. She stands more or less facing him, but looking at the hills. She speaks carefully—to herself as much as to Edgar:

            I want to know what happened.
EDGAR: I told you. We had finished
            in the field. The chores were done.
            He took the colt out of the stall
            and was grooming him to ride.
            He looked at me, and laughed,
            and leaned to pick up the brush
            where he'd dropped it on the ground.
            Just as he took it in his hand
            he got kicked. I hollered
            at him or at the colt.
            I don't remember which,
            but it was done too late.

Edgar's hands open and part, stiffly, and then the fingers lace slowly together again.

ELLIE: And that's all?
EDGAR: It ain't
            much, but it's all.
            If you think about it,

```
           you'll see the way it was—
           how he stood and moved
           and leaned down, looking
           at me, laughing, as he leaned.
           And then the way I carried him
           to the house; I could still hear
           my warning he never heard.
ELLIE:     Yes, my God, I can see it!
           And I can hear your shout.
           I heard it there in the garden
           where I'd gone to hoe the corn
           after the heat of the day
           was past, and bring lettuce in
           for supper. I knew, seems like,
           what you'd be carrying
           to the house.
                        And that's all
           I'll ever have of him.
           And why? Why, at the end
           of his day's work, couldn't
           he have come to me instead?
           Why would it have to be
           danger he would give himself to
           then, and not me?
EDGAR:                   Ellie,
           you're asking for reasons now
           he never had thought of then.
ELLIE:     Carrying him in that way,
           you must have thought whatever
           reasons he had were wrong.
EDGAR:     What I carried in was a burden
           that had been my satisfaction.
```

As he speaks, they look at each other, and for a moment after he has spoken they remain still. The bobwhite calls. The mandolin plays slowly the first two notes of the second line of the tune, as though it might play it through, and then abruptly ceases. With sudden anxiety, even hope, Ellie looks up the road.

```
ELLIE:     Lord, the doctor ought to
           be here by now.
EDGAR:                   I sent
           long enough ago.
           He ought to be here soon,
           or the boy'll be coming back
```

without him. You go on
back in the house now.
I'll wait for him to come.

Ellie turns toward the house. The mandolin starts. Edgar sits with his face raised, his right hand gripping one of the chains that hold up the swing, the other lying palm down on his thigh. Now he hears a horse approaching at a gallop and he listens up the road. At the porch, Ellie too has heard the horse. She pauses, looks back, goes on into the house. Edgar gets up and goes to the gate in the fence between the yard and the barn lot, and waits, resting his hand on the gatepost. Presently, Billy Hardy comes into sight on his way from the barn. He is full of the importance of his errand, yet uneasy, the ground suddenly strange to him. The mandolin stops.

EDGAR: Did you find him, boy?
BILLY: He left town when I did.
           I rode back fast to tell you.
EDGAR: All right. Good boy. I see
           you've lathered the mare right sharply.
           Let her cool some, now,
           before you give her water.
           And when the doctor gets here
           take care of his horse for him.
BILLY: How's Estill?
EDGAR: I don't know,
           honey. Mighty likely
           the doctor can tell us something.
           Look after the horses now.

Edgar rests his hand a moment on the boy's shoulder, and then returns it to the gate post. Billy goes. The cow's bell can be heard quietly jangling as she grazes. Edgar stands without moving. The mandolin plays the tune all the way through. As it plays to the end another horse arrives at a trot, and presently the doctor comes past the corner of the barn. The little pair of saddlebags containing his medicines and instruments is slung over his left shoulder. He is a contemporary of Edgar's, heavier in body, his hair much grayer, his eyebrows bristly and black. His suit is wrinkled, dusty, the inside of his pants legs below the knee darkened with horse sweat. Like Ellie a few moments ago, Edgar now reveals some little reserve of hope.

EDGAR: Evening, Doc.
DOC: Edgar.
           The boy yonder says Estill
           got the daylight kicked
           clean out of him.
EDGAR: He did that.
DOC: Kicked him in the head.
EDGAR: Yes.

DOC (*winces and grunts*):
>How's he seem?

EDGAR:　　　　　　He ain't
>spoke nor stirred since.
>He's breathing, is all.

DOC (*as if to himself*):
>Well. We'll see. We'll see.

EDGAR:　He's yonder in the front room,
>Doc. You know the way.

DOC:　Yessir. Thank you, Edgar.
>I know the way.

Walking with his head down as in thought, he goes to the front door, opens it without knocking, and goes inside. After the door has shut, Edgar stands, looking down a moment. He raises his left hand and smooths it over his hair. He turns in his tracks and looks back at the barn and the field. He gives a sideward shake to his head, and comes slowly back and sits in the swing. Billy comes from the barn and sits in one of the chairs. They do not look at each other. There has been no sound since the doctor entered the house. But now the cowbell is heard again, and one after another the voices of the three birds. After a pause, the mandolin begins.

>*Now Pascal and Bertha Hardy are seen coming around the back corner of the barn, having walked from their house across the fields. As they approach the man and boy sitting under the trees, Pascal allows Bertha to go in front out of respect for her family connection. She is Edgar's sister. She stops beside Billy's chair. The mandolin has stopped. Bertha is looking at Edgar, but she draws Billy over and hugs his face to her side.*

BERTHA:　Billy, you go in the house
>and get your things together
>so you can go back home
>with your pap and me when we go.
>You can come back and stay
>with Uncle Edgar and Aunt Hester
>another time. Be quiet.

Billy gets up and goes, relieved to have something more to do. Bertha waits until he has gone around the corner of the house, and then she says:

>Edgar, what about Estill?
>Billy told us when he passed,
>coming back from town.

EDGAR (*looks up at her; he has been sitting with his arms folded; now he carefully places his hands palm downward on his thighs*):
>He taken the hardest lick
>I ever seen, Berthy—
>right in the side of the head.

It was a killing lick.
He shakes his head.
I know what flesh and bone
can stand.
BERTHA: How is Hester?
EDGAR: I don't know if she knows
how bad it is. Ellie knows.
I didn't say. "I'll send
for Doc" was all I said.
I saddled the mare then
and started the boy to town.
Through these last four lines Edgar's attention has strayed to the distance behind the barn. The final two lines are spoken almost to himself. But now he recovers his presence and looks at Bertha again.
Go in, Berthy. Doc's there
now. They'll need you.
Bertha goes into the house. Pascal sits down in the chair that Billy sat in earlier. Like the others, he is still wearing the clothes he worked in all day. He has begun to feel the discrepancy between his appearance and the austerity of the occasion that has overtaken him. He is wearing a sweated, misshapen old felt hat with a row of diamond-shaped vents cut with his pocket knife around the crown. Now he takes the hat off and with the utmost gentleness and precision places it on the ground beside the front leg of his chair. He smooths his hair back. He crosses his legs and folds his arms. It is a posture of conscientious and uncomfortable propriety, such as a shy, solitary man might assume in a room full of people. Edgar is looking away again, back into the distance, and for some time the scene remains still. And then the cowbell sounds faintly. And then very near and with abrupt clarity, the bobwhite calls once. As though the watcher is now absorbed in expectance, the mandolin does not play.
EDGAR (*recovering his sense of obligation as host*):
Well, Pascal, it's been hot.
PASCAL: Mighty hot. For the time of year.
EDGAR: Did you get your ground in shape?
PASCAL: Oh, not the best, I reckon.
It'll do.
EDGAR: We were in the hay.
We got it all in the barn,
that piece of orchard grass
in the upper bottom. I loaded
the wagon, and Estill and Billy
forked it on. The boy
made a right good hand too—

    to prove a better man,
    I reckon, than we thought.
    He sweated at it, with Estill
    ragging him all the time
    to make him mind his work.
    He would take it from Estill
    because they were buddies, you know.

PASCAL: The way Estill, when he
    was a boy, would take it from me.
    The way, when I was a boy,
    I would take it from you.

Edgar is leaning forward again, looking at the ground, his elbows on his knees. His left hand is clasped in his right, and as he talks he slowly rubs the palms together.

EDGAR: Estill had some wildness
    in him. For a while there
    he had a *lot* of it in him.
    You know it, and I do.
    It was a worry to us
    and a danger to him. We saw it
    and cautioned him about it,
    and yet liked it in him.
    He had to risk and trust
    himself to the world. He had
    to stand close to danger,
    and look away. Who knew
    that better than me and you?
    We knew it in him because
    we remembered it in ourselves.
    I don't know what it is
    that is so fine in a man
    who can turn his head and look
    away from what can kill him.

Pascal shakes his head. Now he is looking back into the field. He has tilted his chair slightly backward so that the front legs are off the ground.

    When he married Ellie,
    I thought he'd settle down.
    And he did, mainly. Settled,
    went to eating and sleeping
    regular, and took hold here
    in the work. He didn't need
    a boss anymore, and we

got along.
            Toward spring,
though, he heard about
this iron-gray colt that nobody
had even been able to handle,
and he went and bought him. Said
he'd break and sell him, make
a few dollars to put away.
But the day he went after the colt,
and led him home, and stood him
yonder in the barn, to look
at him, I saw it wasn't
the money that interested him.
He hadn't wanted the colt
in spite of his wildness;
he'd wanted him *because* of it.
There was still something in him
he had to give to danger.
That's what Ellie knows,
or what she feels. It's why
she's halfway mad at him
for getting kicked. In danger
he found some awful freedom
beyond the reach of love.

The bobwhite calls from farther away, and is answered from still farther. The sunlight has gradually risen up the faces of the hills as the sun has set. Now the sun is down. The sky is white; against it, the house and hills and trees are almost silhouettes. The field in which the grassheads are ripening has taken on a glow as if it is now the source of the remaining light. After a pause of some length, Edgar continues:

So today, when the hay was in,
and we'd put away the team
and done the chores, Estill
went to the colt's stall. I said,
"*Don't* fool with him tonight.
Billy's here. Let's eat
our supper, and then sit
out under the trees and talk."
But he led the colt out
and hitched him and began
to clean him up. I sat
on a bucket by the door
to watch. The colt worried me,

but I liked what Estill could do.
I wanted to see him ride.
Billy sat down too,
beside me, and Estill
went over the colt with the brush
and cur' comb. He was passing
the brush over the colt's rump
when it flew out of his hand.
The colt snorted and jumped—
something Estill liked.
He looked at me and laughed,
leaned to pick up the brush.
He was young and brave, laughing
and looking away. I saw
what I wasn't brave enough
anymore to *not* see.
I hollered either just before
or just after the hoof
struck. I heard the hoof
strike his head, and saw
him loosen in the air
and fall. And saw fallen
what was so quick and fine.

There is a pause. The scene is utterly silent again, and nearly dark. The field still glows, though less than before. And then from the house comes a woman's voice:

Oh! My God!

Pascal slowly lowers his chair. Edgar's hands unclasp and hang downward from the wrists. The mandolin quietly tolls the first few notes of the tune, plays on, fades with the light.

THE END

Five Ives Gets Named

ROY BLOUNT, JR.

Photo by Anthony Loew

ROY BLOUNT, JR., is the author of *About Three Bricks Shy—And the Load Filled Up, Crackers, One Fell Soup, What Men Don't Tell Women, First Hubby,* and other books. Raised in Georgia, he holds degrees from Vanderbilt and Harvard. He lives in New York City and western Massachusetts.

FIVE IVES GETS NAMED

was first presented by Actors Theatre of Louisville on November 1, 1983.

CAST

REED IVES ....Steve Rankin

Director ....Robert Spera
Set Design ....Paul Owen
Costume Design ....Marcia Dixcy
Light Design ....Karl Haas
Sound Design ....James M. Bay
Property Master ....Sam Garst
Fight Director ....Steve Rankin
Stage Manager ....Richard A. Cunningham
Assistant Stage Managers ....Susanna M. Banks, Cynthia A. Hood

The set evokes, minimally, a tony singles bar. In the background jukebox music. At stage center, lit less dimly, is a wall payphone. An athletic-looking man in his early twenties, wearing slacks, bright sportshirt and leather jacket, enters from stage left and strides to the phone springily, carrying a cocktail. He looks a bit foggy but keyed up; his hair looks hastily combed. He sets the drink on top of the phone, fishes for a dime, inserts it, dials ten digits. Turns back toward stage left, winks and makes an unsubtle but engaging be-right-back gesture.

He blurts the first word, then gears down somewhat.

REED IVES: Operator!? Can you uh make this collect, from . . . Reed?

He waits, takes a sip, bounces a couple of times to the music. Then becomes even more animated.

Jim! Me! Calling from the *big* leagues!

You know, them leagues Ty Cobb and Warren Spahn was in! Wooo!

I *know* it's great. Jim, you would not believe tonight. I got a nickname, I—Yeah, I'll call Pop. But I can't tell him all of it. Don't want to disillusion Pop about the BIG LEAGUES.

No, it's not—just let me tell you. It is late, isn't it? Is that the baby crying? Shit, I'm. . . .

You shoulda been up here, Jim. Waiting to show me around. Like you did in Little League and high school. If it hadn't been for your knee. Yeah.

I'm *going* to tell you. Yeah, *sort* of drunk. In New York.

Jim, I ain't going to get mugged. You're worse than Pop. No, I just mean—listen.

I walk in this afternoon, right? Visiting clubhouse YANKEE DAMN STADIUM, Jim. Summoned up by the Mariners.

Yeah, we didn't exactly grow up drooling to be Mariners. There wasn't any then, though, Jim. And if the Dodgers'd held on to me I'd still be in Lodi. Mariners pick me up, this Perridge breaks his leg, and I get a CALL, Jim. Yeah.

Only thing, to get here, I had to grab two buses and a red-eye. Yeah. And I walk into the dressing room with zip sleep. And first thing, this Spanish guy jumps on my back. Yelling, jibdyjibdyjibdy, ninety miles an hour. Then this bald black guy with a big gut, who's stepping real painfully into his pants, he yells across the room:

"Ju-lo get off the man's back! He don't even speak Spanish!"

Above and as we proceed, our man shows a certain, limited, flair for mimicry.

Yeah. "Jibdyjibdyjibdy espik Esponish!?" the guy yells. And he gets off me, like he's pissed I'm not bilingle, and he goes to his locker and I see the name, it's Julio Mindoza! You remember, played second for the Orioles a couple years and bounced around, yeah, and. . . .

Jim, the fat guy is Boom Holmes! "God DAMN my feet!" he goes, and that's my greeting to the Mariners.

Yeah, except just then I meet my Peerless Leader.

Berkey. Yells out from his office, "Who you!" Jesus, who'd he think I was, I'm the only guy got sent up. I go in, kind of salute. Like reporting to duty. Only he don't laugh. He is sitting there eating a—looks like maybe a Franco-American spaghetti sandwich, real wet, and there's a big bottle of Maalox on his desk, and he looks at me like I'm already overpaid. "Can you mbunt?" he wants to know. Is all he wants to know. I don't know whether he can manage, but he has a lot of trouble with his b's.

"Yeah," I say. He's a big sumbitch but a real old sour-looking guy, Jim, looks like Mr. Wiedl used to teach us history and be pissed all the time because we didn't care about the broad sweep of the great human saga. Only Berkey I guess is pissed because the Mariners 'bout got a lock on last place in June. Yeah.

Anyway, what Berkey does, he grabs me by the arm and drags me back out into the dressing room and hollers at everybody, "This guy can mbunt! He prombly can't play, mbut he can mbunt!" And he goes back in his office with his wet sandwich.

And I'm standing there. Clubhouse guy shows me my locker—I'm dressing next to Hub Kopf. Yeah, right. He is talking to Junior Wren. Yeah, used to have the crippled-children commercial. And here's what they are saying:

"Your *niece*! How could you . . . ?"

"Axly it was more my half-niece," says Junior Wren.

"How the fuck . . . ?" goes Kopf.

"Anyway she was adopted I think," Wren says.

"You *think*. You didn't *know*?"

"Anyway she was in these little shorts and halter and she had this raspberry wine . . . and I have her a little bump. Next morning I felt so bad, I quit smoking."

Here I am hearing this shit from guys was All-Stars once, and meanwhile I am *wasted*. I go, you know, "I'm Reed Ives." 'Cause I'm new in this whole organization, they don't know me. "I'm wasted," I say.

"Welcome to the A.L.," says Junior. "Have one." And he gives me a pill.

So—

No, I wouldn't ever depend on it, no.

He takes another sip from his drink.

But . . . anyway I pop this thing, and then I ask, "What is it?"

You're right . . . but—anyway, "Five milligrams," he says.

I never did half that! No. No. And I'm sitting there thinking, "Oh Jesus. Five milligrams."

And the next thing, I'm on the field running all over like I've had twenty hours sleep. Yeah, playing pepper, taking grounders, little b.p.—

Yeah, I got ahold of a couple pretty good. Yeah, and, then, though, the game starts.

And I'm sitting. And I'm, you know, VAW-AW-AW-AWM. There's these billions of dollars' worth of Yankees out there a few feet from my face, and I'm jumping up, getting water, sitting back down, jumping up, taking a leak and thirty thousand people are screaming all up above and behind me, and Junior Wren is looking over and nudging Hub Kopf, and they're giggling, and Berkey is glaring at me. 'Cause I'm not even *seeing* the game. I'm sitting there exploding thinking, "Five milligrams!"

And suddenly Berkey grabs me, drags me off into the tunnel. I can't believe it, I'm about to fly into smithereens and Berkey is yelling, "If you tell anymbody what I'm mbout to tell you I'll mbeat your ass."

I'm going Whaaaat and he's saying, "Mbefore I was mborn my father was hunting with a preacher named Harding Earth. And the preacher stood up at the wrong time. And my father shot him in the temple. Killed him outright. Preacher was to mblame, mbut my father swore right then he'd have a son, and name him Harding Earth mBerkey and have him mbe a preacher. He had that son. It was me. Only he never told me. Till the day he died. He told me then. He told me he had done everything in his power, without telling me, to make me grow up to want to mbe a preacher. Mbut I grew up to want to play mball. That's how much I wanted to play mball. If *you* don't want to play mball, I don't want you *around.*"

And I'm standing there. And he leaves me and I ease back to the bench. With my brakes jammed on. And I'm sitting there dazed next to Roe Humble—yeah, he's okay—Humble says, "He give you the shoot-the-preacher story?"

And I just nod and I have no idea the status of the game and next thing, Berkey is standing in front of me, he's *trembling.* And he says, "Let's *see* you mbunt."

And he's sending me up! I don't even know who I'm hitting for. I'm in the game! Against—you know who pitched tonight for the Yankees?

Tommy Damn John. My first up in the big leagues. Only, I'm not thinking Tommy John. I'm thinking, "Five milligrams!"

He takes another sip and sets the drink back down.

And here comes this pitch—well, you know Tommy John don't waste any time but it seems to me he is idling *very* low, and I'm jumping up and down and "Five milligrams!" and here comes this dippy-do sinker, wandering up to the plate like its heart's not in it, and I square off to bunt, which in my present state means I am holding the bat like it's an alligator, and dum, de dum, Sink, the ball drops and I miss it a foot.

Yeah, I *know* Pop taught us. But—and the same thing happens the second pitch. "Five milligrams!" is blasting in my head and then, oh-and-two, he wastes a fastball up and away. And you know, Jim, I like that pitch. I could even hit you, when I was nine, and you threw me something up there. Went *with* it. And Jim, I got it all.

Jim, I took Tommy John out of Yankee Stadium at the 385 in right center. Two men on, we're only behind one run for some reason, and WOOOM I put us ahead. I'm circling the damn Yankee damn Stadium bases, and you know, on the postgame shows they always ask 'em, "What were you thinking about, rounding the bases?"? I'm thinking, FIVE MILLIGRAMS!

And I cross the plate and Boom Holmes gives me a high five. Boom Holmes gives me one, Jim. Which a *high* five, is appropriate as shit. And he says, "I didn't know you was that *strawng*."

And all I can think to do is—now everybody's slapping at me—is open my mouth and holler "FIVE! FIVE!"

And Junior Wren and Hub Kopf are rolling around in the dugout, and acourse, what the hell, we don't hold the lead, Jim. But in the dressing room afterwards everybody is hollering, "Five!" "The Big Five!" "Five Ives!"

He knocks the drink over.

Oh shit. Nothing. But, yeah, listen, this reporter asks Boom, "Why're you calling him Five?" And Boom says, "Well, that's ghetto talk, you know. That's some *street* talk, there. Means. . . . Means he got the full five faingers on it, you know," and Junior Wren and Hub and Mindoza and everybody else except maybe Berkey knows the truth—they're yelling, "*Full* Five." "F.F. Ives." And—

He turns back toward stage left and waves distractedly.

Well, yeah, I guess it is a shame, sort of. Never know, yeah, whether. . . .

Yeah. Whether I'd've done it just straight, yeah.

His lack of sleep seems to catch up with him for a moment. He shakes it off.

Yeah. But, Jim, you know, if I'd been straight I'd've *sacrificed*.

You're right, that'd been sound baseball.

So, yeah. So, sorry I woke the baby—tell Sharon. I guess I better go, I'm in this restaurant somewhere. I'm *still up*, Jim. And, Jim, there's this honey at the bar—

Yeah, maybe they don't call them honey in New York. I'll call her something else.

I took Tommy John out of the Stadium, Jim!

No, not all the way out . . . nobody ever—yeah, I know. But that's the expression. Uh-huh.

The light is dimming. The music grows slightly louder. The song is "You can get it if you really want."

So. . . . Well, thanks. I will. I'll watch it. Yeah.

He looks back toward stage left.

Hey, Jim, don't, you know, don't tell Pop.

Blackout.

THE END

That Dog Isn't Fifteen

ROY BLOUNT, JR.

Photo by Anthony Loew

ROY BLOUNT, JR., is the author of *About Three Bricks Shy—And the Load Filled Up, Crackers, One Fell Soup, What Men Don't Tell Women, First Hubby,* and other books. Raised in Georgia, he holds degrees from Vanderbilt and Harvard. He lives in New York City and western Massachusetts.

THAT DOG ISN'T FIFTEEN

was first presented by Actors Theatre of Louisville on October 31, 1984.

CAST

IRENE ....Sylvia Short
VIRGINIA ....Adale O'Brien
LITTLE GIRL ....Raye Lankford

Director ....Alan Duke
Set Design ....Paul Owen
Costume Design ....Marcia Dixcy
Light Design ....Jeff Hill
Sound Design ....James M. Bay
Properties Mistress ....Diann Fay
Fight Director ....Steve Rankin
Stage Manager ....Chip Washabaugh
Assistant Stage Manager ....Alan Duke

At stage front, center, is a television set, seen from the rear. It emits a variegated murmur, faint enough not to obscure the characters' lines but audible enough to have a sort of theme-murmur presence, throughout. Facing front, their eyes glued to the screen that we cannot see, are Irene, whose home this is, and Virginia, who is visiting. They are fortyish, unprepossessing. Irene, just to the left of the TV, has her hair in bright plastic curlers. Virginia, just to the right of the TV, is wearing eyeglasses with fancy frames. Both are leaning back in Barca-lounger type chairs. One is nursing a Tab, the other a Fresca. Each sits close enough to the TV that she can reach it by sitting up and leaning forward. Throughout, they look directly at the screen. Never at each other. Never at anything else.

Also throughout, a Little Girl With Glazed Eyes sits on the floor at Virginia's feet, focuses directly on the screen, and writhes and fidgets abstractedly in tune to the TV's hum.

IRENE: Keep the TV in its *place* in the home.

VIRGINIA: Mm.

IRENE: We don't *watch* the TV constantly—we leave it on; you know how you'll do.

VIRGINIA: Mm.

IRENE: But you have to live your life.

VIRGINIA: That's been our feeling.

IRENE: Able to hold a conversation. You know.

VIRGINIA: Can't just be rapt.

IRENE: No.

VIRGINIA: Just glued to it.

Little Girl With Glazed Eyes moves her doll into her lap so that she and the doll are staring at the TV in exactly the same spread-legged posture.

IRENE: But Jim's Mama—

VIRGINIA: That's a new TV, Irene?

IRENE: Ji—

VIRGINIA: Is the hue just right? What happened to your *old* TV?

IRENE: (*Leaning forward to adjust a knob*) This is what I'm telling you. Jim's Mama—

VIRGINIA: With the walnut grain.

IRENE: (*Leaning back*) Had it four years. Never the first sign of trouble. Till Jim's Mama—

VIRGINIA: Your hue is off, Irene. See. Orson Welles's white wine is off.

IRENE: Well. . . .

Irene leans forward again.

VIRGINIA: Was it the old TV you said started having the funny smell?

IRENE: But that was later. See—

Irene leans back.

VIRGINIA: I hate it when the hue's not right.

IRENE: See, Jim's Mama would come over, and she'd watch the TV, and—like when that man comes home?, in the artificial cream commercial?

VIRGINIA: Mn.

IRENE: The grown son, visiting his mother?

VIRGINIA: Mn.

IRENE: *He* gets up so *perky* in the morning, Jim's Mama would say. *He* acts so sweet—'bout his Mama fixing him a big old-fashioned breakfast just like he remembers but with artificial cream.

VIRGINIA: Nmn.

An ominous growling-voice sound from the TV. Little Girl does not change expression, but squeezes her doll so that it appears to be choking.

IRENE: All *we* do, Jim's Mama would say, when *she* makes *us* breakfast, is sip a little coffee and act sour.

VIRGINIA: It's a little . . . fuzzy, too, isn't it Irene?

IRENE (*Leaning forward*): We'd say, Mama, that son on television—that's television.

VIRGINIA: Mn.

IRENE (*Leans back, and scrutinizes TV with narrowed eyes*): That's not life.

VIRGINIA: No.

IRENE: We said, Mama, what they're trying to do is sell you something. That's all. And—

VIRGINIA: Trying to sell you that artificial cream.

IRENE: Uh-huh.

VIRGINIA: That's *what*.

IRENE: We'd say, Mama—

VIRGINIA: We got to where we use it.

IRENE: —that man has probly been up for *hours*.

VIRGINIA: Maybe . . . I think I'd try the brightness knob, too, Irene.

IRENE (*Leaning forward to the TV again*): And, but Jim's Mama, another thing she'd say, there was never a night around here when anybody would announce, "Tonight is kinda special." (*She sits back and gives the TV that narrow look again.*)

VIRGINIA (*Dubiously*): Mnnnn. . . .

IRENE: We'd say, Why Mama, how about the other night when we had you and the Willetses over, wasn't that kinda special?

(*Laughtrack is heard. Little Girl laughs soundlessly, eerily.*)

VIRGINIA: Had that ham.

IRENE: No. She'd say.

VIRGINIA: With the cheese spread?

IRENE: She'd say, our friends didn't ever tell us, "You're beautiful."

VIRGINIA: Ah-*mmmm*.

IRENE: Now Mama, we'd say, Life's just not *like* that.

VIRGINIA: And the TV had the smell then?

IRENE: That was later. (*Leans forward to make another adjustment.*) We'd say, Mama, they're just trying to sell you something. (*Leans back and scrutinizes again.*)

VIRGINIA: (*with worldly wisdom*): Mn.

IRENE: She'd say fine.

VIRGINIA: Hmn.

IRENE: Said she wanted to buy whatever it was.

VIRGINIA: Mn.

IRENE: Said she liked buying things.

VIRGINIA: That artificial cream, you know, is not *bad.* But it's. . . .

IRENE: Said that's what America was built on.

VIRGINIA: It *is* hue, Irene. See her leg?

IRENE: Buying things. (*Leans forward to fiddle again.*) Yes, we'd say, Mama, but don't you want to have something left to leave behind? (*Leans back again.*)

VIRGINIA: Mn.

IRENE: She'd say no, she wanted to give us a big old-fashioned breakfast like we remembered it and see us acting perky.

VIRGINIA: Mm-*hm.*

IRENE: Wanted to get up and make us breakfast even with all the arthuritis in her feet, like the grandmother in the what is it—the arthuritis commercial, you know?

VIRGINIA: Pain commercial.

A burst of frenetic dance music. Little Girl jerks about as if involuntarily.

IRENE: And when she did have us over and cooked, she'd serve something (*leans forward again*) and we'd just barely bite into it—just hardly get it in our mouth good—(*Leans back again, looking dissatisfied*) and she'd say, You don't like it?

VIRGINIA: Mn.

IRENE: We'd say, *Mama,* we haven't *tasted* it yet. She'd say, On TV they taste things immediately.

VIRGINIA: Hm.

IRENE: And they *light up,* she'd say.

VIRGINIA: Maybe it's *not* the hue. Maybe it's the color.

IRENE (*Leans forward again*): We'd say, Mama, you don't give us *time.*

VIRGINIA: See, now, Robert Young is *tanner* than that.

IRENE (*Still fiddling with TV*): Well, maybe he's—

VIRGINIA: At her house would she watch much TV?

IRENE (*Leaning back*): No.

VIRGINIA: Mn.

IRENE: Really, you know, I think that was the trouble. She didn't *have* her own TV. Maybe Robert Young is just getting old.

VIRGINIA: No, Irene, at our house he's real tan.

IRENE (*Leaning forward again*): We'd say, Mama, if you watched it all the time you'd realize.

VIRGINIA: No, I don't think it's that. I wouldn't fool with that, Irene.

IRENE (*Leaning back*): But she'd say no, no, she never had a TV when Jim's Dad was alive.

VIRGINIA: Well. . . .

IRENE: And she had her little motor scooter she'd scoot around on, and all her fish.

VIRGINIA: I believe you said she had beautiful fish.

IRENE (*Leaning forward again*): She'd say people on TV look you right in the eye and smile.

VIRGINIA: No, that's not it, Irene, I wouldn't touch that.

IRENE: Said we were her closest family and we wouldn't look her right in the eye and smile. (*Leans back.*) We said, Mama! She said we wouldn't even look her right in the eye and frown. We said, Mama!

VIRGINIA: No, see that rabbit. You *know* that rabbit is off.

IRENE: People on TV are s' bright-eyed, she'd say. (*Leans forward again.*) Always s' helpful-looking, s' friendly. (*Back again.*) She'd say people on TV have a little chuckle that goes with things they say. A little "huh" laugh before words, to show they're thinking about you.

VIRGINIA: See what I mean?

IRENE: (*Forward again*): And. . . . Well. . . . (*Back again.*) We'd just look at her and look at each other and shake our heads.

VIRGINIA: Mn.

IRENE: But then it started happening.

VIRGINIA: The little smell?

IRENE: That, and—

VIRGINIA: Was it a bad smell?

IRENE (*Leaning forward*): No, no. It—

VIRGINIA: Did it smell like . . . burning?

IRENE: No, it wasn't a mechanical smell. . . . (*Leans back.*) More like an aroma.

VIRGINIA: Mn.

IRENE: Not an aroma. What's the word I mean?

VIRGINIA: Bouquet?

IRENE: No.

A sound suggesting an enormous crowd-roar builds in intensity, to the level of mass frenzy. Little Girl jiggles dreamily, faster and faster, then subsides as the noise does.

VIRGINIA: You know, Irene, too. . . . Your vertical hold. That black band on the bottom? You know how it'll get?

IRENE: And—

VIRGINIA: When it just edddddges up.

IRENE: But—

VIRGINIA: And edddges up.

IRENE: But we'd look over, and Jim's Mama would be on one side of the room, and the TV'd be turned that way. It'd . . .

VIRGINIA: See?

IRENE: We'd look over, and the back of it would be to us. We didn't move it. Jim's Mama didn't move it.

VIRGINIA: Mn?

IRENE: It'd even—it was almost like it was pulling away from us, just singling out Jim's Mama. On its *own.*

The TV hum becomes distinctly erotic. And so do the movements of Little Girl.

VIRGINIA: You didn't get up and move it?

IRENE: No.

VIRGINIA: Jim's Mama didn't get up and move it?

IRENE: No. She'd just be sitting there. Chuckling at it.

VIRGINIA: At—just whatever was on?

IRENE: Jim's Mama didn't care. She wouldn't switch or tune it. She didn't even know how to work it. Jim's Mama couldn't turn a TV on or off, to save her. But it seemed like it gave her a better picture, too.

VIRGINIA: Irene, see, there's more of that black at the bottom.

IRENE (*Leans forward, then back. Forward, back.*): Course, the children complained. You know Dawn and Little Jim. They'll sit there with their noses in the TV and yell at it: "That's stupid!" Listen to a commercial about how some product's so wonderful for you and yell: "Yeah, it probly poisons you!"

VIRGINIA: Hf.

She unconsciously reaches out to pat Little Girl.

IRENE: Lorne Greene'll come on with his fifteen-year-old dog?, you know?, and they'll yell, "That dog isn't fifteen!"

VIRGINIA (*Giving Little Girl another, vaguely nervous, pat on head*):
Children get so critical.

Faint yum yum yum sounds from TV. Little Girl absently peels and engorges an icky pastry of the Hostess line.

IRENE: But they do want to *watch.* "The TV doesn't like us! The TV just likes Nannaw! We want another TV! With Remotronic control!"

VIRGINIA: M-hn.

IRENE: Said they couldn't concentrate on their homework without it.

VIRGINIA: And . . . it was an odor, though?

IRENE: Yes. And anyway, last . . . a week ago Friday night, Jim's Mama was sleeping over—she had baby-sat, you know, while we were at Jim's Elks installation.

VIRGINIA: Mm.

IRENE: And when we got home she and the kids were all gone to bed. And in the night we heard a clattery noise. (*Leans forward again.*)

VIRGINIA: Hm.

IRENE: But we didn't think about it, at the time. . . .
VIRGINIA: Hm.
Shots and pained noises from TV. Little Girl idly whangs her doll against the floor.
IRENE (*Still fiddling*): There *is* a lot of black down there.
VIRGINIA: It's edddging up, Irene.
Irene fiddles some more.
VIRGINIA: You can almost see the color again below it.
Irene fiddles some more.
VIRGINIA: And, Irene, the hue is still not. . . .
IRENE (*Leaning back*): We got up the next morning and Jim's Mama?
VIRGINIA: It's—
IRENE: Was gone.
VIRGINIA: Mn?
IRENE: And the TV?
VIRGINIA: Mn?
IRENE: Was gone.
VIRGINIA: Gone?
IRENE: No note. No trace. No explanation.
VIRGINIA: Why, I-*rene.*
IRENE: We have not seen that TV. Or Jim's Mama. Since. (*Leans forward again.*)
VIRGINIA: Can you imagine?
IRENE (*Leaning back*): Uh-huh. We don't. . . . (*Sits up straight, her eyes wide.*)
    Look!
VIRGINIA (*Also sits up straight, her eyes wide*): Irene! Is that . . . ?
IRENE (*Raising her voice*): Jim!
Now Virginia leans forward to the set. Irene is sitting back in shock.
IRENE (*To Virginia*): Turn it up! (*Louder.*) Jim! Come here!
The TV noise grows louder, Virginia having turned up the volume.
IRENE (*Loudly, to Jim*): Your Mama's on "Real People!"
VIRGINIA (*Peering deeply*): And—Irene! *Peering even more deeply.*
    Irene. . . . Isn't that. . . . There with her. . . . Isn't that your old TV?
Little Girl comes forward, crouching, staring, her eyes bright for the first time.

THE END

Blood Issue

HARRY CREWS

HARRY CREWS is a novelist and non-fiction writer born and raised in Georgia. He teaches at the University of Florida in Gainesville. His works include *The Knockout Artist, All We Need of Hell, The Gospel Singer, Naked in Garden Hills, This Thing Don't Lead to Heaven, Karate Is a Thing of the Spirit, Car, The Hawk is Dying, Body, The Gypsy's Curse, A Feat of Snakes, A Childhood: A Biography of a Place, Blood and Grits, Florida Frenzy, The Mulching of America, Scar Lover,* and *The Enthusiast.* Crews has been a contributor to *Playboy, Southern Magazine, Sewanee Review, Georgia Review,* and *Esquire.*

BLOOD ISSUE

was first presented by Actors Theatre of Louisville on March 3, 1989.

CAST

GEORGE ....John Dennis Johnston
JOE ....George Gerdes
ETHEL ....Nancy Niles Sexton
PETE ....Bob Burrus
MABEL .... Anne Pitoniak
GAYE NELL ....Dawn Didawick
GEORGE JR. ....Alan Pottinger
BUSTER ....Danny Campbell

Director ....Jon Jory
Stage Manager ....Nancy Kay Uffner
Production Dramaturg ....Marcia Dixcy
Scenic Designer ....Paul Owen
Costume Designer ....Michael Krass
Lighting Designer ....Victor En Yu Tan
Sound Designer ....Mark Hendren
Properties Master ....Ron Riall

ACT I

Scene 1

The living room of Mabel Boatwright. The door at stage left leads to bedrooms and bathrooms. Downstage right is a kitchen at the back of which is another door that leads outside the house. Pretty much all of the rear wall of the stage is covered with shelves filled with knickknacks: little plaster ducks and all manner of ceramic animals, including a two foot long black plaster panther with a gold flake chain around its neck. In and among these objects are framed family pictures. Downstage left is a brick fireplace with a raised hearthstone on which rests two vases of artificial flowers. The fireplace is immaculate. This room ought to suggest the place of a comfortably well-off widow who is perhaps overly concerned with cleanliness and having every single thing she owns precisely in its place. As the house lights go up, two men are in the room. They are Mabel's sons, Joe and George Bass. Joe is sitting in a recliner. George is pacing about, moving from time to time to pick up one thing or another from the shelf of knickknacks. They are in their forties and beginning to gray. Joe, the one on the recliner, is five years younger than his brother and he is lean with a square, angular face. He is animated and quick of movement. George is running badly to fat, with a substantial belly.

GEORGE: It was damn shore a hot one today.

JOE: Too hot for me.

GEORGE: Long too.

JOE: A hell of a long hot day.

GEORGE: But the old master seen fit to give us clear weather.

JOE (*Smiling in spite of himself.*): Yeah, the old master did. But thank God today's over.

GEORGE: Ought not to speak like that about a family reunion. Ain't nothing wrong with bringing blood together.

JOE: Is that what we did today, George? Bring blood together.

GEORGE: I caint talk to you, Joe. You've gone off and ruint you mind. Besides, if I remember right, you usually manage to be sommers else every year when it gets time to come together.

JOE: But the weather was good. It was good today.

GEORGE: Yeah, the weather was good today.

JOE: They tell me last year it rained.

GEORGE: Poured. But we made do. Ate good, played some music, got the graves cleaned and all.

JOE: All except our brother's. The one nobody seems to care about.

GEORGE: I caint talk to you.

JOE: Sure you can, George. We're talking right now.

GEORGE: We ain't talking.

JOE: Well, anyway, the old master gave us good weather today.

GEORGE: You ain't even religious. You making fun and you in danger of hell fire.

JOE: Why don't you try to chill out? Lighten up and chill out before you give yourself a stroke.

GEORGE: Chill out? That's nigger talk. You talk more like a nigger ever year.

JOE: George, half the kids on Miami Beach say chill out. You need to get around more, see what the rest of the world is doing.

GEORGE: I ain't in Miami Beach, I'm in Georgia. Florida? A goddamn foreign country. I was there oncet and oncet was one time too many. I wouldn't trust a place wherever tree's got a light in it and a stick propping it up. If Florida broke off and floated across the water to China I wouldn't care. Let the chinks have it.

JOE: You're colorful, George. You know that? Colorful.

GEORGE: You've gone and made yourself sorry. I caint help that. But you leave color out of this. And while you at it, you can just leave all of us—everone of us—out of this. It's what I've been saying—trying to say but you cain't seem to listen, never could as I recall—what I've been saying to you ever since you got home. Some things is better left alone.

JOE: No doubt, George. But it can't be done if you intend to write about it.

GEORGE: You ain't got to write about us, Joe. We doing just fine, thank you.

JOE: Writing is what I do, George.

GEORGE: Go on and ruin yourself if you want to, but don't ruin you blood kin too, don't drag us down with you.

JOE: You seem to keep forgetting that I'm blood too.

GEORGE: You ain't been blood for a long time. And it ain't none of our doin. You done it to yourself. And we don't want you writin about us. I'm givin you fair warnin.

JOE: Don't warn me George, it's not seemly.

GEORGE: You don't know nothin about seemly. And you don't know nothin about decency neither. You quit knowin a long time ago. While we at it, when did you start carin so much about us anyhow? You didn't even come home to Dad Lonny's funeral.

JOE: But we've already talked about that. And it's beginning to bore the shit out of me.

GEORGE: That's a heathen's way of talkin. If you cared about blood, you would have been here, come hell or high water.

JOE: Not blood, George. Ma marrying him didn't make him blood.

GEORGE: (*Snatching a picture off the shelf and holding it up to Joe.*) Dad Lonny, that man right there, raised you, damn it. He loved you like a daddy. He tried to give you the same piece of land he given to me to start farmin when we got out of the service. But you wouldn't have it. Turned 'm down cold.

JOE: I knew I'd never farm.

GEORGE: He never understood it. Hurt'm to the bone.

JOE: I wanted to do something else.

GEORGE: You didn't have to turn'm down like you did. It was other ways to do it. And you let'm go to the grave with that hurt. Sorriest goddamn thing I ever heard of. He loved our daddy and he given mother the best years she ever had. If that ain't blood, what the hell is? Where would you be today if he hadn't of stepped in and been a daddy to us and a husband to mother?

JOE: I don't know where we'd be. And you don't either, George. If you can read goddamn minds, you ought to get yourself a tent and tie a rag around your head and start reading palms too. Raising me didn't make Lonny blood. But that's not the point anyway. The hard fact is I was on assignment in the middle of Alaska, for God's sake. It was too late to come when I got word.

GEORGE: Yeah, you was in Alaska, all right. Workin for a tits and ass magazine. I don't need a tent and a rag around my head to know shit when I smell it. And if you weren't sorry you would have been here and not workin for a tits and ass magazine while we was buryin the man that raised us.

JOE: I was covering the building of the pipeline, George. The one that runs all the way across Alaska. Can you remember that? I was way the hell and gone in the bush before I ever got word he was dead.

GEORGE: Damn you and Alaska both. I read what you wrote. And it was in a tits and asses magazine, too. Somethin anybody decent would've been ashamed to have in his hand. Bunch a naked women touchin theyselves, touching they-selves while they tongues hung out dripping spit like a wind-busted dog.

JOE: You sure do have a way with words, George. Must run in the family.

GEORGE: At least I ain't never had nothin to do with a tits and ass magazine.

JOE: You don't like tits and asses, George? There are people, you know, who would say that wasn't normal.

GEORGE: Don't you talk to me about normal. The only reason I read that damn magazine anyhow is because I found it right here in this house. Our mother somehow got aholt of it. Damnedest thing I ever heard of. Our mother readin a tits and asses magazine!

JOE: I don't think you give Ma enough credit, George, I suspect she knows there's tits and asses in the world. Besides, I didn't give her the magazine and I didn't tell her to read it. If you've got a quarrel, it's not with me. It's with her.

GEORGE: So you just innocent, innocent of everything. Is that it?

JOE: No, I'm not innocent of everything, just innocent of that. My novels won't feed me. I have to work for anybody that'll give me a job.

GEORGE: It's a name for them that'll work for anybody who'll give'm a job. Whore is what it's called.

JOE: If I'm a whore I'll have to make the best of it, won't I? I've been called worse.

GEORGE: I know for a fact you have.

JOE: Look, why don't you sit down and try to relax? I didn't come here to upset you.

GEORGE: Just why did you come? Can you tell me that?

JOE: I came for the family reunion. And to try to find out some things that I don't understand, never have understood.

GEORGE: Understood about what?

JOE: About myself I guess, about myself and the family and . . . I've gone off somehow and got myself turned around, got lost.

GEORGE: Well you ain't lost. You settin right here in you mother's living room.

JOE: I know where I am, George. And if there's anything to find, here's where I'll find it. For God's sake, you're my brother. Try to understand.

GEORGE: If you'd come home more, you'd understand more.

JOE: I have to go where the work is.

GEORGE: Then you oughta git you a good, steady job like other folks. You oughta know what it is to git up when the sun gits up and bust a sweat and keep it all day. Maybe if you did that, you wouldn't want to know so damn much. You'd wanta go to bed at night and sleep, stay in and quit raising Hell like you do. Word gets back to us, you know, about you laying out at night, raisin hell, and otherwise makin a spectacle of youself. My advice to you is to git a job like other folks.

JOE: Is that your advice to me, George?

GEORGE: Damn right it is. And I've got some more advice. You been making a damn nuisance out of youself, is what you doin. Drivin around the county talkin about things that are private and family.

JOE: I didn't do it to upset you.

GEORGE: I stay upset when I'm around you.

JOE: I seem to upset everybody in the whole family.

GEORGE: That's the damn truth.

JOE: Why do you suppose that is?

GEORGE: You git stranger to us every year.

JOE: You think I don't know that, George?

GEORGE: Then dammit, why caint you just do right and be decent.

JOE: Nobody has a lock on doing right and being decent. Not even you, George.

GEORGE: A lock? What the hell's a lock got to do with anything.

JOE: (*Sighing, exasperated.*) Nothing, George. It has nothing to do with anything.

GEORGE: Pretty soon we won't even be able to talk to you.

JOE: I often think that time may have already come and gone.

George comes finally to sit on the couch across the room facing his brother.

Why don't we walk out to the car, George? Get a little something to loosen you up.

GEORGE: Do you have to drink here in Mother's house?

JOE: Ma knows I drink, George.

GEORGE: Yeah, she knows you drink and it's killin her and I wisht you'd show a little respect and call her Mother and not Ma.

JOE: Damned if I can keep up with everything you wish. Maybe you ought to make me a list.

GEORGE: Just go ahead and keep on. You been doin this all day and I'm about sick on it.

JOE: Yeah, you're sick on it.

GEORGE: What's that s'posed to mean?

JOE: You said it, I only repeated it.

GEORGE: You know you do that a lot? You don't have to go and say what I say right behind what I say.

JOE: It's just a bad habit. I've got a lot of bad habits.

GEORGE: You by youself too much. But it don't have to be that way. Get you some dogs, and run foxes with you friends. Have some good, wholesome Christian fun oncet in a while. Square dances and things such as that.

JOE: Jesus, why didn't I think of that?

GEORGE: It'd be a damn sight bettern spendin all you time with you mouth glued to a whiskey bottle.

JOE: It's true. I do need a taste from time to time.

GEORGE: Time to time my ass, all the time is what you mean. Why in the hell do you drink so much?

JOE: I drink to make it all go away.

GEORGE: To make what go away?

JOE: It.

GEORGE: Damn it, I heard that. I said make what go away.

JOE: Look, try to get out of your own skin and into mine for a minute. You did that, maybe you'd understand.

GEORGE: Get out of my own skin into yours!

JOE: If you just tried.

GEORGE: That's the nastiest thing I ever heard of, getting out of my skin into yours. You caint say nothin without turnin it into somethin shameful and indecent. That's right out of some porny film which I'm sure you know all about.

JOE: Lord God help us all now and at the hour of our death.

GEORGE: You leave God and dying out of this.

JOE: All right, no more God and no more dying.

GEORGE: You don't even believe in God and you'll die soon enough and you gone have to do it right by youself.

JOE: Precisely. Which is what we were talking about: Being alone.

GEORGE: All right then, how come you're alone so much if you don't like it?

JOE: You're not going to understand this but . . .

GEORGE: Quit tellin me what I'm gonna understand. I'm a high school graduate, got the prettiest crops in the county and a decent family, and I damn shore ain't alone.

JOE: I didn't plan it for myself. I just looked around one day and that's the way it was.

GEORGE: Seems like to me you a little weak in the plannin department.

JOE: That's the stone truth.

GEORGE: The stone truth?

JOE: Right.

GEORGE: Thought that's what you said. And I don't know what stones is got to do with it but I do know this, you alone so much because you best friend's the bottle. I've known your kind before. The bottle's you wife, you children, and you blood. That still ain't you biggest trouble though. You know you biggest trouble?

JOE: I don't think I want to hear this, but lay it on me anyway.

GEORGE: What'd you say?

JOE: Lay it on me.

GEORGE: Thought that's what you said but I'm gone pretend I didn't even hear it. You biggest trouble, boy, is I went to work and you went to college. You think you bettern me. And sooner or later you gonna let it overload you ass. That's you biggest trouble.

JOE: Is that my biggest trouble, George?

GEORGE: See you doin it agin, right there, repeatin what I say.

JOE: Sweet baby Jesus, you give me a case of the screaming red ass.

GEORGE: (*Looking as if he might come off the couch.*) Don't you profane in my mother's house, goddammit!

ETHEL (*Enter Ethel Locker, sister of their mother. She is very old, very fat, and very vivacious. Her extreme, almost hyper vitality gives the lie to her age. Her vitality, like almost everything else about her, is an affectation. She moves with a surprisingly light step for one so heavy.*): You boys having a nice talk out here? My, my. Just look at you two. This is a happy day. What a glorious day! All of us together, just singing and talking and eating and having us a big old time.

GEORGE: Mother go to sleep all right, Aint Ethel?

ETHEL: Sleep? Like a baby. Dead to the world. Poor thing. She just loved to see her two boys together today. But it's all about wore her out. Joe, your mama told me you was working on a new book.

JOE: I was, Aunt Ethel, but I finished it. Be out in the Spring.

ETHEL: You know I'll never understand that as long as I live. People taking and giving you good money for something they known to be a lie. Well, not a lie, I didn't mean it like that. But they know it never happened, made up, you know. But it's a lot in this old world I don't understand.

She turns and takes a framed picture from among the knickknacks on the shelf behind her and holds it up for them to see.

Member this? Just look at you two. Standing there, hair combed down so sweet, all dressed up for church, purty as puppies. Member this?

George stares at the picture and seems to relax into himself there on the couch where he has been sitting angry and rigid since she came into the room. Joe does not look at the picture but continues staring straight ahead.

GEORGE: Yes, mam, I member that real good, Aint Ethel.

ETHEL: Joe, you member this?

JOE: I remember.

ETHEL: Who would've thought that sweet little boy would go off in the big wide world and write books and git his name in the paper and the TIME magazine and everthin? Now who would have thought such a thing?

GEORGE: And who would've thought the other one would've rode out his life on a tractor?

ETHEL: Now, George, we all travel different roads to the throne of God. You got yourself as nice a farm as it is in the county, and a good tight house on high ground. God has truly blessed us all, praise his name, and I think we ought to have us a little something to eat.

JOE: Nothing for me, thanks.

ETHEL: Now, son, you've got to keep you strength up. Slice of ham, maybe, some patatoe salad, a little piece of pie?

JOE: Aunt Ethel, I've eaten more today than I usually eat in a week.

ETHEL: And that's why you nothing but breath and britches, son. You need to put on more flesh like you brother. I bet he'll have a little something.

GEORGE: I believe I could eat me a piece of pound cake with just a drop or two of that good choclate surp on it.

ETHEL: I'm gone fix that two times, one for you too, Joe.

JOE: Thank you, but I don't think so.

GEORGE: Is Uncle Pete already gone to bed?

ETHEL: Lord no. He ain't one to sleep much. But that man washes more'n a woman. He's back there right now soakin in the tub. Soakinest man I ever seen. He'll be out torectly though. Let me git on in that kitchen.

She exits to kitchen where we see her open the refrigerator and bend to it, etc.

JOE: Get on in that pig trough, she means.

GEORGE: You a goddamn unholy man, Joe Bass, even if you are my brother, and you gone pay for it. She loves you like you was her own son.

JOE: You're right, it was a shitty thing to say. My head has changed up on me today. Anyway, I'm sorry, man.

GEORGE: My name is George. Don't *man* me. More nigger talk. You gone off, like Aint Ethel says, and got you name in the paper a few times and you forgot where you come from.

JOE: You've had your own name in the paper a few times if I remember correctly.

GEORGE: I never been convicted of nothing. For as I'm concerned, whoever fixed them uppity niggers was doing the Lord's work, just tryin to keep things the way they was meant to be.

JOE: One of them was fourteen years old, George.

GEORGE: A fourteen-year-old uppity nigger grows up to be fifty-year-old uppity nigger. He got off on the wrong track and somebody got him back on the right track with a rope and a whip. But Aint Ethel's blood. Don't you care about blood?

JOE: Yeah, as a matter of fact, I do care about blood. And something's gone bad wrong with it and whatever it is I mean to run it to the ground now. Driving around the county these last few days talking to the old people who must remember my brother—our brother—they act strange when I ask about him. Now why is that, George? Why would that be?

GEORGE: First thing that comes to mind is that you might of been drunk.

JOE: No, I wasn't drunk. I'll grant that I'm drunk enough, often enough, but I wasn't drunk. And it did seem passing strange.

GEORGE: Strange. How do you mean strange?

JOE: It's not as though they don't remember, or at least remember *something*, but rather as though . . . as though it makes them . . . nervous. Maybe even ashamed.

GEORGE: Bullshit. They aint nervous and they aint ashamed. It aint a goddamn thing to remember. It was born dead. It aint even got a name.

JOE: Or a marked grave.

GEORGE: Or one of them neither. No name. No marked grave. Born dead, dammit!

JOE: It's more than that. I can see it in their faces. Born dead or not he was my brother. The same strange look comes on them when I bring up Lonny Boatwright and Daddy, too.

GEORGE: It's some things we weren't meant to understand.

JOE: Maybe.

ETHEL (*Calling.*): Here it comes, honey.

JOE: I'll walk out to the car for a minute. I don't think I can watch this.

Joe crosses downstage and exits as Ethel comes out of the kitchen. Holding a plate in either hand, she turns to watch him go.

ETHEL: Joe stepped out for a breath of good fresh air, is he?

GEORGE: He's stepped out to his car for a snort is what he's done.

ETHEL: A snort! Naww, he ain't stepped out for no snort.

GEORGE: He has to have him a drink a whiskey.

ETHEL: Oh, George, I don't think so.

GEORGE: (*Going after the cake in great gasping gulps.*) He's been drinking all day. Don't see why he ain't fell down yet. I known him to be a drinker but I didn't know him to be the kind of drunk I seen today.

ETHEL: Why, I didn't know he drinks. If he does like you say.

GEORGE: He does. Believe you me.

ETHEL: Seems like I heard sommers, or read sommers writers was bad to drink. Say they git to be drunks cause they writers.

GEORGE: Writers git to be drunks just like everybody else. They drink too much.

ETHEL: I caint believe that.

GEORGE: I can.

ETHEL: You want some more of that good pound cake?

GEORGE: I believe I could eat me one more piece.

ETHEL: Surp, too?

GEORGE: No Mam, I got to watch this weight of mine.

ETHEL: (*Getting up for the kitchen with George following.*) We sure had us a time today. I wish we had us a reunion everday.

GEORGE: Joe sure as hell don't.

ETHEL: You mama didn't raise you to cuss, son.

GEORGE: Didn't raise Joe to be a drunk neither for all the good it done. He's about ruint this whole thing for me. And if I don't watch him close, he's gone ruin it for mother, too.

ETHEL: How on earth would he do that?

GEORGE: It's about the baby.

ETHEL (*Distracted, fussing with the cake, half hearing.*): Baby?

GEORGE: Mother's first born.

ETHEL: Oh, God! (*Her attention definitely focused now.*) Lordy, lordy! Then what I been hearing's true. He don't want to do that.

GEORGE: Do what?

ETHEL: What he's been doing.

GEORGE (*Waits for her to continue, but she does not.*): Well, what is it? What has he been doin?

ETHEL: I don't know.

GEORGE: Aint Ethel, you ain't making much sense. Or maybe it's me. I talk to Joe for ten minutes and nothing makes sense for the rest of the day.

ETHEL: It was born dead.

GEORGE (*Exasperated.*): I know that, Aint Ethel. Everybody know *that.*

ETHEL: Then why's he going on about it? Talking to folks and such.

GEORGE: You'd have to ask him.

ETHEL: I don't want to ask him. I want him to leave it just the way it is, just the way everybody remembers it. It was born dead, that's all.

GEORGE: I told him. My exact same words, but he already known that.

ETHEL: (*Taking enormous bite of cake.*) God, things like this make me start eatin and I caint quit. How's your piece, son?

GEORGE: Good as the last piece Aint Ethel.

ETHEL: It's just the way they done it in them days. A baby born dead, and deformed besides, liver on the outside of its body. Maybe now Joe's got older, he just feels bad about . . .

GEORGE: Well, hell, I feel bad about it too. I don't take a backseat to nobody in feeling bad about a dead baby. That's Joe for you, though. He always thought he could do everything bettern me. He even thinks he can feel bad bettern me. It ain't my fault they fixed that damn dead youngun the way they did.

ETHEL: Be easy, son. In that day and time, they just took one all messed up like that and put it in a box and covered it up. No ceremony, nothing to mark it by. Purty soon everybody forgot whereabouts it was even bared.

GEORGE: I bet mother aint forgot where.

ETHEL: No, I guess she ain't. But I know for a fact she wishes she could, wishes she could forget everything about it. Mabel was always willful and headstrong, did what she had to do, went her own way and the devil take the hindmost. She'd do as she pleased and never give two hoots in hell for the rest of us. We all thanked God ever day of our lives Lonny Boatwright was there for her.

GEORGE (*Shaking his head.*): Dad Lonny, I'll tell you. They won't make another one like him. (*Smiling fondly.*) He was a good man, but he weren't blood. Joe's right about that if he ain't right about nothin else I know of. Everything would've been different if daddy'd lived. (*Shaking his head.*) Dead of a heart attack and him thirty-one-year-old.

ETHEL: God works in mysterious ways his many wonders to perform.

GEORGE: It do make a man wonder.

ETHEL: Well, God works in . . .

GEORGE: I know, Aint Ethel, I know. You already said.

ETHEL: And now she's had to put another husband in the ground. Her near eighty-year-old, too.

GEORGE: You know good as me she's seventy-six.

ETHEL: You don't need to bark, son. I dent mean no disrespect.

GEORGE: I dent mean to bark neither. It's just this whole day and Joe out there drinking the heart out of the night.

ETHEL: Oh, I don't think so. He just stepped out for some good fresh air.

GEORGE: Jack Daniels sour mash is what he stepped out for.

ETHEL: I do wish you two could be closer, like you was when you was boys.

GEORGE: It's been a long time since we was boys. And Joe has fell in with the wrong crowd and ruint his mind with them books he writes.

ETHEL: Son, blood is thicker than water.

GEORGE: I don't want to talk about blood just right now.

ETHEL: Why don't we make us some coffee? You Uncle Pete is bound to quit soakin sooner or later, and you know how he is about his coffee.

GEORGE: Les make it in this Jap pot Lonny bought Mother just before the old Master called him home.

ETHEL: I misdoubt the thing's ever been used.

GEORGE: Looks more like something to add up figgers on than it does a coffee pot.

ETHEL: And it looks some more complicated to me.

GEORGE: Anything a Jap can make, I can figger out. Just let me git at it. Make some, maybe we can pour it down Joe.

George starts in on the coffee. The pot has lights and switches and a timer, etc.

ETHEL: I was here the day that coffee pot come in the house.

GEORGE: I know you was, Aint Ethel. I heard.

ETHEL: You just heard. I seen it. I was *here*. Mabel didn't even want it.

GEORGE: I heard.

ETHEL: You ain't heard. You just think you heard.

GEORGE: You want to tell it, I want to hear it.

ETHEL: Les see, him dead now two months . . . this had to be right at six months ago, a Saturday it was.

GEORGE: I don't believe I need to know the day.

ETHEL: (*She turns to look at George and she is going to tell this story the way she wishes.*) It was of a Saturday and Lonny's mind had already started to go bad on him by then. Not enough air gittin to it, the doctors said. Nothing they could do about it, the doctors said. And, well, you know he *was* eighty-seven-year-old. It was time, don't you know, for somethin to break down, and what broke was his brain.

GEORGE: I already known about his brain.

ETHEL: I'm telling this story. I want you to have the straight of it.

GEORGE: Dent mean to be short. But I don't need all the details.

ETHEL: Details is all that matters. That coffee gone make?

GEORGE: It's a running now. Them Japs is right smart about things like this, even if they eyes ain't right and they all look like they come out of the same mama.

ETHEL: Well, like I say, it was of a Saturday.

GEORGE: Aint Ethel, don't tell me the day no more. I known the day from the start.

ETHEL: That coffee smells good. Why don't you pour us a cup and come set down.

George pours two cups, puts 4 spoons of sugar in his, and he and Ethel go into the living room and sit on the couch.

It was of a Saturday and you mama wanted to go to the store for groceries and Lonny just put in to go too and him with his mind already gone bad, what with no air gitten to his brain and all and . . .

GEORGE: I believe you already told that, Aint Ethel.

ETHEL: I caint tell the story without telling the story.

GEORGE: If you want to tell it, I thought to hear it.

ETHEL: Thought that's what you said and I'm tryin. This Jap coffee ain't got a bad taste.

GEORGE: It's a Jap pot. You drinking Maxwell House. Japs make pots, but I don't magine they even know what coffee is.

ETHEL: Anyway, Lonny had just the week before bought that coffee pot for you mama. Went all the way to Macon to get it. She tried to git him not to do it. Said she already had a good one. Which she did. But his brain had already broke down and . . .

GEORGE: I heard about his brain breaking down already, Aint Ethel.

ETHEL: But his brain had already broke down and he went and got it anyhow. And I bet you Mabel ain't used that thing the first time since it come in the house. Anyhow, we come back from the store that Saturday with the groceries and when we walked in the kitchen to set'm down, Lonny took him one look at that Jap pot he went all the way to Macon for and he said, 'Why, Mabel, I believe they got them a coffee pot just like ourn.' Well, you mama didn't blink a eye or miss a beat. She just said, 'Yes, Lonny, they do.' And then he said, 'How long you think they gone let us live here?' Son, when he said that—broke brain or not—if I'da had false teeth I'da spit'm from here to yonder. Cause he built this house hisself.

GEORGE: I *know* he built the house, Aint Ethel.

ETHEL: You mama was tried and was not found wantin, praise His name. She said, 'Lonny, I have talked to them and they said we could live here as long as we like.' Well, Lonny just relaxed all over and said, 'Thank God for that.' He lit up his pipe and went to set on the back porch easy as a baby. Four months later he was dead. That broke brain of his . . .

GEORGE: I don't need to hear no more about his brain, Aint Ethel.

ETHEL: But you mama was a miracle. I don't know what I would've done if Lonny had said that to me.

GEORGE: She's a great woman, a good and great woman, Mother is.

ETHEL: She's done what she could, the best she could, and like the Good Book says, Judge not, that ye be not judged. So I just try to keep everthing to myself. Jesus on his throne knows I don't understand Joe or what he does. But I understand this much: I love him but I wish he'd go home.

GEORGE: He'll go home.

ETHEL: I just hope it's soon enough.

Enter Ethel's husband, Pete. He is tall and skinny with the thin brittleness of the very old. Ancient of days this one. He's wearing khaki pants and shirt and his face has the high color and the ravaged lines of a drunk. His thin wispy hair is damp. Though he moves slowly to accommodate his fragility, his bearing is almost military, head up, back straight, and while his body may have failed him, his mind is sharp and still focused on matters of the flesh.

GEORGE: Uncle Pete! I thought you'd gone to shit and the hogs'd eat you.

ETHEL: George, for shame!

PETE: Soakin, George, just soakin. Man needs to soak. Keeps his pencil sharp. Just ask you Aint Ethel if it don't keep my pencil sharp. Ain't as sharp as it once was—what is?—but it can still write. Write in the light, write in the night. Rain or shine long good letters to please everybody concerned.

ETHEL: Pete, sometimes I despair of you.

PETE: I shore God hope so.

ETHEL: You gone talk nasty, I'm gone go to bed.

PETE: Ain't nothing nasty about a sharp pencil. Leastwise it was a time you didn't think so.

ETHEL: I was always a lady.

PETE: It ain't never too late to change that. It ain't much but it's bout the only hope I got to hold onto these days.

ETHEL (*Smiling. She's heard all this before.*): George, what am I gone do with this old goat?

GEORGE: Don't look like it's much you can do, Aint Ethel.

PETE: Good for you, son. I'm shore to git worse before I git any better.

Enter Joe, a slight drunkenness in his walk, gestures, voice, etc.

JOE: Get through soaking did you, Uncle Pete?

GEORGE: He was soakin but he ain't a old soak, like some I could name.

(*Joe watches him for a beat and then walks right up into his face. The tension is palpable. Pete feels it, sees it, and is confused by it.*)

JOE: Why don't you back off and cut me some slack?

GEORGE: Cut you some slack? More nigger talk. And git away from me. You smell like a liquor barrel.

JOE: At least my heart's not rotten.

GEORGE: What the hell would you know about a heart?

JOE: (*When he starts to talk we see and understand two things: he is drunker than we thought he was, and he has been outside in the dark with a bottle eating his liver over the problem at hand, a problem which he is wrestling with but does not understand. He counts it off on his fingers.*) One, I don't need a four platt cow whip to argue my case. Two, when I do argue my case I don't need the dark of the moon to do it. Three, there's a lot I'd like to change, George. Your opinions for instance. But, four, while I'd like to change some things, I can't think of any bones I'd like to break. And five, finally five, my heart's not rotten enough to confuse bones with opinions.

GEORGE: (*Looking at Pete and Ethel.*) Now did y'all hear that? Can somebody tell me what the hell he's talkin about? He left his mother's house a Christian man and come back home a crazy heathen. Hearts and bones, my ass! Everybody knows it ain't no bone in a heart.

PETE: This ain't no way for brothers to be talkin in their mama's house here at the tag end of a family reunion.

JOE: I don't have a family.

GEORGE: You brain's so soaked you ain't got good sense either.

ETHEL: I'm going to bed myself. 'Slate, and tomorrow's another day.

GEORGE: Good night, Aint Ethel.

ETHEL: G'night, son.

GEORGE: Sleep good, darlin.

Exit Ethel to rear of house.

PETE: Is it fresh coffee back there? Cause that's what I think I smell.

GEORGE: I don't smell nothing but a drunk.

JOE: Go to bed George. Go on to bed before you get yourself into a trick of shit.

GEORGE: What you mean is before I git sick.

JOE: What I mean is what I said.

GEORGE: I ain't even gone remark on that.

George exits.

PETE: Son, what was that all about?

JOE: Nothing. That was about nothing.

PETE: I been too many miles to believe that. Lemme git a cup of that coffee.

JOE: To hell with the coffee. I got a bottle. Will you take a drink with me?

PETE: You know how you Aint Ethel feels about me and my drinking.

JOE: She's gone to bed, and I need a drink. Is it yay or nay? You have a drink with me?

PETE: I believe I could stand me a taste.

JOE (*He pulls a bottle out from his jacket.*): As luck would have it I can oblige.

PETE: You oughten to have that whiskey in the house. You mama wouldn't like it and George couldn't stand it.

JOE: Ma will never know it. And George? With him it's a problem of mind over matter. I don't mind and he doesn't matter.

PETE: That's no way to talk about a brother.

JOE: I guess. You want ice?

PETE: Never wanted ice in my whiskey. It needs to be the temperature of you guts to make the leap to you blood. Ice don't do a thing but make the whiskey wait.

JOE: Will you want a little water behind this?

PETE: What I want is a drink now that you brought it up. But I guess we could stand here and talk it to death. (*He takes the whiskey.*) The neck of the bottle's always done me just fine. (*He drinks.*) My, my, that do taste good. (*Hands the bottle to Joe who drinks.*) Man wouldn't want to cut that with water if he could help it.

JOE: Cutting whiskey is lightweight, very lightweight.

PETE: Profane is what it is.

JOE: That, too.

PETE: You daddy never would of done it.

JOE: I don't know what he would or wouldn't do. I wish I could have but it wasn't in the cards. I don't know anything about the man.

PETE: What might you want to know about'm?

JOE: Everything.

PETE: Myself, I never wanted to know everythin about anythin. Be too damn scary, overload my fuse box, so to speak.

JOE: All right, forget about everything then. Just tell me how he felt about the baby.

PETE: Baby? Which baby you talking about?

JOE: His first born. The one dead at birth.

A look of pain and bafflement passes in Pete's face as he watches Joe a long slow time before he finally hits the bottle.

PETE: What brought this on?

JOE: Something I've been thinking about. Working on actually.

PETE: You'll have to do bettern that for me, son.

JOE: I can't do better than that. I don't understand it all that well myself. But I've decided I will. I realized a while back that I had been thinking about it a long time.

PETE: But why come up on it now?

JOE: Give a writer something he doesn't understand and he'll write a book about it.

PETE: You gone and write a book about a child that didn't live?

JOE: That's part of it. There's other things.

PETE: What other things?

JOE: I don't know.

PETE: Well, shit.

JOE: Yeah.

PETE: You mind if I go ahead on and kill this bottle?

JOE: Hell no, Pete. Go on and kill that soldier.

Pete turns up the bottle and takes down the remaining two swallows. While Pete's drinking, Joe crosses to an end table by the couch, takes a folded white cloth out of a drawer and unwraps it with a flourish, as if doing a magic trick, and produces another bottle.

PETE: Dammit, son, how many of them you got in this house?

JOE: I've got'm planted like wildflowers in a field. Never like to be where I can't put my hand on a bottle.

PETE: You drink too much, son.

JOE: Yeah, I drink too much. But never as much as when I'm here in this house. Even *thinking* about coming home can make me get on the outside of a quart of Jack Daniels. I wasn't in Alaska when Lonny was buried, I was in the bottle.

PETE: (*Taking the bottle and starting to uncap it while he talks. Once he has a taste, he's as bad a drunk as Joe.*) The truth is, I never trusted a man who could git through this world cold sober. And in my time I shore as hell missed a few things over whiskey myself. Just let it lie. What you said will stay right here.

Pete looks at the uncapped bottle in his hand from time to time as he speaks. Raising the bottle to look at it through the light.

PETE: But we got to be quiet about all this. Wake up Ethel and I won't be drinkin nothing but grief. That woman's got enough grief for the whole world and she does like to share it.

What he has been wanting to do all this time is go on and take a drink, but since he had the last one, courtesy dictates that he pass the bottle. He hands it to Joe.

PETE: Here, press this to you face, boy, you'll feel better.

JOE (*Taking the bottle.*): I wish to God I could believe that, but the whiskey's not working either. Won't check in. Falls on my stomach like so much water.

PETE: It was sometimes like that with you daddy. He could drink some. And did.

JOE: What else could he do? What kind of man was he?

PETE: He was as good a man as ever shit behind two shoes. And work? He was a working sumbitch. He had the fever as a child and it done something to his heart, hurt it. He known it was gone kill him. There a year or so before it did, he'd sometimes fall in the field.

JOE: When he did, what would he do then?

PETE: Only thing he could do. He got up and went back to it.

JOE: Hard worker?

PETE: I'm here to say.

JOE: Good husband?

PETE: How's at?

JOE: I said was he a good husband?

PETE: Good husband and a fine man.

JOE: Ma love him?

PETE: What kind of thing is that to say?

JOE: Did she?

PETE: Thought he could walk on water is all she thought.

JOE: And did he lose a testicle like they say?

PETE: Lose a testi*what?*

JOE: A nut. Did he lose one of his balls?

PETE: I don't think I want to git into this. It ain't seemly.

JOE: Uncle Pete, you been around a block or two, and we got a bottle. Can't we talk?

PETE: It's talk and it's talk. But my wife's you mama's sister and that makes me blood.

JOE: Yeah, it makes you blood. And blood can ask anything of blood. Did he lose a nut or not?

PETE: You stay up nights thinking of shit like this, Joe?

JOE: It doesn't keep me up at night, but I do think about it.

PETE: You ought not think on blood thataway. That . . . that *trouble* you Daddy had, it happened before he ever met you ma. He's dead and gone now, and no good can come of blamin the dead for anything.

JOE: I'm not *blaming* him, Uncle Pete. You ought to know that. With the life I've led, I'm the last one to point a finger. Besides, I know what clap could cost in them days.

PETE: Hell, it weren't his fault, young buck like he was, off down there in that swamp. He'd woulda never laid with that Seminole gal had he known she was tainted. But she was, she was tainted. Could of happened to any man.

JOE: Way I heard it, he was told he'd never have children.

PETE: That's doctors for you. You here ain't you?

JOE: Yeah, I'm here.

PETE: George, too.

JOE: George, too.

Pete gets up and goes to stand looking at the picture he replaced earlier.

PETE: The world does smell of shit ever now and agin.

JOE: It does that.

PETE: But the thing is, boy, the thing is . . .

JOE: Yes sir?

PETE: You have to act like it don't.

JOE: I don't *have* to do a goddamn thing.

PETE: You ain't gone commence to being crazy are you?

JOE: I wouldn't worry about it if I were you.

PETE: I don't wanta worry about it, God damn it, I want *you* to worry about it.

JOE: Now, wait a . . .

PETE: No, by God, you wait. I shoulda said this to you a long time ago. Me or somebody else, because you caint seem to see it you own self, understand how much pain you've caused everwhere you go. You come in the front door and trouble walks in with you. Ever kin you got loves you. But it's limits to what even blood can do, what blood can put up with. We ain't made out of iron nor steel nor run by 'lectricity, God damn it. We got feelings too. If you daddy was here, he'd tell you the same thing.

JOE: Well, my daddy's not here, never has been here. And where the hell did all this come from anyway? Maybe you better bubble this bottle again yourself.

PETE: Hell, I'll drink with you til we both fall down and caint git up. But before that happens I'm gonna have my say. To have so much school learning, you blind in one eye and caint see out of the other. How about that car you wrecked the last time you was home? How about us finding out ever month or so you laid up in some hospital full of broke bones? How about opening them books of yours and finding ourselves on ever other page. The names in there—what you call them people—don't mean a God damn thing. They us all the same. For Christ sake, Joe, that ain't even decent.

JOE: That's what George tells me, but if you want decent, find a preacher. I'm a writer. Decent's another word I never got much mileage out of. It just came with the package. I didn't ask for it. It's just there like the color of my eyes. To ask me to be what I'm not is like asking me to have different colored eyes. I don't have to like it.

PETE: Then you just gonna go on and ruin this for you mama and everbody else, is that it?

JOE: I don't plan on ruining a damn thing.

PETE: Lemme put it this way. You think you can just git through the rest of this without causin no trouble. You think you can do that for me?

JOE: For you?

PETE: Listen, I was close to you daddy, a hell of a lot bettern just good friends. Now, if blood means anything, you'll promise me.

JOE: Promise you what?

PETE: Not to cause no more pain.

JOE: I can promise I'll do my best.

PETE: I guess that'll have to do. You bout ready to turn the lights out on this and go to bed? You know how you mama is.

JOE: Yeah. Oh God! I wish I was anywhere in the fucking world but here.

PETE: You don't mean that.

JOE: I mean that.

PETE: Understand, in this house you surrounded by blood, son.

JOE: I don't need to be surrounded by a goddamn thing. I made it this far. I'll make it the rest of the way.

Pete hands him the bottle; Joe drinks long.

PETE: Son, you got to understand . . .

JOE: Oh, I understand. I understand only too well. This goddamn people! This god-damn blood! Reserved among strangers, generous to a fault, and violent enough to kill each other over a bird dog or a fence line. My fucking brother! He'll sir you to death and then take you out back and butcher you without blinking.

He drinks again from the bottle he's been holding.

If I'd known where it'd take me I never would have gone.

PETE: Where what would've took you, son?

JOE: What I do with my fucking life, such as it is. Other people allow scabs to heal over and and scar up. Not me. Not people like me. We pick at the scabs, non-stop scab pickers, keep'm bleeding. The sight of issuing blood is our only joy. If we can make it bleed—whatever *it* is—we can stay alive. Jesus, Jesus. (*He drinks again, openly crying now.*)

PETE: (*Trying to lighten up.*) You gone just set there with that bottle and let a old man die of thirst?

Joe passes the bottle without looking up.

JOE: (*Getting hold of himself, but still shaken.*) A stranger in my own goddamn country. A stranger everywhere. People I grew up with—even my own kin— look at me like I've come back from the moon carrying death on both shoulders.

Reaches to take the bottle from Pete without asking, drinks.

Well, to hell with it. I can't be what I can't be, do what I can't do. Least this whiskey is finally checking in, thank God.

PETE: Good. I'm glad it's checking in as you say. But try to hear this. What you after runnin all over the county talkin to everbody. It's cripplin your mama's blood and it's makin you brother dangerous. You trying what you ain't got no business trying.

JOE: I've got to try as hard as I can to do the best I can. I don't have a choice.

PETE: (*Takes a kitchen match out of his shirt pocket, chews on it, looks at it a reflective moment, looks at Joe.*) Let me tell you a little story you daddy—Lonny, that is to say—use to tell about trying. *His trying-too-hard story*, he used to call it. You mighta heard it.

JOE: That old bastard could tell a story.

PETE: Well, when him and Frank come back from the swamp, Lonny got him a job with the Rural Electric Asosaytion, people that brought 'lectricity to folks out in the county. Had a buddy out there that was as close to him as somebody that ain't blood is likely to be. Feller's name was Jake. They both had the same job, climbing and topping trees and they was both damn good at it. Thing about Jake though, he was bad about winning—winning at anything—bad as a pig is about slop. Damn boy had to win. And Lonny and him got to talking out there one day, and Lonny must've said he was faster or some such thing and Jake said it ain't but one way to find out and to goddammit come on. Lonny said he tried to back out two or three times but Jake put in to try'm. You see, they'd put up poles down the middle of the right-of-way they'd cut, but it weren't no crosspieces on them yetawhile. Nothin'd do Jake but the two of'm go on out there and both of'm git at the bottom of two different poles. First one to the top was the winner. They put on their climbing rigs, big thick safety belts that loop around the pole, inch-and-a-half climbin jack-spikes buckled to their boots. A feller clapped for'm and off they went. Before Jake's spikes hit the pole six times, he was already two foot ahead of Lonny. See, he meant to win, so he was holding onto the safety belt that went around the pole with both hands and he was a climbing, puffing, his feet pumpin, hittin that 'lectric pole with them spikes driving up it, and when his feet would come up to take a fresh hold, he'd flip that leather belt with both hands and he was looking down, straight down between his pumpin knees, and never looking up and flipping that belt and driving with his feet, and when he got to the top of the pole, well, bless God, he didn't do a thing but flip that leather belt right over the top of that pole and come sailing back down on the back of his head and broke his neck. Dead 'fore Lonny could git down to'm. (*Pause a beat.*) That'as Lonny's *trying-too-hard* story. What do you think.

JOE: (*Pauses a long beat staring into his whiskey glass. He's good and drunk now.*) Well, this guy Jake you're talking about wanted to do it, wanted to do it bad, it was in him to do, and he did it. (*Pause a beat.*) If I had to guess, I'd say that at the exact moment Jake hit the ground and broke his neck, he was as happy as he had ever expected to be in his entire life.

Fade to black with Joe drinking, the bottle raised.

END Act 1, Scene 1

ACT I

Scene 2

Back porch. Next morning. Mabel is sitting in one of the chairs at a round metal table. A walking stick hangs on the chair arm. She is dipping snuff and from time to time drains her mouth into a cup. Off stage there are the sound of voices and a game of horse shoes.

MABEL: (*Calling.*) Git a ringer, honey! Git a ringer! Ahh, shoot. You gone mess right around and let that sorry thing whup you.

The back door opens and Gaye Nell, George's wife, comes onto the back porch. She wears an apron and her hands are white with flour. She is short and not so much fat as square, square thick body and square thick legs—what Southern women mean when they say a lady is "stout."

GAYE NELL: How we doin out here?

MABEL: How you doin in there?

GAYE NELL: Well, I . . .

MABEL: I hope you rolled them dumplins long enough. You never roll them dumplins long enough, and they lumpy. You dumplins is lumpy. But make extry like I told you. Even lumpy, we gone need extry.

GAYE NELL: You just leave everythin to us. This is your day.

MABEL: This is *my* kitchen and *my* house, too.

GAYE NELL: Now, you old honey, you.

MABEL: Don't be old honeying me. Is Joe come out yet?

GAYE NELL: Nome, he ain't. You'd let me bang on that door he'd . . .

MABEL: I told you to let'm lie.

GAYE NELL: I jus said *if.* I ain't done it. But if you . . .

MABEL: Well, I won't. Let'm be. He needs his rest. Brain work is mighty tirin.

GAYE NELL: I'm sure I wouldn't know.

MABEL: I know you wouldn't. Some got five talents, some got only one. Then it's them as don't have none atall.

GAYE NELL: I do the best I can.

MABEL: You just like Godamighty made you. You got nothing to be ashamed of. You weren't never the purtyest thing in the world and the bloom is gone off the rose, but you caint help that.

GAYE NELL: You talk hateful to me sometimes.

MABEL: It's only the truth and I try to tell it when I can.

Enter George from the yard carrying a horse shoe. He's wearing khaki pants and a sweaty T-shirt.

GEORGE: It's another hot one today.

GAYE NELL: Could you drink you a glass of good cold ice tea, George honey?

GEORGE: Die if I don't, and I believe them boys could, too.

GAYE NELL: Them younguns thirsty, too?

GEORGE: We been pitchin all morning and that ain't cool work.

GAYE NELL: I know you a fool about a good game a shoes. Too bad you caint git you brother out here and . . .

MABEL: Joe needs his rest.

GEORGE: He wouldn't pitch no horseshoes if you made him king for a day. Mindless is what he says it is.

GAYE NELL: Mindless? You mean . . .

MABEL: Git that tea, Gaye Nell.

Gaye Nell exits.

GEORGE: You speak kindly short to her sometimes, Mother.

MABEL: I never believed in keeping my mind a secret.

Enter Joe on last line, carrying a glass of tomato juice.

JOE: Keep what a secret, Ma?

MABEL: Anything. Speak you mind, I always say. Did the baby sleep all right?

JOE: I slept fine, Ma.

GEORGE: Was that the baby I heard stumbling down the hall just fore good daylight?

JOE: You won't live long enough to hear me stumble, Pooter.

GEORGE: My name's George.

JOE: I been calling you Pooter since second grade.

GEORGE: I know how long you been calling me Pooter and I don't like it. Mother, he knows I don't like Pooter.

MABEL: It's only a nickname, George. I do wisht you could have a sunny disposition like you brother.

GEORGE: Ridin a tractor for thirty years in good weather and bad don't tend to give a man a sunny disposition.

JOE: I hope I don't have to hear too much more about that tractor.

MABEL: Now, son.

JOE: I'm telling the truth. And you just said how we feel in this family about the truth.

GEORGE: (*Calling.*) Gaye Nell, you gone bring that ice tea?

GAYE NELL: (*Off-stage.*) I'm coming with it, honey.

GEORGE: (*Calling.*) Well, then come on, dammit!

JOE: Is dammit your pet name for your wife now, George?

GEORGE: Don't start in on me agin this morning.

JOE: Just a little joke, Pooter.

GEORGE: Mother, he's startin in on me again.

MABEL: We all called you Pooter.

GEORGE: I know what you all called me. But I'm grown now and a grown man don't prechate being called a Pooter.

GEORGE JUNIOR: (*Calling off-stage.*) Daddy, you gone finish this game of shoes or whut?

GEORGE: You mother's bringin us out some tea.

Enter Gaye Nell with tea on a tray.

GAYE NELL: (*Calling.*) George Junior! Buster! I got good cold ice tea for them that wants it.

GEORGE: Git on over here, boys.

Enter George Junior and Buster, 19 and 17 yrs. old respectively, medium height, heavy boys, slow of movement and speech, a little loutish, dressed more or less like their father.

GEORGE JUNIOR: Gimme a glass a that. I ain't nothing if I ain't thirsty.

BUSTER: Uncle Joe, you look like mother-I've-come-home-to-die.

MABEL: Shut you mouth and drink you tea, Buster.

JOE: I'm not used to being up quite so early, son.

GEORGE: Shoot, me and these boys usually got half a day's work done by this time a the morning.

JOE: Good for you, George. I think that's admirable.

GEORGE: You think that's what?

JOE: Admirable.

GEORGE: I thought that's what you said.

JOE: I think *you're* admirable, George.

GEORGE: (*Looking at Mabel.*) He's startin in on me again.

JOE: There's nothing wrong with being admirable George, and having two admirable sons.

GEORGE: You ain't doing a thing but making fun.

JOE: Not really, George.

GEORGE: You . . .

MABEL: Drink you tea, George.

GEORGE: Well, he . . .

MABEL: You chirrun will be the death of me yet.

JOE: You don't mean that, Ma. Children are a blessing, a blessing from God.

GEORGE: That's real funny coming from somebody don't believe in God or children neither one.

MABEL: George, don't git on my nerves.

BUSTER: Shoot, you believe in children, don't you, Uncle Joe?

JOE: Sure I do, son.

GEORGE: But you don't have none do you?

JOE: Not that I know of, Pooter.

GEORGE: Hell of a thing to say, in front of you own mother and my children to boot.

MABEL: George, I want you to git back out there and finish that game of shoes.

GEORGE: I don't want to set here no how. Come on, boys.

GEORGE JUNIOR: Let's get to it.

BUSTER: I'll show you how it's done.

Exit George and sons.

MABEL: Nobody'd know you and George was even brothers.

JOE: I guess you're right.

MABEL: You ought to try not to be so rank with'm.

JOE: I don't try. It just seems to happen.

MABEL: You have to remember he never had your advantages.

JOE: My advantages?

MABEL: Going to college and such.

JOE: He could have, had he wanted to. The government would have sent him the same as it sent me when we got back from Korea. He chose to do something else.

MABEL: Chose? Chose, you say? If you believe that, you ain't as quick as I thought you was.

JOE: I believe everything. I'm the world's champion believer. My life proves that.

MABEL: You've got above you raisin is what you've done, boy. And you think you know what you don't know. George does what he can. It ain't his fault he caint do much.

JOE: He sure as hell knows how to get me ragged.

Offstage: Whoooeee, hot damn!

MABEL: (*Calling.*) Top that ringer, Buster! Top that'n with one of yorn.

Offstage: How bout it, Grandmother? Is that a topper or what?

JOE: God, he's raising two more Georges, two more just like himself.

MABEL: (*Calling.*) Whup you daddy! Buster. Whup'm! (*To Joe.*) Men always raise theirselves all over again. A woman's vanity is in her face, a man's vanity is in his son. If you had a son, you'd know that.

JOE: Maybe that's why I don't have one.

MABEL: It's times when I wondered why you didn't have chirrun. Chirrun usually ain't in this world cause men and women wanted'm. Chirrun's in the world cause men and women wanted each other. Don't look at me like that, son. The trouble with you is the only thing you can see is what you can see.

JOE: I see better than you think I do, Ma.

MABEL: All you see is a old woman with bones like a bird settin here. Bones like a bird and a mouth full of snuff. But it was a time when these old bones carried the finest flesh in the county. I turned a head or two in my time, and don't you forgit it.

JOE: Ma, try to believe me when I say I know that's the gospel truth. And I've always known it.

MABEL: I've seen ever way a day can do.

JOE: You've lived to a good age, Ma.

MABEL: Age ain't got a damn thing to do with it. Did you hear me say something about age?

JOE: I can't remember ever hearing you talk like this.

MABEL: It's a lot you ain't heard.

JOE: I've always known that, too.

MABEL: You don't know nothin. You too young to know anythin. It's been trials in my life would've broke your back ten times over.

JOE: I know you've had a hard life, Ma.

MABEL: I didn't say it was hard. Did I say it was hard? All I'm sayin is it's been what it's been and I've done the best I could with it. Purty damn good, too, if you ask me. Course you didn't ask me, did you? Nobody ever asks a old woman nothing.

JOE: You feeling all right, Ma?

MABEL: I feel my age hard on me this mornin. I always do when it's one of these.

JOE: One of these? One of what?

MABEL: Anythin that marks the calendar. Reunion, birthday, marriage, birth . . . death.

JOE: Ah, yes, the ticking clock. I know it well.

MABEL: When you going back to Florida?

JOE: I don't know, few more days I guess.

MABEL: Stay as long as you will. Won't be many more of these for me.

JOE: You'll be here when I'm dead and gone.

MABEL: I might if you keep drinking like you do.

JOE: Jesus! I wish George would live his own life and leave mine alone.

MABEL: George don't need to say nothin to me about your whiskey drinking for me to know it. I been around drinkin men all my life. I can tell a drinkin man from as far away as I can see him.

JOE: Ma, I'm not a drunk.

MABEL: You ain't drawed a sober breath since you been here.

JOE: If you say so. I don't want to argue.

MABEL: Be the first time you didn't. What you need is a wife. Wife'd take some of the starch out of you.

JOE: I had a wife, Ma. Remember?

MABEL: Git another one then. A man without a woman is unnatural.

JOE: I figured one was my fair share.

MABEL: Talk straight and mind you mouth. I won't be made sport of.

JOE: I was talking straight, Ma. And I have come to think one was my fair share. There was nothing wrong with Tish. She didn't cause our marriage to go sour. It was me. All me. She was a good woman, and after it all busted up, it came to me that if I couldn't live with her I couldn't live with anybody.

MABEL: That's what come to you, did it?

JOE: That's what come to me.

MABEL: A man caint make a family without a woman, a wife.

JOE: I think I know that, Ma.

MABEL: You think! Think? You ain't thinking, you just think you thinking. A family's all a man's got. A man that ain't got a family ain't got nothing.

JOE: I've got family. I've got blood kin all over this end of Georgia.

MABEL: It's blood and it's blood. Tell you a little story, son, I think you need to hear. Up in Jeff Davis County, just about where I was born and raised, a woman's husband was killed. She weren't nothing but a young thing too, young and seven months pregnant to boot. She was the only one seen the killing, seen it and knowed who done it. Sheriff come out there to the place and tried to git her to name the man that done the killing. She didn't want nothing to do with the sheriff. Know the only thing she ever told him?

JOE: No, Ma, I don't.

MABEL: Never done nothing but point to her pregnant belly and said: "He knows who done it, and when the time comes, he'll settle it." That's what she told the sheriff. You got blood like that? You got blood like that right today?

JOE: I don't guess I do.

MABEL: You don't guess? Guess? Think? You better stop guessing and thinking and try somethin else. You got to make blood to have blood. Like a lot of folks you think you got what you ain't got.

JOE: What you say is true, but knowing something and being able to do something about it is two different things. The only record I'll leave is the one I leave in print.

MABEL: Then that's purty damn sorry is all I can say. The only record that counts is the one left in blood. I don't even believe it's a right record or a wrong one no more. I once did, or thought I did, but I don't no more. It's just what's left after a life's passed on. Life leaving life. And somebody a lot smarter'n me, and a lot smarter'n you think you are, has got to figger that out. Figger how, out of all that, the world gits made.

JOE: I may not be able to leave a record of blood, but I can leave a record of the blood that was left. For some of us, that's the best we can do.

MABEL: Or the worst. You mean to do it?

JOE: Yes.

MABEL: I thought you might. It's been talk. You ain't exactly been quiet about it.

JOE: You mind?

MABEL: Mind what?

JOE: What I'm doing.

MABEL: Would it matter?

JOE: Maybe. Maybe it would.

MABEL: You mean it wouldn't matter. That's what *maybe* means, and that's what I thought. Just git it right.

JOE: I'll try.

MABEL: I known you'd try. I didn't say *try*. I said git it right. You man enough to do that?

JOE: I don't know . . .

Enter Pete, hungover.
PETE: Mornin, mornin.
MABEL: Did you git you nap out, Pete?
PETE: We stayed up late, Mabel. Talked 'til real late.
MABEL: Hep me out of this chair, Joe. Anythin that upsets me more than a young
    drunk, it's a old drunk.
PETE: We didn't have but a taste. For God's sake I hope you don't git Ethel started
    this morning, Mabel.
Mabel struggles out of the chair with Joe helping her.
MABEL: Hope in one hand and shit in the other. See which one fills up first.
Mabel exits.
PETE: Now she's probly gone go in there an git Ethel started too.
JOE: I'd count on it if I was you.
PETE: I caint stand none of that this morning.
JOE: You don't have a choice. And everything gets easy when there's no alternative.
Enter George and his boys.
GEORGE: These boys beat me. Beat me bad. But a man don't mind bein beat by
    his own sons.
BUSTER: I can pitch them shoes.
GEORGE JUNIOR: Buster, you know you caint pitch no shoes with me. I beat
    you ever time. You might as well go on and say it, I beat you ever time.
BUSTER: George Junior, you ain't got sense enough to come in outten the rain.
    And God given a billy goat sense enough to come in outten the rain.
GEORGE: Hush about rain, Buster. (*Looking up to check the sun and sky.*) This
    weather ain't gone hold. It's gone start rainin before long and it ain't gone quit.
    We oughta be home in the field with them corn pickers. Rain gits the jump on
    us, it's gone hurt us bad. But by damn I meant to do this out the way we always
    done. Have a big meal in there in a while for Mother, talk some this afternoon,
    and git a early start in the morning. But I can feel rain in this heat, it's coming
    and that damn corn still in the field.
PETE: (*Rubbing his hip.*) Might. I don't feel real good in my bones this morning.
GEORGE JUNIOR: Don't think twice on it, Daddy. That corn ain't goin
    nowhere but in the silo. You ain't even got to think twice on it.
BUSTER: (*Cuffing George Junior on the shoulder.*) Damn if you don't manage to
    say something right now and then, old son, even if you ain't got good sense. We
    going home, Daddy, and whip that corn, whip it like a baby.
PETE: I'd say you got all the help you need, George.
GEORGE: (*With great and serious pride.*) Even if they are my sons, these boys is
    workin fools. It ain't another man in the county that can work'm down.
GEORGE JUNIOR: It is one man that can put us in the shade.
Putting his hand on his father's shoulder and looking at him fondly.

And he's done it more'n oncet.

GEORGE: It was a time when I could do it, son. But that time's gone forever. (*Looking from Pete to Joe.*) It's been more'n one time I raised my head up from the pillow and looked out the winder in the middle of the night and seen these boys—the lights on on the tractors—plowing right on through the night, plowin like it was the end of the world. Damn boys can do some work. It ain't no quit in'm.

GEORGE JUNIOR: I reckon we know where we got that.

BUSTER: Cept you the runt of the litter. I got most of it.

GEORGE JUNIOR: (*Raising his closed fist to Buster.*) You don't be still, I'm gone let you smell you daddy's fist.

Enter Gaye Nell.

GAYE NELL: You boys git on in here and git washed up. It's gone be on the table before you can say turkey-in-the-straw.

GEORGE JUNIOR: Turkey-in-the-straw, les eat. Har, har, har.

BUSTER: Whailin the daylights outa George Jr. at horseshoes all mornin's made me so hongry I got a sick headache.

GEORGE: You make any of that good banana puddin?

GAYE NELL: Now you know I did, George, honey.

GEORGE: Dog'd if I don't believe I could live on that banana puddin of yorn.

GAYE NELL: Honey, you say the sweetest things about my puddin.

Gaye Nell exits with George and the boys follow.

JOE: I'm damn glad it's his and not mine.

PETE: What?

JOE: Gaye Nell's banana pudding. I think one night of eating her pudding would cure my hunger forever. Like coal mining, eating Gaye Nell's pudding must be dark and lonely work.

PETE: Sometimes I wonder about you, boy.

JOE: I am not a kind man. But whatever. I need another drink.

PETE: I'd ruther you didn't. I wish you'd try to think about what I was trying to tell you last night.

JOE: (*Draining the last of the glass.*) Oh, that. That's all I did think about. You don't have to worry about a thing.

PETE: (*Starts to get out of his chair.*) Well, praise the Lord.

JOE: I don't think we can put it on the Lord. I had a dream about a blood issue last night.

PETE: (*Sitting back in his chair.*) A blood issue?

JOE: Dreamed about the baby. My dead brother.

PETE: DAMN! (*Then quieter, more reflective.*) Well, dreams don't mean nothing.

JOE: Probably not. But it won't leave me alone. And if it won't leave me alone, I can't leave it alone.

PETE: How much of that you had?

JOE: Not nearly enough, I suspect.

PETE: What is it you want? Just tell me that, what is it?

JOE: Find that baby.

PETE: You caint do this, Joe.

JOE: Get him a slab and a headstone. Then I'll go from there.

PETE: (*Despairing.*) Do and be damn then. (*Starts to get out of his chair.*) I ain't gone listen to this.

JOE: I mean to cut his name on it. I mean to do it.

PETE: (*Slumps back into his chair.*) He ain't got no name. Nobody knows what his name is.

JOE: I'd think Ma could help me out on that.

Blackout.

ACT II

Scene 1

Living room, same as first scene. Later the same morning. Pots and pans of various sizes are on the stove in the kitchen. Cakes and pies with portions cut out of them, and a mounded plate of biscuits, and a whole uncut turkey, etc., still sit on the serving counter by the stove. Maybe through an open door leading off the kitchen the ruined remains of a meal rest on a long dining table.

Mabel is sitting in a rocker draining her mouth from time to time into a spit cup. Joe and George are sitting where they were when the play opened. George Jr. is standing in front of the shelf of knickknacks, looking, picking up first a picture, then a ceramic animal, turning it in his hands, examining it. Buster is in a ladder back chair. Ethel is making noises at the sink in the kitchen. Gaye Nell is moving about the room with a pot, topping off everybody's coffee cup. Only Joe is drinking from what appears to be a glass of iced tea.

MABEL: Ethel, leave all that alone and come on in here and set down.

ETHEL: I ain't giving it nothing but a lick and a promise. I'm so full I don't believe I could set down no how.

GAYE NELL: I'm gone hep you Ethel. Just let me finish pourin this coffee. That was a mighty fine meal if I do say so myself.

MABEL: Them dumplins was lumpy. They could a used rolling a time or two.

GAYE NELL: Now you old darlin, I rolled them things till I was plumb give out.

GEORGE: Dumplins ain't Gaye Nell's best point, but godamighty she's got some banana puddin, believe she could make that stuff with her eyes closed and both arms broke.

GAYE NELL: You say just the sweetest things, George Honey. You want you another little taste of my puddin.

GEORGE: I got to watch this weight of mine. But I do believe I could stand me another small heppin.

GAYE NELL: Joe, you sure I couldn't pour you a cup of this good Maxwell House?

JOE: Thanks, no. This tea is fine.

GAYE NELL: You join you brother in a little of my puddin?

JOE: I don't think so. There was enough food on that table today for a platoon of North Vietnamese to march on for a month.

Gaye Nell goes to get the pudding and brings it back over the following exchange.

GEORGE: Now how in the hell did you git from banana puddin to Veet Nam?

JOE: I guess all that food just stunned me, George.

GEORGE: Stunned you?

JOE: Stunned me.

GEORGE: You don't reckon it's that tea you drinking that . . .

MABEL: Shut up George. I don't feel like you chirrun gittin on my nerves. Let a old woman set here and rock and dip.

GEORGE: Joe's gone . . .

MABEL: Rock and dip, I said!

Enter Pete, his hair damp and uncombed.

ETHEL: (*Turning to look from the kitchen.*) Well, that didn't take long. I thought you was probly lost to the world for the rest of the afternoon.

PETE: Even a short soak restores my juices.

MABEL: I wish to God you wouldn't talk about juices. Besides, you like me, you ain't got no juices left.

PETE: Ethel, tell'er if I got any juices left or just whut.

ETHEL: You ole thing, you hush about them juices.

PETE: Juices or not, I'm here to tell you, I'm one stuffed youngun.

BUSTER: We didn't even touch that second turkey.

GEORGE JUNIOR: (*Turning from the shelf.*) The one we did touch weren't hurt bad. I've seen turkeys hurt worse than the one we cut git up and run off.

PETE: But we done a job on that ham.

GEORGE: (*Finishing the pudding Gaye Nell's given him.*) Only thing better'n Gaye Nell's honey-glazed ham is her banana puddin.

JOE: Leave it alone, George. I've heard about enough on the subject of pudding.

GEORGE: How would you know what's enough? You didn't even touch it.

JOE: You've already said it was good. I believe you, George. Now let it rest a while.

MABEL: You chirrun don't git on my nerves.

GEORGE JUNIOR: (*Taking the black ceramic panther off the shelf.*) This shore is a purty thing. I member wantin to play with it when I was just a youngun.

MABEL: You still ain't nothin but a youngun.

GEORGE: Put that back 'fore you break it.

GEORGE JUNIOR: I bet this right here is oldern me.

JOE: I know it's older than you are, son, because I wanted to play with it when I could only crawl myself.

MABEL: I'd a let you, you'd a broke it. Bring it over here to me, George Jr.

George Jr. brings her the panther, and she holds it in her lap.

BUSTER: How long you had that thing, Grandmother?

MABEL: Forever.

BUSTER: Shoot, even I know it ain't no forever.

MABEL: You right, Buster, it ain't no forever. Just seems that way. I weren't nothing but a yearling girl when I got this. (*She looks fiercely about the room.*) And hard as it is for some I know to believe, I oncet *was* a yearling girl.

GEORGE JUNIOR: We got proof of that right here. (*He takes a framed picture off the shelf.*)

MABEL: (*Turning to look at him.*) Put that back.

JOE: Let me hold that son. It's all right, Ma, I'm not going to drop it.

MABEL: Did I say you was gone drop it? (*She's stroking the ceramic panther in her lap as though it were a kitten.*) Look at it if you want to.

George Junior brings the picture to Joe and stands looking over his shoulder at it.

GEORGE JUNIOR: My goodness, would you look at that!

MABEL: It's so faded now you caint hardly see it.

JOE: It's not faded bad, ma.

MABEL: Probly just my eyes. Old age ain't but one humiliatin thing after another.

Buster comes over to look.

BUSTER: Where is that you was settin?

MABEL: I was settin in a pea patch. It was of a Sunday and I was in my finest dress and my best bonnet. I wisht you coulda seen it when it was new. I wisht you coulda seen me when *I* was new.

GAYE NELL: (*From the kitchen where she has gone to help Ethel.*) Now you honey, you still a glory and a wonder.

MABEL: (*Stroking the panther faster, almost furiously.*) I'm a old woman that caint even see her own picture when she was a yearling girl no more.

GEORGE JUNIOR: Whereabouts did you get that painther?

MABEL: (*Stops stroking panther, stares at it in her lap as though surprised to find it there.*) You granddaddy won it for me at the fair. Frank and Lonny'd just come back up here from working that job down in Florida (*Starting to stroke the panther again.*) Been down there nearly three year. (*Looks down at panther, strokes faster, staring.*) And it was hard, dirty work, masquiters, alligators, mud . . .

JOE: And Indians. Don't forget the Indians. Seminoles.

MABEL: (*Not looking up, not stroking the panther now either, gripping it instead.*) It's where they live, them Seminoles, down there in the Everglades swamp. But they didn't have no trouble with them. They was tame indians, even back then.

JOE: (*Shortly, coming right under her last line.*) Real tame is the way I hear it.

PETE: (*Struggling up from his chair, and crossing to Joe.*) Let me get you some more tea, Joe.

Takes glass and as he's about to turn toward the kitchen, raises the glass just a bit above his belt line and his nose wrinkles, sniffing. Looks back at Joe.

But maybe you had enough . . . of tea. This coffee's mighty fine. How about it, son?

JOE: Sure, coffee's o.k.

GAYE NELL: (*From kitchen.*) Me'n Ethel's just finishing here. We gone have a cup. I'll bring the pot.

Ethel and Gaye Nell come into the living room. Gaye Nell pours coffee.

(*To Mabel.*) Could I git you something? Some coffee? Co Coler?

MABEL: (*As though she had not heard the question, causing Gaye Nell to put the pot down and take a seat. Everyone is looking at her now, the matriarch holding court.*) My, my, they was both dandies when they come back here to the county, Frank and Lonny both. Frank had bought him a Model T Ford automobile and they had both bought them a white suit a piece. And when you seen one, you seen'm both, like brothers they was. Fine young men, both of 'm, showin off as young men's subject to do.

GEORGE JUNIOR: How old was you here in this pea patch, Grandmother?

MABEL: Sixteen year old. Just turned too, the month of May, nineteen and twenty-eight. Them peas was just up good, greenest things you ever seen. The whole world was green in that May of nineteen and twenty-eight.

BUSTER: I wish I could run up on a girl like you was then, purty and ripe as a mushmelon.

GEORGE: Watch your mouth, boy. That's you grandmother in that picture.

MABEL: George, I sometimes think you older'n me. The sap's beginning to rise in Buster. It's the natural way of a young man to recanize a ripe mushmelon when he sees one. And I'm here to tell you I was naturally ripe in the spring of nineteen and twenty-eight. Had everthin that was comin to me, my eyes, my hearing, and my teeth. An young men ain't the only ones the sap begins to rise in either. Am I right or am I wrong, Gaye Nell?

GAYE NELL: I wouldn't know a thing about that I don't believe.

GEORGE: You embarrassing her, Mother.

MABEL: More's the pity, too.

PETE: (*Something between a shout and a laugh, a kind of yip.*) And you talk to me while ago about not havin no juices left. It ain't what it sounds like to me.

ETHEL: I believe we can do without that, Pete.

PETE: Don't try to ruin my fun, Ethel. God knows, it's little enough fun in this ole world the way it is.

MABEL: Not for Frank and Lonny it weren't. It was fun everwhere they went. They didn't have to find no fun, they cared it with'm. From the minute they got back to the county they was bad to lie out with dry cattle.

GEORGE JUNIOR: Dry cattle?

JOE: Son, working with you daddy as you do, and him the anxious teacher he is, I thought you'd know cows don't give milk until they have a calf.

GEORGE JUNIOR: Yeah, but . . .

MABEL: Dry cattle's what they called maiden girls in that day and time.

GAYE NELL: Certainly not a flattering way to put it.

JOE: It was not a flattering time.

GEORGE JUNIOR: I still don't git it.

GEORGE: Try not to act afflicted, George Jr.

JOE: You got to have a talk with that boy, George.

GEORGE: (*To Pete.*) I think I can take care of my own fambly, thank you very much. (*Then to Mabel.*) What's got into you, Mother?

MABEL: Like Joe said to me just this morning, I hear the ticking of the clock.

GEORGE: Well, I don't know what that's supposed to mean, but it's just like Joe to say something to upset you. (*To Joe.*) Do you have to upset Mother ever time you come home?

MABEL: I ain't upset. Did you hear me say I was upset, Pete?

PETE: (*Laughing.*) No, but then I coulda missed it. I still got them juices on my mind.

ETHEL: Yore mind stays on juices.

MABEL: For yore sake, Ethel, I hope so, but somehow, I misdoubt it. But, anyhow, as I was saying, they come back from that swamp and quicker'n you could say it, they known ever purty young girl in the county.

PETE: I member it well.

ETHEL: Shut up, Pete.

JOE: And so you got to know'm too.

MABEL: One of the first to know'm. They had that Model T Ford automobile and a pocket full of money. And everbody in the county thought the world of them, including Daddy, so when the fair come through he let'm take me. (*Stroking the panther again.*) You daddy won this painther with a baseball.

PETE: Frank was a rock-throwing fool. He could slap throw a rock. Anything close as twenty yards to'm, if he could see it, he could hit it.

MABEL: Thrown a ball is what he done. Hit a board and dropped a nigger in a barrel of water. That nigger'd been dry all day til you daddy showed up.

BUSTER: And you got the painther for wettin a nigger?

MABEL: That was the prize.

GAYE NELL: I thought Lonny won that painther.

MABEL: What?·

GAYE NELL: Seems to me like I member him sayin that. Back when me'n George was courtin, Christmas time it was, and Lonny—Lord rest his soul—had him a drink or two, and he said that painther . . .

MABEL: Gaye Nell, you caint even member to roll dumpins.

GEORGE: Now, Mother, Gaye Nell only meant . . .

MABEL: I know what she meant. Thinks my mind is going bad is what she thinks. Well, I'm here to tell you my mind is good, good today as it was the day I was born.

GAYE NELL: I didn't mean nothing, you old honey. It just seems like to me he said . . .

GEORGE: You said he'd had him a drink or two. A man drinkin ain't thinkin. (*Next four lines delivered very rapidly.*)

GEORGE JUNIOR: Daddy, you a poet and don't know it. (*Laughs.*)

BUSTER: An two big feet to show it. (*Laughs.*)

GEORGE JUNIOR: They longfellers. (*Laughs.*)

GEORGE: You boys shut up an try not to act afflicted.

JOE: I thought that was clever, George. You've raised two clever boys.

GEORGE: You'd think a dead hog was clever.

JOE: That's clever too. You're a clever man with two clever sons.

GEORGE JUNIOR: You gone have to put us in one of them books of yourn.

JOE: I might do that.

GEORGE: You do and you know what'll happen.

JOE: What'll happen, George?

GEORGE: You know.

MABEL: George, for God's sake!

GEORGE: Go ahead on, take his part.

MABEL: I ain't taking nobody's part. I'm trying to rock and dip.

JOE: It's all right, Ma. I don't mind. I'm used to George trying to keep me decent and on the right track.

GEORGE: I ain't said nothin about that. But what I ain't never been able to understand is why you let our mother see that stuff . . .

JOE: I think we been over this before, Pooter. It's her business to read what she wants to read. If you've got a problem with that, she's right there in front of you, straighten her out.

ETHEL: I think what we all oughta do is have another taste of Gaye Nell's puddin and talk about something pleasant.

MABEL: I ain't innerested in puddin and pleasant. George is gone straighten me out.

GEORGE: I'm sorry I even mentioned them damn books. The last thing in the world I wanted to do was ruin you day, Mother. And them books of Joe's would ruin the best day God ever made.

JOE: You know just how to rescue a day, George.

A BEAT of strained silence before Pete bounces out of his chair in false heartiness and good cheer and goes to the shelves of knickknacks and takes down a picture.

PETE: *This* weren't a bad day. (*Picking up a photo from the shelves.*) Now this over here was a great day, too, a day that brought us to the day we celebratin. Good Lord, how would've it all a been if Lonny hadn't brought Frank to see you?

JOE: Lonny brought Daddy?

PETE: Frank was sweet on you mamma. Hell, whole county known it. But that boy was shy as the day is long.

JOE: Shy, you say.

PETE: Backward is what the boy was when it come to young girls. Stayin down in that swamp so long I reckon. And right here in this picture is the day Lonny hog-tied'm and brought him to see you mama.

MABEL: Bashful and shy, he was, but sweet too. Sweetest man I ever known. Ittas me that put Lonny up to gettin him to come. Ittas me that wanted it.

PETE: Musta been him too, or he wouldn't a come. He was a man that known his mind.

MABEL: I reckon. We tuck to each other right off.

PETE: Damn good thing I'd say, or George and his boys and Joe wouldn't be setting here right now, nor Gaye Nell neither. Funny, life is. Life and the passin of it. Seems like yesterday, don't it?

MABEL: Not to me it don't. Seems like somethin that happened to somebody else.

PETE: I'm gone git you spirits back up if it kills me.

MABEL: It ain't gone kill you. And I ain't got no spirits left.

GEORGE: Joe's got enough spirits for all of us.

JOE: That's more than clever, George. That's gone all the way to cute.

Buster and George Junior have come to stand behind Mabel's chair to look over her shoulder at the picture.

GEORGE JUNIOR: You caint hardly tell'm apart.

BUSTER: It's them white suits. Wish I had me a suit like them they wearin.

MABEL: (*Just now really looking at the picture.*) They was proud as peacocks.

GEORGE JUNIOR: Man had him a suit like that he'd naturally be proud.

MABEL: They was proud of everythin they had. It was their nature to be proud.

JOE: Of you too?

MABEL: What?

JOE: They were proud of you too, I guess.

MABEL: They was young bucks with the sap rising and I was a yearlin girl. That don't seem hard to figger.

JOE: No, that's not hard to figure.

MABEL: Frank and Lonny was close as brothers. (*She looks from George to Joe.*) Closer than if they was blood kin. And it was a good thing for me they was. (*Glances again from George to Joe.*) Good thing for you boys, too. They known how to have fun if they didn't know nothing else.

PETE: But what started off as fun didn't always end up that way. Damn boys could cause a ruckus in the county. It was a young buck name of Fletchum that made the best corn whiskey in the county. One day after we got done plowing, Lonny and Frank and me walked back there to Fletchum's still to git us a taste and what we done was played a little joke on him. Lonny took the sign of Tweek Fletchum's shotgun to the grave, marked like a speckled puppy. They coulda got killed together. Hell, I coulda got killed too and it weren't even my idea.

GEORGE: Them was killin times in them days. It was many a fool set right with a double-barreled shotgun. Set right in his burial shroud and put in the ground.

JOE: So many to kill and so little time, right George?

GEORGE: I don't know as I was talkin to you.

BUSTER: Dog I wish I could have lived back in that day and time.

PETE: No you don't son. You just think you do.

GEORGE JUNIOR: Buster's right. He do somehow manage to be right now and then. It ain't much such as that goin on these days.

ETHEL: And I say more power to that, praise God. It ain't nothin good about making whiskey.

PETE: Now, Ethel, don't go on talkin about somethin you don't know nothin about. Makin whiskey's like most other things in the world, it's some good and some bad in it.

ETHEL: I don't know how you can set there and say it's anythin good about makin corn whiskey. Don't do a thing but make men leave home and be sorry. Go out and run dogs in the woods all night, howling at the moon their own-selves.

PETE: It was a time when half the county would have starved to death if it hadn't of been for whiskey stills. And it given work to Government men who weren't good for anything else much. A damn Government man was never much better than an egg-sucking dog, and near about as smart too. If they'd of been smarter so damn many of 'em wouldn't of got killed.

ETHEL: You hush up about egg-sucking dogs and men gittin killed. That ain't something you know a thing about.

PETE: Ethel, after bein married now goin on a hundred years to me it's still a lot you don't know. I shot at my share of Govament men in my time, missed some and hit some.

BUSTER: Uncle Pete, you didn't really shoot no Government man, did you?

PETE: Well, let's all just pretend I didn't so Ethel won't fall into a fit.

ETHEL: I ain't gonna even remark on that. Say what you want to, I'll not remark on that.

MABEL: Well, that's a blessing anyhow. The fewer remarks I have to suffer this morning the better off I think I'll be. I know how it was in that time. I didn't live through it for nothin.

JOE: I always thought Ma'd forgot more then the rest of us all put together ever knew. She's been around a few blocks in her time. Whatever can come down she's seen come down.

GEORGE: Try to make sense, Joe. Come down? Come down from where? It ain't nothin ever come down on our mother that I didn't know about and if it has then by God I'd like to know about it right now.

JOE: I'd explain it to you, George, but it's already Monday and I got to probably go back to Florida at least by Friday so I don't see there's time to do it.

GEORGE: Did you hear that, Mother? Now is it any wonder to you how come I stay so put out with him? Sometimes, Joe, you make me so mad I caint see straight.

JOE: Well, now that you bring it up, I've wondered more than once just how straight you see anyhow.

MABEL: I despair you boys ever growing into men. You daddy would've lived you might of ended up with more backbone.

GEORGE: (*Staring at Joe.*) Ain't a damn thing wrong with my backbone. I earn my bread by the sweat of my brow like the Good Book says.

JOE: Is that what the Good Book says, George? Read it a lot do you?

GEORGE: Keep the Good Book out of you mouth. It ain't a fittin subject for such as you.

BUSTER: (*Goes over to stand behind his father's chair and puts his hand on his shoulder.*) Now rest easy, Daddy, he didn't mean nothin. Did you, Uncle Joe?

GEORGE: He don't never mean nothin except to get me fit to be tied.

GEORGE JUNIOR: Uncle Joe, I love you, but I think me and Buster'd be obliged if you'd try to watch how you speak. That's our daddy you talkin to.

JOE: I didn't mean anything by it. Me and George go back a long long way, you know. We were once boys ourselves.

MABEL: You'd never know it to hear the two of you talk these days.

PETE: Ah, Mabel, that's just brothers for you. Brothers is always at each other like that.

MABEL: That may be, but I'm about tired of listening to it.

GEORGE: Well I know one thing, we don't have to set here in this living room and go to tellin stories on each other. Daddy and Dad Lonny might of made a little whiskey in their time but I don't see why we have to tell it on'm.

MABEL: Weren't nothin wrong with moonshinin. I stirred many a barrel myself.

GEORGE: I ain't never heard you say such a thing!

MABEL: It's a lot you ain't heard. The night you daddy was bared, somebody went in the smokehouse and stole all the meat that was hung and curin in there. It was nine middlings of meat hangin, and sausage in boxes, and headcheese in muslin cloth and somebody taken it all, everythin but one little piece of side meat bout big as my hand hangin in the back. I know who done it an I could call his name, but he's lying hisself today in the same graveyard you daddy's in and no good can come of naming him. It was a hard time in the county and a lot of men done things they was ashamed of and suffered for the rest of their lives.

GEORGE: I ain't never seen the day I'd steal nothin.

MABEL: That's right. You ain't never seen the day. Cotton that year was selling for three cent a pound and you could buy a quarter of beef for four cent a pound. The rest of the country was just startin to feel the real hurt of the Great Depression, but it had been livin here in the county for years. Some folks said it's always been here. I seen the day you daddy'd git up before daylight and walk five miles and plow another man's land all day and come back after dark with fifty cent in his hand. Then plow his own crop by the light of the moon. No, George, you ain't seen the day.

GAYE NELL: (*Defensive, defending George.*) George is honest as the day is long. He knows right from wrong.

MABEL: Right and wrong, right *from* wrong? Right from wrong when everthing in your house has gone wild? Right from wrong when you children's starvin and you own stomach's growing to you backbone? Right from wrong when one of the old folks starts to laugh and ends up strangling on their own blood?

ETHEL: Myself, I believe we ought to stop this kind of talk. I think we ought to look on the bright side.

MABEL: (*Musing voice.*) For me, Ethel, this is the bright side. Today I'm lookin on the only side I know.

BUSTER: But you ain't never stirred no mash have you, Grandmother?

GAYE NELL: Of course this old honey ain't done no such thing, Buster.

MABEL: Me and Lonny kept the younguns alive makin whiskey. Thank God Lonny was there to step in and be a daddy to you boys when Frank died. A woman with two chirrun and no man was lost and dead in that day and time.

PETE: (*Trying to lighten the talk.*) Well, I've drunk some and I've made some, and I'd a lot ruther drink it than make it.

ETHEL: I don't even want to hear you talk about drinkin.

MABEL: It's people today think it was easy work, makin whiskey, but it weren't nothin easy about it.

PETE: And I never known nobody who made it that thought it was anythin wrong with doing it.

MABEL: It was somethin to work at when it was no other work to be had.

GAYE NELL: I still wouldn't think that'd make it right.

MABEL: Here in my old age I've got some tired of hearing about right.

GEORGE: I know what I'm gone do. I'm gone go out there in the backyard and shoot a game of shoes. Come on, boys.

GAYE NELL: I'll come out there with you. I ain't cared for any of this talk one bit.

MABEL: Set back down, George. You ain't gone shoot no shoes. This ain't finished yet. Is it Joe?

GEORGE: I ain't got to set here and listen to him run his mouth and make a fool out of hisself.

MABEL: I said set down. You may be a grown man with chirrun of your own but you ain't got so old you won't set down when I tell you to.

GEORGE: Mother, I didn't mean nothing like that. Course I'll set here if you want me to.

MABEL: Then set.

ETHEL: Well, I ain't your son or your daughter neither and I know what I'm gone do. I'm gone go lie down on the bed. I have taken me a sick headache with all this. I'm gone go on back there and take me two BC headache powders and put a damp rag over my eyes.

PETE: Then I guess it ain't no use in me going on back there with you then is it?

ETHEL: (*She stands and pauses to look at him a beat.*) Ever time I think you caint say nothin no sorrier, you go right ahead on and do it anyway.

Ethel exits to rear of the house.

MABEL: (*Looking at Joe.*) Well, get on with it, son. Speak you mind.

JOE: What am I supposed to get on with, Ma? Maybe you know something I don't know.

MABEL: You got somethin on you mind you want to finish. You been wantin to finish it since you got here.

JOE: All right then, I guess what I was thinkin is that you sound like you and Lonny and Daddy were close.

MABEL: We was real close.

PETE: (*Nervously, half getting out of his chair.*) You want another cup of coffee, Joe?

JOE: (*Ignoring him.*) All three of you then, real close.

GEORGE: Just what in the hell you gittin at, Joe?

GEORGE JUNIOR: Just be easy, Daddy.

MABEL: Yeah, I meant all three of us. Close as three people could git. Lonny and Frank and me. Lonny stood up for Frank at the weddin. It was Lonny led the shiveree that night. Frank and me in a big feather bed cause it was so cold out the ground was froze. And Lonny was out there howlin and laughin and ringin a cowbell, him and the other young men of the county, bangin on pots and singin and drinkin and me and Frank like two children in that big feather bed gigglin and cuttin the fool. But some time after midnight it quieted down except for the fiddles. (*Her voice has gone dreamy.*) Them fiddles sweet as angels. Then after some long time—or maybe it weren't so long—it's hard to know when Lonny started singin, his voice comin right in with the fiddles, so pretty and so soft it was in the fiddles before you ever known he'd commenced to sing. When Lonny was a young man he could sing the birds right out of the trees. A voice that went right into you bones and stayed there til you whole body was quick with it. (*Catching herself up, almost as if being startled from sleep.*) That big fool! It was him that put everbody up to setting Frank's wagon on top of the house.

Laughter that is a little forced from having to turn from the beauty of Lonny's voice.

Frank come out of the house next mornin and there was his wagon straddlin the house with the shaves tied to the chimney, but Lonny showed up just like magic and we all eat the first breakfast I cooked as a wife, laughin and jokin, them pokin fun at my biscuits, and then Lonny helped Frank get his wagon down. Them two!

JOE: I find that strange. Strange and unusual.

MABEL: (*Feisty.*) You think it's strange, do you?

JOE: Marriages usually push men apart, not bring them closer.

MABEL: How would you know?

JOE: I lost more friends to marriage than any other way. You see less and less of them until sometimes you don't see them at all. It's even struck me that the closer a man is to one of his friends, the more the wife seems to dislike him.

GEORGE: Joe, I think it's about time you shut you mouth about this.

JOE: (*Ignoring him.*) Well, you got even closer than that finally, didn't you?

GEORGE: I'm not gone tell you agin.

MABEL: (*Ignoring him.*) I can only thank God for it. I was without a man. I had a need and Lonny seen the need. It was Lonny went for Miss Emily Johnson, the midwife at you birthing.

JOE: Did he go for her when my brother came?

PETE: (*Comes out of his chair, almost upsetting the saucer he's holding. Too loud, too urgent.*) I got to have me some more of this good coffee! Joe, let me have you cup son! You can drink another cup!

Neither Mabel or Joe have looked at Pete. Their eyes are locked, balanced in an unblinking gaze.

MABEL: (*Calmly.*) He went for George's birthin too.

JOE: Not George. My other brother. The first born.

MABEL: (*Interrupting him but in a calm, deliberate voice.*) No, when he was born, it was Frank went. Baby didn't have no chance. I never looked at it but once. The birthin blood wasn't even cleaned off.

JOE: And he was dead?

MABEL: No, not dead.

JOE: I thought he was born dead.

GEORGE: You gonna have me to fight, damn you!

BUSTER: Easy, Daddy.

MABEL: (*Ignoring Buster.*) He . . . I held him. I just held . . . it weren't no more than minutes til . . . I held'm til he was dead. I weren't no more than a yearlin girl myself . . . it looked liked . . . It was like lookin at my own death. Frank, he . . . Frank was there.

PETE: Mabel, don't.

MABEL: Miss Emily Johnson, she tried to take it from me. She never wanted me to see. But I held it till it died lyin right agin me . . . and the birthin blood . . . its liver . . . the baby's . . . its little liver was on the outside . . . blue . . . but it never cried . . . once.

GEORGE: Oh my God, Ma. Oh my God, please . . .

MABEL: (*Interrupting.*) Frank dent leave the house for . . . even to see it put in the ground. He never cried but . . . Lonny set with'm . . . and then he went and bared that baby. It was Lonny bared that baby . . . and bared Frank. And I got the slab . . . and I . . . we, Lonny and me . . . got the headstone.

JOE: I know you did, Ma.

MABEL: Pete?

PETE: What is it, Mabel?

MABEL: Take this painther and put it back.

Pete gets up and takes the panther and puts it back on the shelf.

Now hep me outen this chair. I'm tired.

Pete goes to her and helps her onto her walking cane. She walks to the door, looks back one brief time at Joe, and EXITS to the rear of the house. Pete turns to look at Joe. George has been sitting on the couch, his sons on either side of him standing with a hand on each of his shoulders. George's face is very red, his teeth are bared, the veins are standing in his neck. With an anguished cry, a sound that might have come from an animal, he lunges from the couch and onto Joe taking him by the neck and screaming something unintelligible as he attempts to strangle him. George Junior and Buster manage to drag their father away from Joe.

GEORGE JUNIOR: Daddy, don't . . .

BUSTER: Get'm off . . .

GEORGE: You a low life, self-made, son-of-a-bitch, Joe Bass.

Fade to black.

ACT II

Scene 2

Living room, in the middle of that night. With the house dark, a blues guitar comes on, a grieving, string-bending, Mississippi John Hurt kind of blues, and then a voice, the voice of Mabel Bass, old but still high and pure and sweet, singing the gospel song WAS YOU THERE WHEN THEY CRUCIFIED MY LORD, which—at least in the version I know—is a lament, a moaning lament.

MABEL: (*Singing.*) Was you there when they crucified my Lord / was you there when they crucified my Lord/ oh Lord/ it set the world a tremble, tremble, tremble / was you there when they crucified my Lord.

A small lamp comes on at a table by the shelf of knick knacks and pictures, lighting the stage dimly, showing Mabel in a long white nightgown. She takes her hand from the switch of the lamp and lifts it to let it rest on the black panther. Over all of this she has continued to sing.

Was you there when they spierced him in the side
was you there when they spierced him in the side
oh Lord

it set the world a tremble, tremble, tremble
was you there when they spierced him in the side.
Her voice finally fades to silence on the chorus, but the grieving blues guitar continues for maybe a minute and then it too fades and dies.

God, Frank with that guitar and Lonny singing. All gone now. Gone forever. Well, we made it the best we could. The only way we known how to make it. Let them that's settin down marks agin us or settin down marks for us, set'm down. We had what we had. (*She strokes the panther.*) Lonny bout busted his britches when he won this painther. And Frank too, proud as if he'd a won it hisself. By rights he should a won it. By rights he should a . . . should a . . . by rights. (*Her voice has been soft, gentle but now even more gently.*) By rights. (*More harshly.*) To hell with rights! Rights ain't never fed me and rights ain't never kept me warm.

She moves away from the panther and picks up a picture farther down the shelf. Gentle laughter.

First house we ever called ourn. No queen ever thought her palace was purtier. And Frank and Lonny built it with nothin but gut and grunt.

A recliner that has been sitting with its back to her and to the audience moves almost imperceptibly, so tiny a movement at first that any of the audience that has seen it wonders did it really move. During what follows, though, the recliner moves again, swiveling, coming slowly around, until Joe is revealed sitting in the diffused light watching his mother who is facing the shelves. Joe has a drink in his right hand resting on the arm of the recliner. So still does he sit through the entire monologue that he does not seem to be breathing.

MABEL: (*Laughing.*) Oncet it'as finished you could smell the turpintine outen that green pine from a mile away. Godamighty, how many folks in this day and time'd even think two men could take that many trees down with a crosscut saw, much less snake'm out'n the woods with a mule an split 'em with nothin but wedge and mallet? Not many I reckon. (*Pauses.*) Not many coulda or woulda done it. But they both thought I oughten to have a fitten house to have my baby in. That baby. No screens and wooden windows and a shotgun hall. Ten by ten rooms and one special for that baby. That baby. Les see now. What we brung to the marriage, weddin presents. Yes. A fry pan, a iron wash pot, four plates and four knives an forks and one big spoon for dippin, a iron bedstid with slats and cornshuck mattress, four quilts, four sheets. Frank and Lonny built a little cook table and a bigger table to eat offen with a bench on each side instead of chairs, a chest, a drawers, a plank ironin board wrapped in striped bed tickin an two flat irons. Yes. An the proudest thing of all, a Home Comfort, Number 8, wood stove with a hot water reservoir and four eyes on top. God of us all it was gone to be good hot water for that baby. That baby. Mis Emily didn't want me to see it. Didn't want Frank to see it. But I seen it. I held it agin me til it died and Frank held me holdin the baby and him cryin cause it wouldn't cry 'til it died. And Lonny helpless just standin there helpless as everbody else an finally him holdin the three of us with that baby dead amongst us. And Frank would not be comforted. Would not be comforted. Would not believe it was not some taint in his blood. Crying, the sin of my life is in my blood, tainted, all tainted. My poor sweet Frank. My poor sweet Lonny. Oh, Lonny, what can we do for Frank? With Frank. Love him. We can love him. And we did. We did. Love. Oh, God. Oh, my Savior.

She stops, turns her head as if to listen as the grieving, stringbending blues guitar comes up softly again and softly she sings a bit of the gospel the scene opens with and when her voice dies there is silence for a beat.

JOE: (*Softly.*) Ma.

She stands as if she has not heard but we know she has, her worst dream come true.
   Ma?

MABEL: (*Without turning.*)
   Joe?

JOE: I couldn't sleep

MABEL: (*Turning to regard him a beat.*) I didn't mean for you . . .

JOE: I just came out here for a drink. I thought a drink might . . .

MABEL: It don't matter. Sometimes it ain't nothin wrong with a drink a whiskey. Why don't you pour a little some of that for me?

JOE: (*Unbelieving.*) You want a whiskey, ma?

MABEL: (*A little of old feistiness coming back, getting herself together.*) I asked for one didn't I?

JOE: You want anything in . . .

MABEL: Just a little in a water glass'll do me fine.

Joe pours the drink and when Mabel turns it up she drains the glass.
   Always been careful not to drink too much of that, seemed to me I was too fond of it. It do help at times though.

JOE: That was a great story about Lonny and Daddy building you that house for the baby.

MABEL: For the baby. Yes, that baby. But that ain't why they built it.

JOE: But, you . . .

MABEL: They built it cause they loved me.

JOE: I've known that all along.

MABEL: You don't know nothing.

JOE: I've known more than you think I knew. But this is no time of night to talk about it. Go try to get some sleep.

MABEL: Sleep's dead for me this night.

JOE: Just close your eyes and try to relax. You'll drift right off.

MABEL: I'm heavy with thoughts. It's no sleep for me.

JOE: Today's just upset you. I didn't mean . . .

MABEL: It ain't today. Today ain't upset nothing.
She turns to regard the shelf of knickknacks and pictures. She waves her hand to include it all.

　All that . . . all that . . . *stuff.*
JOE: A lifetime. A whole lifetime on that shelf.
MABEL: (*Softly.*) Garbage.
JOE: What?
MABEL: (*Enunciating each word slowly, deliberately.*) Leavings. Droppings. Garbage. (*Abruptly.*) *Lies!*
JOE: You don't have to do this, Ma. I know now what I need to know.
(*Mabel goes to the shelf and slowly picks up the panther and turns to face Joe.*)
MABEL: I said lies, goddammit.
JOE: Not anymore, Ma.
MABEL: It's what I said ain't it?
(*She hurls the panther against the wall, shattering it, tiny bits of it spraying Joe, where he does not flinch, but slowly takes a long drink from his glass. In the silence that is heavy and total, they regard the broken panther over the floor, Mabel breathing heavily, her face twisted in what looks like the approach of tears.*)
　Starting with that. I've watched it all these years setting up there. At least now I won't have to see it no more.
Enter Pete wearing a thin cotton robe. The robe is damp, clinging to his thin erect body, his wispy hair wet and hanging.
PETE: What? I heard . . .
He sees the broken panther.
　Who? How did . . .
MABEL: (*Calm now.*) Just cleaning up a few things, Pete. Set down before you give youself a heart attack.
PETE: I was . . . soaking. Couldn't sleep, thought a little soak might . . .
His voice trails off to silence as he drops onto the sofa.
Enter George with a pump shotgun, wearing boxer shorts, his hair tossed, his eyes full of sleep.
JOE: Put the goddamn shotgun down, George.
GEORGE: What's going on out here? I thought I heard somebody breaking in.
MABEL: Not breaking in, George. Just breaking. We breaking a few things.
GEORGE: (*Turning to glower at Joe.*) Joe, damn you, I . . .
MABEL: Me, not him.
GEORGE: What?
PETE: She broken the painther.
GEORGE: Ah, Mother, I'm sorry.
MABEL: You shit, put that gun down like Joe said and set down.
GEORGE: (*Amazed.*) You . . . you *cussed* me.

MABEL: Set down, before I do worse than that.

George sits, the gun across his knees. Enter Ethel, her hair in rollers, her face a mask of cream, and angry.

ETHEL: (*Loudly.*) How am I supposed to sleep with . . .

PETE: She broken the painther.

ETHEL: (*Calmer, confused.*) The painther?

PETE: (*Pointing.*) Right there on the floor, what it is left.

ETHEL: It's the middle of the night. Have you lost you mind, Mabel?

MABEL: I've lost all I'm gone lose.

Enter Buster and George Junior, dressed as their father, in boxer shorts, knuckling the sleep from their eyes.

GEORGE: You boys git on back in there and go to sleep.

MABEL: Set down. Set down and shut up.

They sit.

ETHEL: (*Nervously.*) Me'n Pete's going to bed. It'll be bright and better day tomorrow.

Ethel moves toward the door. Pete does not move on the couch.

MABEL: You leave, Ethel, you'll die curious.

ETHEL: Have you lost you mind, Mabel? Curious? Me curious?

MABEL: Oh, you curious. The whole damn county's been curious forever. Now set down.

GEORGE: Mother, for God's sake, what ails you?

ETHEL: (*Moves again toward the door.*) Come on, Pete.

MABEL: You never could listen, could you Ethel?

Mabel goes to George, surprisingly fast given how infirm she has shown herself to be thus far, and snatches the shotgun from his lap. She expertly jacks a round into the chamber and blows down the shelves of knick knacks.

PETE: Whoa!

GEORGE: Git down!

ETHEL: (*Screaming.*) Don't Jesus! Don't!

Ethel collapses onto Pete where he sits bolt upright on the couch. The silence following the blast is as loud as the shotgun. Nobody seems to be breathing. Joe, who is half in a bag anyway, slowly raises his glass and drinks.

JOE: I believe you got her attention that time, Ma.

MABEL: Why don't you go ahead on and drown yourself in whiskey. Just cause you write books don't mean you got good sense.

JOE: (*Taking another drink.*) Truest thing I heard today.

MABEL: Shut up! I'm talkin and I got the gun.

Mabel jacks another round into the chamber and blows off what's left of the shelves on the wall. Gaye Nell screams from offstage.

You don't hear good.

JOE: I do now, Ma. You've got the floor.

MABEL: And you've got a shitty life.

GAYE NELL: (*From offstage.*) I heard . . . I heard . . .

MABEL: You bound and determine to tear open a wound that's been tryin to heal for bettern forty year . . .

GAYE NELL: (*From offstage.*) My God, guns . . .

MABEL: . . . nothin would do you but to see if it's any blood left to spill.

Enter Gaye Nell, in a long cotton nightgown. Her eyes are wide and wild and she has her hands caught in her hair just above her ears and she is straining as though she means to pull it out. Then she speaks:

GAYE NELL: We gone be kilt everone.

She trips over George's feet, rises, falls over a coffee table but regains her feet, grabbing her two sons by the heads searching through their hair with her hands.

Are you hurt? Is it either of you hurt cause I heard . . .

George reaches out from his place on the couch and drags her down beside him, but she continues thrashing about, trying to get up, resisting him. He finally shakes her hard by the shoulders. Then George speaks:

GEORGE: You hush, woman. Goddammit, it's trouble enough already. Hush now.

GAYE NELL: (*Calmed down some now.*) I thought the whole fambly was being kilt out here and . . . (*Her eyes fall on the shotgunned shelves.*) Oh, sweet Jesus be with me now!

MABEL: I'm with you now, you young heifer. (*Pause.*) And I've got the shotgun in case you ain't noticed. Be still or be sommers else. I ain't got time for you. But I'll tell you what time it is, time to bury the black talk that's been in this county before they bury me. It's time to break and bury.

PETE: Don't, Mabel. Not here in front of you younguns. Please.

MABEL: Here in front of the younguns and God and Ethel. Mainly Ethel. I caint tell the whole county, but I can tell Ethel, and then the whole county'll know.

ETHEL: You've never loved me.

MABEL: You've had a wicked tongue that talked out of a wicked heart. You think I can forgit and forgive just cause you blood?

ETHEL: I never said a thing that everbody else didn't say.

MABEL: And ever bit of it twisted as a goat's guts. And I cared it all these years. Nothing else I could do *but* care it. Now I'm breakin it and droppin it. You can care it from here on and you will. You'll know the truth. Even if you don't tell it. It's something in God's creatures that don't like the truth and I ain't no different, no different from anybody else.

GEORGE: Will somebody please tell me what's goin on?

MABEL: Scandal. I was a scandal in the county.

PETE: Mabel, please.

MABEL: Lonny and me and Frank . . . and the babies.

ETHEL: But it's gone. It's all gone now?

MABEL: It ain't gone. Is it Joe? You been talkin and the people here abouts been talking to you. It ain't gone. Tell'm it ain't gone.

Joe looks into his drink, says nothing, finally raises glass.

PETE: Mabel, this won't do. What brought this on?

MABEL: (*Mabel points to Joe, sitting staring into his now empty glass.*) That brought it on. That drunk who has to come talkin of dead babies.

PETE: You happy with what you've done, goddammit?

JOE: I'm not happy. But that was never the point. The point is that I don't have to eat my liver anymore wondering who the hell I am.

MABEL: (*As though she had not heard him.*) No man is a scoundrel in his own heart. But looking back maybe we was, Lonny and me and Frank. But if we was, it was out of love. We all loved each other. (*Her voice has gone musing, almost as if to herself.*) Can you love right on into something else . . . to evil. Maybe we poisoned the blood of this fambly. But it was what Frank wanted, and I've thought many a time it's what killed him. Or maybe . . . maybe it was thinking he cared the sin in his own blood . . . he had tainted his blood hisself. I don't know. I'll never know.

ETHEL: I caint stand this.

GAYE NELL: (*Her hands pressed to her ears where she has had them during the last few exchanges.*) I ain't hearing this. I caint hear a thing. Not one thing have I heard. And I think we all ought to go back to bed.

Joe has stood up and wandered to the debris on the floor where the shelf of knick-knacks have been shot off the wall. He moves some of it with the toe of his shoe apparently searching for something.

MABEL: It's too late to go back anywhere now. Frank wanted chirrun. He wanted a fambly. In that day and time it was about all a man could hope to have. Then he thought his tainted blood killed that poor baby, deformed it and killed it, and killed the only hope he had of a fambly.

JOE: (*Turning to look at his mother from where he is standing looking through the broken ceramic and splintered glass on the floor.*) Ma, you don't have to say anymore.

MABEL: No, you wanted it said. So I'm here to say it for you. To tell it all. Frank asked me would I?

PETE: Oh, Jesus! Mabel don't, please.

MABEL: He asked me would I with Lonny.

GEORGE: Oh, God damn you, Joe! God damn your soul to hell!

MABEL: And then he asked Lonny. And Lonny said yes he would if that was what Frank wanted. And I said yes too. When Frank died, Lonny taken and married me and raised you boys. Everbody said we married before Frank was cold in the ground. They started talking and never stopped.

GEORGE JUNIOR: They can all go straight to hell.

GEORGE: George Jr. you shut up and . . .

GEORGE JUNIOR: (*Suddenly on his feet, now.*) No sir. I don't think so.

GEORGE: What did you say?

GEORGE JUNIOR: I said I don't think I'll shut up. I got something to say. I'm a grown man and I mean to say it. It ain't no taint in *my* blood and it ain't none in yours. (*He moves to Mabel and takes her thin shoulders in his hands, looking into her eyes.*) I never known Grandfather Frank but I known Grandfather Lonny. If it come to that, I got two grandfathers on my daddy's side. And I got you and I love you. (*He hugs her.*) Anybody says anything about you, Grandmother, they got to come by me to do it. That's everybody outside this room (*Pauses, looks around.*) and everbody inside it too.

MABEL: (*Her back going straighter, eyes brighter, looking at Joe.*) There, that's blood talking. You ain't got nothing to hold on to but a empty glass of whiskey.

Joe bends down, brushes away a little debris and picks up a broken frame with a picture in it.

MABEL: (*Softly, almost frightened.*) What is it you got there, son?

JOE: (*Looking at her, almost smiling, almost happy.*) I thought I'd take this picture of Dad Lonny on home with me when I go.

Joe exits.

MABEL: (*Shattered, maybe even defeated and it shows in her voice.*) I wonder if that painther can be put back together?

GEORGE: (*George goes over and slowly, with seeming great tiredness, picks up part of the panther.*) We'll put back together what we can.

BUSTER: (*Getting out of his chair and going to his father and lightly putting his hand on his father's shoulder.*) Shoot, me and George Jr. will have this thing back together before big daylight. We good at such as this.

MABEL: (*Still in a small voice.*) Maybe I can hep you.

GEORGE JUNIOR: (*Drawing her to him again.*) Shore you can, you darling. You can help us put it back together as good as new.

THE END

Head On

ELIZABETH DEWBERRY

ELIZABETH DEWBERRY grew up in Birmingham, Alabama, and received her doctorate in twentieth-century American Literature from Emory University in 1989. Her novels include *Many Things Have Happened Since He Died* and *Break the Heart of Me*. *Many Things Have Happened Since He Died,* which she adapted for the stage with Tom Key, premiered at the Horizon Theater in Atlanta in 1994.

HEAD ON

was first performed by Actors Theatre of Louisville on March 31, 1995.

CAST

ANNE ....Adale O'Brien
ANNE'S THERAPIST ....Dee Pelletier

Director ....Shirley Jo Finney
Scenic Designer ....Paul Owen
Costume Designer ....Laura Patterson
Lighting Designer ....Brian Scott
Sound Designer ....Martin R. Desjardins
Properties Master ....Mark J. Bissonnette
Dramaturg ....Michael Bigelow Dixon

The green room of the Oprah Winfrey show, ten minutes before taping. The therapist paces anxiously, looking at her watch. Anne enters, in shock, and the therapist runs over to her.

THERAPIST: Oh, thank God you're here. (*Doubletake*) Anne? What are you doing here?

ANNE: I'm sorry I'm late. I saw a wreck.

THERAPIST: But you're not multi-orgasmic.

ANNE: No, I'm fine.

THERAPIST: Oh God.

ANNE: I wasn't *in* the wreck. I just saw it happen. I was so afraid I was going to be late. I've wanted to be on *Oprah Winfrey* forever, it's my most recurrent fantasy, and now here I am.

THERAPIST: *Are* you?

ANNE: What?

THERAPIST: Multi-orgasmic.

ANNE: I don't think so.

THERAPIST: Who told you to come here?

ANNE: Your receptionist. Do I look bad? I brought another outfit if you don't like this one. This all happened so fast I didn't have time to buy anything. If it hadn't been for the wreck . . .

THERAPIST: What did she tell you?

ANNE: You were going on Oprah to talk about your book and the client you had coming on with you canceled and would I go on instead.

THERAPIST: Oh God.

ANNE: What? I know I just started seeing you, but you've already been a big help to me, dealing with Jerry's death. I have a lot to say.

THERAPIST: It has to be somebody who's multi-orgasmic.

ANNE: Jerry had a bad heart.

THERAPIST: Were you ever multi-orgasmic, even by yourself?

ANNE: I never had *one* orgasm. I can't say that on TV. I've never told anybody that before.

THERAPIST: We go on in eight minutes. I can't replace you.

ANNE: It's not my fault. There was a wreck, a head-on collision. But I can do this.

THERAPIST: I know it's not your fault.

ANNE: Two people died. Traffic's still backed up for miles.

THERAPIST: I'm not blaming you. I'm sorry.

ANNE: I'm an official witness, in the police reports. That takes time. Everybody was late to everywhere they were going. Have you ever witnessed a wreck?

THERAPIST: Yes. I have. Can we talk about this later? Right now . . .

ANNE: Of course. I'm sorry.

THERAPIST: I mean, there's nothing we can do about the wreck.

ANNE: Of course not.

THERAPIST: This was such a great opportunity, *Oprah Winfrey*. I could have been a best-seller. I had this client who was perfect, at age fifty-seven after three months of therapy with me she became multi-orgasmic.
ANNE: Why isn't she here?
THERAPIST: She broke her hip.
ANNE: You can break your hip?
THERAPIST: No, she fell in the bathtub.
ANNE: That's too bad.
THERAPIST: It's not the same if you don't have somebody, a real person, to say it works.
ANNE: I'm sorry I haven't read your book, but tell me what to say, and I'll say it. What's the book about?
THERAPIST: Post-menopausal sex.
ANNE: I just wanted to meet Oprah Winfrey. I wanted to talk to her. Sometimes in my imagination I think of her as my daughter—not by Jerry, of course—and I just wanted to shake her hand. I thought maybe after the show we'd hug. Is that asking too much?
THERAPIST: No.
ANNE: I bid on a dress of hers once at a charity auction. Somebody else outbid me, though. I wanted to go twenty dollars higher but Jerry said it's a used dress, we can get you a new one for less than that. Then, of course, we didn't. That's how things went with him.
THERAPIST: And he never brought you to orgasm.
ANNE: Well, I don't know about that.
THERAPIST: Yes you do.
ANNE: I might have had one and forgotten.
THERAPIST: You wouldn't forget.
ANNE: I think sex is overrated anyway. I can't imagine writing a whole book about it. What did you say?
THERAPIST: Have you ever just wanted to ram yourself into something?
ANNE: You know I have. Maybe I could read a chapter real fast. If only that wreck hadn't happened. Look, I'm still trembling.
THERAPIST: You can't read it in six minutes.
ANNE: Right, so tell me. I once heard my mother say it feels like a sneeze between your legs. Should I say that?
THERAPIST: Why don't you focus on the spiritual dimension of sex? Two human beings coming together, each giving their body over to the other, moving out of themselves into the other . . .
ANNE: It sounds like a head-on collision. (*Beat*) I'm sorry. I'm wrong.
THERAPIST: No, you're right. It does.
ANNE: Both drivers died. The debris was so bad the ambulances almost hit each other. (*Beat*) What was the wreck you saw?

THERAPIST: My husband and his girlfriend.

ANNE: Oh.

THERAPIST: He was sitting in the car on a country road waiting for her and she plowed into him at sixty miles an hour.

ANNE: Did they die?

THERAPIST: No, they both had airbags.

ANNE: Those things are amazing. I wish I could go through life wearing airbags in my clothes. I don't think they had airbags this morning. I don't have them, my car doesn't.

THERAPIST: Right after she hit his car she jumped out of hers screaming, "You can't do this to me. I love you. I thought you loved me." Can you imagine?

ANNE: Amazing.

THERAPIST: I can still hear her saying that. I remember thinking that was what I wanted to yell at him, and she'd taken that too.

ANNE: (*Touching the doctor gingerly*) I'm sorry.

Short silence.

THERAPIST: Five minutes. This is awful.

ANNE: Tell me something to say. I wish I'd read the book. I really ought to read more.

THERAPIST: It has exercises you can do with your partner.

ANNE: But Jerry's dead!

THERAPIST: Maybe you could do them with Oprah.

ANNE: Sex exercises?

THERAPIST: No, it's just ways of developing intimacy, touching each other's inner selves.

ANNE: I already know her inner self. I watch her every day. I know every outfit she owns. I wonder if she's ever going to sell any more of her dresses.

THERAPIST: Why do you want one?

ANNE: Because I want to know what it feels like to be her. Maybe I'll never know what it's like to be rich or famous, but I could know what it feels like to step into the dress of a woman who's beautiful, who knows how to talk to people and how to listen to them. I'd zip her zipper up my back and feel her sleeves on my arms and close my eyes and just for a minute, I'd let myself pretend I was not just in her dress, I was in *her* and I'd become her and she'd become me. I want to do that before I die.

Short silence.

I think they died instantly. They would've had to. They were completely smashed together. You couldn't tell one car from the other.

THERAPIST: I would imagine.

ANNE: Jerry took several days. He went into a coma. He had tubes hooking him up to every kind of machine there is. It was awful. And then the trial lasted for months.

THERAPIST: Can we try to put that off for an hour, talk about it as soon as the show is over? Would you do that for me?

ANNE: I'm sorry, you're right, I'm obsessing.

THERAPIST: That's not what I said.

ANNE: You actually saw your husband's wreck happen?

THERAPIST: I told you.

ANNE: My heart was pounding so hard and so fast I could feel it all the way through my body and my skin went tight and hot and I had to fight to keep my eyes open and it was coming and coming, I knew what was going to happen, I knew. And then it did and I felt the impact in my teeth and the whole world was crashing noises and echoes of crashing noises and spinning and then I heard my voice, my own voice above all the clatter, and I realized I'd been screaming and I stopped. (*beat*) Is that how it was for you?

THERAPIST: I was hiding behind a tree. I had a camera with me and I was going to take pictures of them having sex and then I was going to divorce him, and when I saw her car coming, I saw what she was going to do, and I hoped he'd die.

ANNE: You were lucky.

Therapist looks at her in a question.

ANNE: I think if Jerry's girlfriend had tried to kill him, even if she'd failed, I could have gotten what I needed from that. Then I wouldn't have had to do it myself.

Pause while Therapist looks at her watch.

THERAPIST: We can't talk about this right now. In two minutes . . .

ANNE: I know, I'm sorry.

THERAPIST: Don't talk about Jerry on the show.

ANNE: I promise.

THERAPIST: Not a word.

ANNE: Nothing.

THERAPIST: He never existed. You're just beginning therapy . . .

ANNE: I had therapy in jail.

THERAPIST: No, you never went to jail. You're a widow beginning private therapy and you're a typical post-menopausal woman in the sense that you have deep longings for human connection inside you that you don't know how to address because you haven't read my book, and I'm going to tell you what you should do, and you're going to sit there and say I'm right, okay?

ANNE: Okay.

THERAPIST: And after the show, right after you hug Oprah, we'll get in our cars and go to my office and we'll have a long session.

ANNE: We'll get in our cars.

THERAPIST: And go to my office.

ANNE: I don't have airbags.

THERAPIST: It's time to go.

ANNE: Do I look okay?

THERAPIST: You look beautiful. Right now, you're wearing the dress of a beautiful woman.

ANNE: Jerry died in a car crash. I ran into him with my car in the yard before I hit the house.

THERAPIST: It's okay.

ANNE: I wasn't trying to kill him. I was just trying to get him to listen to me. Afterwards I got out of the car and my head was bleeding so bad I could hardly see but I made my way over the bricks to him and I held him in my arms, my blood dripping on his face, and I said, "When this is all over, can we talk?"

THERAPIST: You and I, we'll talk.

ANNE: What did you do after the girlfriend yelled at your husband?

THERAPIST: I took pictures of them. Then I told them to go fuck themselves and filed for divorce.

ANNE: You look beautiful too.

THERAPIST: Come on.

ANNE: Do you have airbags?

THERAPIST: Yes.

THE END

Digging In
The Farm Crisis in Kentucky

JULIE CRUTCHER AND VAUGHN MCBRIDE

JULIE CRUTCHER was the literary manager at Actors Theatre of Louisville from 1981 to 1986. She is the author of *Approaching Lavendar,* which premiered at Actors Theatre in the 1983 SHORTS Festival and was produced by PBS as part of ATL Presents in 1984. Her other one-acts to premiere at Actors Theatre of Louisville include *Type Casting, Home for the Holidays, What Happens After,* and *The Son.* Following its ATL premiere, *Digging In* was presented at PepsiCo's Summerfare. Crutcher continues on staff as a dramaturg with Actors Theatre and most recently worked with Marsha Norman on her premiere of *Trudy Blue.* Crutcher also coordinated the first short story contest for *Louisville Magazine.*

VAUGHN MCBRIDE began his professional writing career in the Humana Festival of New American Plays at Actors Theatre of Louisville. His plays have been performed in regional theaters across America and at the Manhattan Theatre Club in New York. His works for young actors are presented throughout the country and abroad. His plays include *Elba, The New Girl, Let's Us, My Name Is Linda, Echoes, The Baby Unicorn,* and *Pass My Imperfections Lightly By.*

Material from interviews conducted by Mary Jennings and Andrew Stahl. Copyright © 1900 Julie Crutcher and Vaughn McBride. Development and production supported by a generous grant from the National Endowment for the Arts. Reprinted by permission of the Authors, care of Actors Theatre of Louisville, 316 West Main Street, Louisville, KY 40202-4218.

DIGGING IN: THE FARM CRISIS IN KENTUCKY

was first performed by Actors Theatre of Louisville on March 21, 1987.

CAST

YOUNG FUTURE FARMER OF AMERICA ....Doug Hutchison
OLD FARMER, CHRISTIAN COUNTY ....Jonathan Bolt
OLD FARM WOMAN, HART COUNTY ....Adale O'Brien
OLD FARM WOMAN, HENRY COUNTY ....Marilyn Rockafellow
OLD FARM WOMAN, BUTLER COUNTY ....Suzanna Hay
OLD FARMER, HENRY COUNTY ....Dana Mills
FARMER, MCCRACKEN COUNTY ....Patrick Husted
FARMER, CALDWELL COUNTY ....Steve Hofvendahl
FARMER, BUTLER COUNTY ....Adam LeFevre
CONGRESSIONAL AGRICULTURE ADVISOR/BANKER ....Dana Mills
RADIO STATION FARM REPORTER/SHERIFF ....Frederic Major
FARMER, CHRISTIAN COUNTY ....Andy Backer
SECOND FARM WOMAN, HENRY COUNTY ....Marilyn Rockafellow
FARM WOMAN, CHRISTIAN COUNTY ....Suzanna Hay

Director ....Larry Deckel
Set Coordinator ....Paul Owen
Costume Coordinator ....Ellen MacAvoy
Lighting Coordinator ....Jeff Hill
Sound Coordinator ....David A. Strang
Property Coordinator ....Charles J. Kilian Jr.
Stage Manager ....Michael B. Paul
Slides ....Carson Jockell

Lights up, revealing a young boy standing center stage. He is reciting the Future Farmers of America creed. He looks as if he is pledging allegiance to the flag. The light on him gets brighter.

YOUNG BOY: I believe in the future of farming with a faith born not of words but of deeds—achievements won by the past and present generations of farmers. I believe that to live and work on a good farm is pleasant as well as challenging for I know the joys and discomforts of farm life. I believe in leadership from ourselves and respect from others. I believe in my own ability to work efficiently and think clearly. I believe that rural America can and will hold true to the best traditions of our national life and that I can exert an influence in my home and community which will stand solid for my part in that inspiring trust.

At the end of the creed there is a pause.

OLD FARMER: I started farming—1928. Course when I started in—dagone it was something else. I had it my own way and I thought it was real hard. But it paid off. If I earned a nickel, I got paid a nickel.

OLD FARM WOMAN: Some people say they want to go back to the old type of farming. I don't know why anyone would want to go back. It was very difficult. Yes, slow, hard work. They would cook on a woodstove. You would bring in chips to start the fire with. I wouldn't want to go back to that. I love farming but I don't want the drudgery. I like the conveniences of town.

OLD FARMER: I had me four mules and, uh, no tractor. I had 265 acres to work. See, my father died so they had me tied in with 700 acres I said, how in the world am I gonna do, work 700 acres, by gosh, with four mules? But then I pitched around then and got hold of me a tractor which I like to never paid for. They had to take it away from me several times. Those little tractors ran about I'd say, about 22 to 23 hundred. That same tractor today is $50,000.

OLD FARM WOMAN: We talked about selling once and one of the nephews, Minnie's boy, was in the army, when I wrote to him I mentioned to him that it was on the fence and that we didn't know whether to sell. Owee, I got a letter just as quick as he could get one back to me. He said, oh please, don't sell. That's home to me. So we didn't sell. He died in World War II.

OLD FARMER: Back when I was younger, we killed our own meat. Even slaughtered the cattle. We'd kill maybe a thousand or nine-hundred pound calf and if we didn't want it all, maybe one of our neighbors would take part of it, and then when he killed, if ours was gone, then we'd divide up again. We lived pretty high on the hog, as the fellow says. We'd kill that beef and you wouldn't think it would keep, but we'd kill that beef and we'd hang it up in the smokehouse. I call it the smokehouse and cover it with a plain old bedsheet. You'd cover that up and that meat would keep. You wouldn't have to worry about it at all. You kill it in the fall and it would keep. Of course, you know the best meat in the world's got mold on it, you can eat all you want of it 'cause they's good. Molded meat is all right. Isn't that where you get penicillin?

OLD FARM WOMAN: In the old days farmin' wasn't what they called a profession, that was, you just was, if you were ignorant you, or if you really didn't know enough to do anything else, you just farmed. And that was the way farmin' was looked up in for a long time. I mean, and of course I've always felt like and I still think it takes all kinds of knowledge. You've got to know how to take care of the livestock, you've got to know how to be a business person, as far as managing your finances. Buying land and tools, you've got to know how to manage a household and, uh, really you have to be kind of a jack of all trades, I mean an electrician, a plumber. Now my husband wasn't that good.

OLD FARMER: But they, oh people had to, they, they had, where people now have coffee breaks, you know? Well, uh, they loved their brews back in those days. They got together every morning and they had their mint juleps. And yeah they'd have their whiskey, 'course I don't remember too much about it. But they'd have their dogs and all their horses hitched out there. And they had a time. I remember my father talkin' about them. But uh, they had a mint bed. Each fella had a big mint bed. That mint bed is still there on it. Still got it. When they went to tear the house, remodel the house—take one room off— that was the room where they had all gathered. And I think they was, I believe if I remembered right, there was nearly a wagon load of whiskey bottles. And I remember 'em right well. They was a brand of whiskey they used as Old Taylor. Oh, it's good.

OLD FARM WOMAN: And we made the light bread. I can remember mother baking that. Just loaf after loaf of light bread. And now I don't serve two kinds of bread at a meal. Then there was corn bread, biscuits and the light bread. We didn't always have biscuits and light bread but we always had corn bread and biscuits or light bread.

OLD FARMER: There's a terminology that goes around today that I had no idea what is. I've heard people talk about being bored and that wasn't in my vocabulary. They talk about kids being hyper. I never knew a hyperactive kid growing up on the farm. It was just the way the family was.

OLD FARM WOMAN: During the war—couldn't get hands and Charles was little. Mother (Stahl) never was no help to you about taking care of the children. She said there'd be some of them unloaded on her the whole time, but she kept Charles for me to get on a horse and I went to hunt a hand and couldn't find a hand and I took Charles in my arms and plowed the corn and I never will forget—Mr. Thomas said I wish I had my camera, I'd take your picture— plowing up to our barn almost. And I told Mac, I says, I can't find nobody, everybody is gone to the war. Mac didn't think I could help him, and he says, what will you do with the baby and I says, well, I'll take him with me—he was a great big boy—he was 4 or 5. I plowed two rows at a time.

OLD FARMER: I won't farm with the attitude like a lot of people. I just got a philosophy that's not in that realm. This is my life. It's not an occupation. My life. And this land, it's part of me. And if I don't take care of it, then I'm the poorer for it. As long as I take care of this dirt, it'll take care of me. And I'll tell any young farmer, if he'll take care of it, he can live. He won't have the standard of living he may have had. But when he chose to be a farmer, he didn't choose to have the standard that a lot of people like.

OLD FARM WOMAN: We didn't take the daily paper, we couldn't afford it. And we didn't have electricity. And we had a coal oil stove that we cooked on. You just never thought about saying, "I don't like this, I don't want that." You thought it was just a way of life you had.

OLD FARMER: I don't think a young person can come out here and establish themselves into farming and make it today with this, "I've got to have this, I've got to have that." You can't do it.

OLD FARM WOMAN: In lots of ways people have changed. Well you never heard of such a thing as a vacation but now you hear they want to go to Louisville to hear something. Why even this yard sales or flea markets. Why even some people from around here went all the way up there for that. A couple of them sell antiques. One of 'em is a preacher too. Always thought he was a sissy but he has three children. Can't be too much of a sissy with three children, can he?

OLD FARMER: Back there then we had hogs and cattle and we had our grain crops and if one failed, the other would come along with us and uh, so that way, but we had to raise a lot of hay. . . . My father had 28 mules when he died, 28 mules, that's what he had. But, uh, oh we, we had a lot of fun back in there. Chewing and huntin'. We'd hunt. It wasn't no rat race then like it is now.

OLD FARM WOMAN: I crochet, piece quilts, sew, read. I've been reading trashy books. I just want something to entertain me. I don't want that heavy reading. I do my Sunday School lessons and sometimes I read something educational but lately I've been reading trash.

OLD FARMER: I sold right at a good time. I was 72 years old when I quit.

OLD FARM WOMAN: This must be dogwood winter. There's a bunch of winters they've named. Dogwood, blackberry, witch's winter, they've got a lot of them but dogwoods are in bloom. I've got about four trees in the yard. They call it dogwood winter because the dogwoods are in bloom and it's cold. I had a pink dogwood tree but it died. It didn't bother me much because I don't think it was going to be what I thought it was.

I had about 700 acres. I have but about 52 acres now. I'm losin' this, you know. Old as I am, I'm losin' it—the farm, the home, all of it.

OLD FARMER: It bothers us that we're a forgotten people. There seems to be an attitude that nobody really cares. Of course that wasn't always the attitude. That's what happens when you become a minority. We were the majority for years and years and years. As far as the country's concerned, they can do without us. That's where they're wrong. They can't do without us.

Music fades out, slides remain on. Lights up on Farmer, McCracken County.

FARMER, MCCRACKEN COUNTY: I will never forget Herbert W. Armstrong out of Pasadena, California. We'd listen to the radio, all of us truckers know what to listen to in the hour of the night when we're up working and other people is in bed sleeping. Herbert W. Armstrong was saying that there was going to be a famine in this country—people were going to starve to death by great multitudes like they was in Africa at that time. They showed a film and I don't remember just what part it was—I don't remember if it was Ethiopia at that time or not—but somewhere over there—and they showed the black people—just the horror of it. America was just going to have to feed the world. I listen to Secretary Butz say that we had to feed the world. Plant to the fence-rows. My sons believed this, and I believed this.

So, farming was my life so I come back. I said, hey, I love trucking, but I don't like being gone from home, my nerves are getting bad, seeing too many wrecks every week—at that time we had 70-mile-an-hour speed limits—and we had these little Volkswagens coming out and you had to put the mirror on the side of the truck where you could see down at your wheels, or you just cut over and squashed one of them. So after so many years and so much of that, my nerves got to where sometimes I just wanted to get out beside the truck and run around and scream for a while. It got to me, I was having a nervous break-down, so I quit. Went to Mayfield and I said, you know my sons are farming and we want to be part of the American dream.

Slow fade to dark. Slide of Auction Sign remains for a few seconds. Snap to black. Lights up on all ten characters. Aunt Daisie and Old Farmer sit off to one side. Banker must be dressed in Reaganomics-regulation-navy-blue suit. His shoes shine. He sits at a very nice office desk whose top is clean except for a telephone. It's all very neat and tidy. His space, as well as the radio station farm reporter's are higher than the seven farmers'. Radio Station Farm Reporter sits in a big over-stuffed chair. The kind that reclines. To say he is portly is to put it kindly. This man always has something in his mouth—or is always on the verge of putting something in his mouth. Use it as punctuation.

The other six characters are farmers. Farmer, Christian County and Farm Woman, Christian County, are married and occupy the same space. They all define their own spaces just as farmers define their own boundaries. It's relatively unconscious. One idea would be to have carpet of five different earth tones laid on the stage floor. (Think in terms of an aerial photograph of South Central Kentucky and how the fields look.)

FARMER, CALDWELL COUNTY: Personally, well, I grew up on a farm and I went to the U of K and and graduated in Agriculture in 1964–65, and spent my whole life learning how to produce food. From the time I was a six-year-old until I graduated from college, my whole life has been spent learning how to farm. I lost everything that I had committed to and had dedicated my life to. I lost everything, the whole shooting match. Now, you're talking to a real-life casualty now. You're talking to a sure-like casualty. In 1984, we liquidated, and then I spent a year reconstructing my life.

FARMER, BUTLER COUNTY: I think the good old days for me were the early '70's. Seemed like everything prospered and went along good and really there wasn't much you could do wrong. Prices got better—land prices strengthened and interest was reasonable—moderate inflation rate that would more than pay the interest bill.

The early '70's have been the best time of my life. Farming was just something that kindly come natural, I feel. I kindly knew what to do, and it worked out pretty good.

FARMER, MCCRACKEN COUNTY: We got in it just before it all went to hell, about 1977, but we actually really got started—you know, you buy a gilt and you got to breed her, and she's got to have pigs and then her pigs goes on the market, so actually eighteen months before you get into the flow of things, you see. So we really got started in about—the loans completed and everything— really got started in 1978 or 79. This was Federal Land Bank. We invested about $200,000 here in hog buildings, and we come in here and we got with it, me and the two boys. Our goal was to try to sell 4,000 to 5,000 hogs a year, that is what we wanted to do. And in 1980, hogs went to 27 cents a pound, which we was getting $57 a head for them, and it was costing $90 a head to produce them, so we lost $90,000 that year. Well, we knew, hey, we can't produce anything at a loss, you know what I mean, so we got too big for the local banks, so we went to the Farmers Home Administration after we lost all that amount of money. And of course there was all kinds of money to get from FHA. In fact, Federal Land Bank just rolled out the money out in a wheelbarrow for us, and we asked for $60,000 that year, and they ended up sending us:

BANKER: $160,000 . . .

FARMER, MCCRACKEN COUNTY: They came out and they said:

BANKER: It's a hog farm and we talked it over, and uh, well, the way for you to overcome this thing is to get bigger. You raise 100 acres of corn and you need to be raising 400-500 acres.

FARMER, MCCRACKEN COUNTY: And I said it looked to me like the way to overcome it is to get something for our products, and then we could pay our debts. Their theory of how to overcome the situation we was in was to plant 4 times the corn we were planting.

And we bought a bulldozer in the meantime ready to clear our land, and, well, I could get 400 to 500 acres over here on a farm that a doctor owned and they encouraged me to buy it. Then we bought 61 acres and give a land contract on it, and then I went over there and made a fool out of myself contracting and talking to people and then I went to FHA for two weeks, and everytime I would go in, the supervisor wouldn't be there or he would disappear, and then I realized he was avoiding me.

RADIO STATION FARM REPORTER: Forty years I been a farm director at the radio station. I took the job temporarily, I'm still here. Forty years ago you could go out and see an old, beat up tractor, some of them still with cleats on the wheels. Today you drive down and you see a farmer, and this is what I'm telling you—they're driving air-conditions.

FARMER, MCCRACKEN COUNTY: And I said, hey something is wrong here. So, I go in there one day and they say he is not there, and I know he is there. I said, well, I am going to sit here until you close and I am going to be here in the morning. Sometime or another this man is going to have to come in this building. There is something wrong here. And then he comes out. I go in and I talk, and he has done a reversal, see. We bought a big dual tractor, we are obligated, and he is supposed to come through with the money, and he never did come through with the money. And all this land he told me to contract and buy, it took me a year to get the money for the 61 acres. He hid out from me— now I am talking about the FHA supervisor—and what had really happened, I can see it now—was that Ronald Reagan came in and he started cutting programs and shut the money off and the man didn't have enough guts to tell me the truth. He played little schoolboy games and he hid from me. And they are the most lying, deceitful people that I have ever met in all my life.

RADIO STATION FARM REPORTER: I'm for the farmer, and I know a lot of them haven't been done right, and they blamed somebody else probably. But the farmer that has farmed, used old machinery, kept improvising, and doing all these different things, well, you check this out and see if I'm wrong, I'll eat my hat. But check it out and see. They improvise, use baling wire, bale it together, have come out smelling like a rose.

FARMER, MCCRACKEN COUNTY: Then when things got so bad, you borrowed all you could borrow and there was no more equity and things started going the other way and then they put us on a supervised bank account, and when you sold a load of hogs or anything, you went in. You gave them the money, and they turn around and give you the money to pay your bills and you crawl to them.

RADIO STATION FARM REPORTER: Now these that have bought, and I say I'm not agin that because I sell that equipment, they have bought the 80 to 90 thousand combine, big 50 to 60 thousand dollar tractor, air-conditioning tractor, and I can't say that I'm not for it, and probably some of 'em thought they *had* to buy, you know, to farm the size farms they have, but I just don't know if they can afford it.

FARMER, MCCRACKEN COUNTY: We did this for about six months and it was the most outrageous, horriblest thing that ever happened in my life.

FARMER, CHRISTIAN COUNTY: Used to be, the man went in there and bought his chemicals, his fertilizers, and he charged it until he sold his crop. And then you paid. PCA come in and says, well, we can charge you this, you can buy, instead of buying two cows, you can buy fifty and pay for it in a few years, and then the interest—soon, instead of just PCA charging interest, elevator charges interest, every parts house charges interest, and we're talking about 18% interest.

FARMER, MCCRACKEN COUNTY: My house and 234 acres of land and five big hog buildings which cost $200,000 sold for $94,000. $94,000. That was two months ago. I could not believe this. I could not believe it. Now they are asking $133,000 for it. But we got to pay the difference between the $155,000 that we owed Federal Land Bank and the $94,000. We got $70,000 deficiency against us. We owe FHA over $500,000 feed bill. And it's not being told to the American people just what is wrong. It's not being told.

RADIO STATION FARM REPORTER: Never owned a farm, and I don't want to. I think today farming is a right depressing, at this particular time, a very depressing business. Machinery has changed is one thing and then we had a . . . you know farmers are like everybody else, they're kind of greedy.

FARMER, CHRISTIAN COUNTY: Yeah, we had liens on the farm, and the other people we owed had to be paid off so that if there was anything left over, they got it. But there wasn't anything left over. They were so blind and so stupid, they couldn't see that. I come in March 1, at lunch time and walked around the sale up there, and I come in and told my wife, I said, we lost $20,000 today. She said, well, you ain't done nothing. Well, the way farm and machinery prices have fell today, I've lost $20,000. Every time they would foreclose on somebody and have another machine sale on them, you'd be losing money. From March 1 till October or November when they got all the sales going, I'd lost somewhere between $40,000 and $50,000 on paper. Now, that's what's killing us. When your cattle prices kept going down, machinery prices, and land prices. They keep blaming me, and all this, and other farmers for it.

FARMER, BUTLER COUNTY: It started with the embargo and a lot of people wouldn't agree, but I think the Nixon embargo in 1973 or 1974 when he embargoed the soybeans to Japan really was the most critical because it showed people—our customers—that we weren't going to be a steady supplier and Japan and other nations just simply poured money into Brazil and Argentina and other countries—and are still doing it. That's when it started. Up until that time they had never, I don't think, considered developing other areas to grow crops for them. Then we went on when Carter put the embargo on because of Afghanistan. I think all that done was just reinforce their fears. Of course, that was mainly against Russia, but still it showed all of the other nations what we were willing to do and then other nations got to pouring money into Brazil and Argentina to assure an adequate supply.

FARMER, CALDWELL COUNTY: There were 14 embargoes in 1972 through 1981—when Reagan was elected whether we know it or not, we had a continuing embargo. Nobody is aware of that fact. The way it was was that the value of our dollar was so high and so great compared to the foreign currencies, that they could not afford to buy anything American—be it food, steel, or whatever.

FARMER, BUTLER COUNTY: They tell me there is a strip of ground in Brazil that is as large as Iowa, Illinois, and Indiana all put together—and it is virtually untapped. That is probably as close to—as far as the grain—those three states are probably close to half of all the grain produced in the U.S.. When you've got a potential like that to be developed and you've got a record like the U.S. of not being a reliable supplier—if I was sitting in the seats of power over there in some of those embargoed countries, I would be looking for alternatives. I wouldn't let my people be at the whim of the U.S. government. So Japan is building one of the largest soybean processing plants in the world, just so they can process Brazilian soybeans. Japan's the one that developed Brazil.

FARM WOMAN, HENRY COUNTY: It really started in '82—the drought year. We didn't have enough feed to feed with, so we had to buy feed, which is real expensive, especially after a drought year when nobody had any corn to sell, that makes it real expensive. And we lost so much money on the hogs. Hogs are so unpredictable. One day they're $50, the next day they're $20. And we bought when they were high. And when we sold, they were cheap. So they didn't even pay the feed bill. So we decided that we would put in a dairy in here. And we already had the basic barns and we did all the work ourselves. Poured all the concrete. I've never been so sore in my life. I would hate to have to do that for a living—pouring concrete. We just had to keep up. So the next year, it was the year after the drought. We still had the crops on my Dad's farm, and my husband had leased some more corn ground, so we raised about 300 acres of corn and some soybeans. This was in '83. I mean, he just planted everything he could find everwhere—and we combined for days and nights and days and nights and days and nights. And we paid off our note that year to under $100,000. And we were so proud. But see, the way we did that is at the beginning of the year—well, our banker told us:

Banker moves down to woman's space. Alternatively, he could simply step out from behind his desk.

BANKER: You turn in everything you make to us this year. It'll look real good on your record and that you're paying as you go along.

FARM WOMAN, HENRY COUNTY: Well, that made sense to me.

BANKER: O.K., then at the end of the year, what bills you have—your fertilizer, feed, whatever you have, you bring 'em in and we'll settle.

FARM WOMAN, HENRY COUNTY: We believed that. So we had a $19,000 fertilizer bill and a $5,000 feed bill. I got a staph infection, how, I don't know. But anyway, I had to go in the hospital for fifteen days running tests, so we had a big hospital bill. I mean, we just had all kinds of bills 'cause we didn't pay any, and we were telling these people, at the end of the year, we're going to pay you. So we got all of these bills together after we sold our tobacco and everything.

We'd just given the bank. I mean, we hadn't kept copies of the checks or anything. We didn't put the money in our account and write the bank a check. We just, every time the warehouse gave us a check for our tobacco, we'd go hand it to 'em. So we go over there and I had all the bills itemized on paper, and I had all the actual bills, and I handed it to our banker, and said, well, you know we need to settle up and get these people paid. And he looked at me real funny-like, like . . .

And I looked at my husband, and I know he was holding his breath because he was afraid I was gonna yell, and I said, what do you mean? What are you trying to say?

BANKER: Well, we can't do that. The money went on your note. We can't take it back off the principal you paid.

FARM WOMAN, HENRY COUNTY: What do you mean you can't take it back off the principal I paid?

BANKER: Well, that's just not a bank policy. We can't do that.

FARM WOMAN, HENRY COUNTY: And then I got too mad to even say anything. And I kept looking at my husband, like, you're the man, say something. And he just . . . he was in shock I think.

FARMER, CALDWELL COUNTY: The farmer cannot change the direction he is going overnight like a retailer can. He can't change his menu. If hamburgers become unacceptable, he can't take them off his menu—he is committed to raising hamburgers.

FARM WOMAN, HENRY COUNTY: We never did pay the big fertilizer bill and the big feed bill. We got sued over those. I mean, the people had to. And one of them has gone under since then, and you know, I feel kind of responsible, but it wasn't just us.

Banker moves back to his usual place.

FARMER, MCCRACKEN COUNTY: Here's an article in the local paper entitled "On The Hill: Farm Crisis Must Be Addressed" and it's by our State Rep. and I'm going to read a little of it:

"Compared to Governor Collins' Toyota giveaway of 300 million, 70 million dollars is a small amount. But 70 million is the total amount that will be available in low interest loans for farmers under a bill passed by the house of Reps last week. Under House Bill 150, which is designated to provide emergency relief to the state's world-weary agricultural industry, loan money would be earmarked for crop production, a maximum loan would be $50,000 and the lending limit would be one year."

Well, I saw this yesterday in the paper and I picked up the phone and called our rep, just to talk to him about this, and I said, "I want to congratulate you and your contemporaries on passing this bit of legislation, and although it is a small amount and although it will not adequately solve all the problems of everybody, it is a step in the right direction. How do I make application for this money?" He said, "Huh, well, yeah, that is, yeah, you're right things are in bad shape." I said, "You're not kidding things are in bad shape. How do I participate in this?" "Uh, well, I'll just have to find out and let you know about it." I hung up the phone, and I said to my wife, "Here's a man in the legislature here, he doesn't even know what I'm talking about. One of his aides probably wrote this and he's referring here to Governor Collins' Toyota giveaway, and the Governor's a democrat, he's a republican, and all in the world he's doing is making political hay at the expense of the farmer." And I resent that, because the average fella, you pick that up, read that in the morning, what woulda been your reaction? You would have said, "Oh, here's our government giving 70 million dollars to the farmer."—right? Wouldn't you have said, "Here's some more of my taxpayer money going down there, a handout, to keep the farmer in business when he can't help himself."

BANKER: The government spends $50 billion on agriculture programs—$50 billion—we have mountains of surplus food. We have warehouses full of excess cheese and butter, dry milk. We have mountains of grain, so what if a few farmers go out of business? Probably be good because we have too many out there producing too much now and the taxpayer is having to pay the bill for it. So I don't see why we should have to pay more money to keep these farmers in business when we have already got too many in business that are producing too much now.

FARMER, BUTLER COUNTY: I can't make enough money out of my operation to overcome the difference that my land has devalued since 1980—I tell a lot of people this and they kind of look at me like I am crazy—but the value of the real estate that I own has gone down $800,000 and that's just the same as I put it out here in the ground and lose it to the backwater—it's gone. Then you take a financial statement into the bank and you value your land at what you think it will be worth this year, and it's maybe 10% less than what it was worth the same period last year—the banker looks your financial statement over and he says, hey, you are in worse shape this year than you were last year.

FARMER, CALDWELL COUNTY: Angry—you damn right—I'm one angry gentleman. I am angry for this reason—for 22 years I worked seven days a week, 365 days a year committed to my industry and to my business. I never once took a day off for vacation, not one hour of vacation time. And I was pretty damn good. When you go broke as a farmer, you're subjected to economic terrorism, it's that plain and that simple. It's no different than being held a hostage in a real-life situation with people with guns and knives.

FARMER, BUTLER COUNTY: And then you have to go through the same thing every year—try and explain where you've got it, but when you take a $2 to $3 million investment in land and devalue it 10%. You're talking about $200,000 or $300,000, and when you do that three or four years in a row, you're talking about a bunch of money. That's what has happened to me.

FARM WOMAN, HENRY COUNTY: I have been, oh, for five years now, I have been saying something's not right, 'cause we had no control of our finances. It was like, well, we'll loan you the money to put out your crops for this year, and you pay us back everything you make off of it. I mean, you know, they don't care whether you eat, live, I mean, it didn't matter. And it would make me mad, real mad, and to the point that I would want to go punch them in the nose. But it depresses my husband—it depresses him, and he withdraws and he just gets real quiet and withdrawn and he just goes out on the farm and stays for hours and hours and hours, and it makes me want to go slap 'em.

FARMER, BUTLER COUNTY: I don't mean to sound conceited or anything else. But I think I am as good a farmer as there is in Butler County, or in this part of the state as far as that goes. I won the Jaycee's Outstanding Young Farmer Award for Kentucky, and I won the Farm Bureau's Outstanding Young Farmer in Kentucky, and I placed seventh in the nation that year. I do a good job with what I do, but still when you know that you've done that good job, then you look back where you were five years ago and look where you are at now, and you've used up a lot of your net worth through, I feel like, no fault of mine whatsoever, and there is nothing in God's world I can do about it. I had a chance to sell my operation in 1980, and I could have put enough money in the bank that I could have lived comfortable for the rest of my life on the interest and never had to hit another lick if I didn't want to, and I didn't choose to do that. I wanted to farm.

Slide change.

RADIO STATION FARM REPORTER: They don't know how to manage, it's just one of those things. Let me give you an example. Eight years ago, I went into a place right here in town, and the guy's sitting in here, a farmer, and he's sat in there a little while, and he said, "All the drinks and eats are on me in here tonight." I'm just like everybody else. Yeah, I ate a steak off of him. He bought everybody—"Everything's on me"—and I told my wife, I said, "Honey, that guy'll go down the drain." He was among the first to go down the drain here. The farmer's gotta think more before they buy things, can I do without this? They're going to have to.

FARMER, BUTLER COUNTY: A man on television last week, well, it was Dan Rather, he was saying why should I care whether you farm or not. He was interviewing a farmer out in Iowa. The farmer said, "Well, for one thing I might come and get your job." And I witnessed this all through college. A guy coming off the farm, if you're a farmer, then you can do anything. And you have a lot of integrity, you know how to keep records and finances, you do a good job, you work without having someone look over your shoulder, etc., etc. This fellow said, "I understand that if I go back East and look for a job, I can get a job anywhere. They'll hire me before they will anybody else."

FARM WOMAN, CHRISTIAN COUNTY: Tommy and I, when Tommy was first born, we were at the house all the time, at the trailer by ourselves. I taught him to read by the time he was a year old. He was always real bright. We were at the grocery store or shopping somewhere, and he was sitting in the cart, and he talked up a storm, and he'd sing commercials, but I was in a store and people were "He's such a pretty little baby," and he said, and I don't know what possessed him in the store, but people were standing around and he said, "Mom, am I going to see Daddy again?" and I said, "Yeah, it's getting close to the weekend, and I think maybe you'll be seeing him." And a lady was standing beside me and asked if my husband was in the military, and I said, "No, he's a farmer."

FARMER, CHRISTIAN COUNTY: March 1985. That's when we just kind of dug in and held on to prove that they couldn't starve us out. And they didn't starve us out. It was the milk cows that kept us going. But we had to hire a lawyer to keep it all above board, and so they wouldn't do anything to us. We had gone to them with the lawyer and we asked them—you know—we want to get this debt clear, we want to operate, we want to go ahead and try. But they didn't want that. They wanted to go through the legal system and see if they could get everything. They saw that there was some equity left in the cows and equipment—they thought. There wasn't any. So, to make a long story short, I guess it was about 30 days before the process come—they had to run an ad in the paper. But that was not done in our best interest either. They run it in the back of the paper, didn't tell that there was a house on the place—that there were grain bins, that there were barns or anything. So we—up to two weeks—we were showing the house to different ones that were interested. But November 24, it went up for sale on the courthouse steps.

Slide change-sequence maybe. Music under to lead into next bit.

FARM WOMAN, CHRISTIAN COUNTY: So now, instead of sitting there, he's worrying about what he should be doing or could be doing or won't be doing, and when he's there he's still worried about what he needs to be doing that he can't be doing. He ain't got the money. It's just a circle. You're just like in a grain bin running around for a corner to sit in, and you never find a corner. You never. It went from January to December—it was just continuous since 1981 and you make the full cycle every time. I thought we were through all of this— the equipment and everything was gone. I was sitting here trying to feed the kids supper one night, and I was feeling an inner peace that I had not felt in a long time, and this was, what, last month—February, March—I was sitting in here trying to get supper done and get it right on the table at 5:30, and someone knocked on the door and I went over and opened up the door and there was the sheriff—and I thought I'm in this cycle—why did I feel the peace if I'm in this cycle again. But he said:

SHERIFF: I'd like to speak to your husband.

FARM WOMAN, CHRISTIAN COUNTY: My husband's not here, he's at work.

SHERIFF: Where does he work?

FARM WOMAN, CHRISTIAN COUNTY: You won't find him because his job is all over this place. What do you have?

SHERIFF: I have a subpoena for your husband—Federal Land Bank has subpoenaed him for depositions in your lawyer's office.

FARM WOMAN, CHRISTIAN COUNTY: We knew about this yesterday, why is he being subpoenaed?

SHERIFF: That's the way they do it.

FARM WOMAN, CHRISTIAN COUNTY: O.K., give it to me. Give me his subpoena. (*SHERIFF doesn't.*) You don't have to do this, you don't have to be this way, it can be a whole lot easier, just give it to me, serve me.

SHERIFF: Lady, I am just doing my job.

FARM WOMAN, CHRISTIAN COUNTY: I've had this done to me before and you can make it simple or you can make it hard, and you've made it hard. (*Sheriff turns his back to her.*) And it just unnerved me—I started shaking and the kids—I'm trying to make it as peaceful as possible for them—they hurt too much. And I just shook like a leaf, and I busted out crying—well, no, I couldn't cry. I just shook. As soon as he walked in the door, I just busted out crying and at 1:30 I fell asleep—because you don't ever—the cycle—you just in the cycle. You run around that grain bin trying to find a corner. There ain't no peace— there ain't no peace even when it's all gone.

FARMER, CHRISTIAN COUNTY: No, 'cause I ain't got nothing to look forward to. What you wanted and what you wanted to do—it's all gone. You can't do what you wanted to do.

FARM WOMAN, CHRISTIAN COUNTY: When I got pregnant, we sat down and decided we wanted to bring our family up the way it should be. You know, the mother's place is in the home. And that's what we wanted. And now I resent it, and I guess that's why I stay so angry. I want to be a mother, that's what I want to be. I resent the fact that they have not only put him out of his job, but they've put me out of mine.

Slide change.

BANKER: We have some farmers who are doing fine, and then there are a lot of farmers that are having some tough situations through no fault of their own. And it is going to be a difficult transition into a different kind of agriculture, but those that are able to hold on are going to learn to be better managers. They are going to be better marketers, better equipped to the kind of agricultural environment that is going to pervade in the late 1980's and beyond.

FARMER, MCCRACKEN COUNTY: Well, you know for years Purina has produced chickens cheaper than we can raise them on the farm. Bought chickens a year or two ago, and paid 35 cents a piece and then the feedbill, it was ridiculous and then you'd go to the grocery and buy a chicken ready to go on your table for next to nothing. But, hey, how did they do it? Their chicken industry is a write-off for the dog food. Get out of paying taxes. It's a write-off. Their chicken business loses them money, but it makes them money. See where I'm coming from?

Slide sequence of corporate farms.

FARMER, CALDWELL COUNTY: Now the farmer has never had a solidified voice, a unified voice. He has always been segmented, fragmented. That's because we are not all the same. Each one is different and unique. But he has basically the same fundamental needs—he has a price—he needs a fair price. He needs his cost in relationship to this price. He needs a level corn field. Those are the things that he needs. But he is not getting them.

BANKER: The farmer comes up here and says I need for the government to bail me out and keep me in business. The other taxpayers are going to say how much more do you want?

FARMER, CALDWELL COUNTY: Let's take, for instance, if the American public was aware of the fact that our federal government subsidizes production of grain; they do in fact subsidize the production of grain by the American farmer, which in turn then is traded by five major grain companies—90% of the grain traded in world grain is traded by five grain companies—they take subsidized grain, funded by public dollars and make a profit from it. Now is it fair to the American taxpayer and the American public and the men, women, and children of this country that are having to struggle even to have an adequate diet, is it fair to tax them and then in turn let these companies make all the money? Hell no. It is not fair. If it was fair, I would agree with it, but it's not fair.

FARMER, BUTLER COUNTY: We were being told that we've got to feed a hungry world. The government was telling us, "You're going to have to plant from fencerow to fencerow—there will never be another food surplus." Looking ahead, you could see that even and really today—that bothers me as much today—we've got people literally starving to death in the world, and yet we've got such food surplus here in the U.S. that we can't pay our farmers enough for them to survive. That just doesn't make sense to me whatsoever.

FARMER, CALDWELL COUNTY: And if you stand there 24 years old and Earl Butz raised his fist and shook it at the crowd and said, "You produce it and we will sell it," what the hell would you do? You'd produce. And produce we did. And we believed it. See, we were misled by the political system, we were misled by our university systems. See, we could produce it—you're damn right—there is no nation, no people in the history of mankind has ever produced so much and received so little. I guarantee it.

Slide shift.

FARMER, CHRISTIAN COUNTY: In 1983 when we had that drought, I had them beef and milk cows over there, and there was no corn in Kentucky, so there was nothing for them to eat. In 1984 I checked around on this government supplied corn they was talking about. The closest place I could find it was in New York. It would have cost us a fortune to have it brought down here. New York—now they had it in Texas and other places—but the trucking route was the closest in New York. But the people at the AFC office said you have to do one thing—check and see if the cows can eat it. If a cow won't eat it, nothing else will. It was such a bad quality. This was the surplus the government keeps. Something a cow won't eat. And if a cow won't eat it . . . if you can grind it up and put molasses on it, a cow'd eat a brown paper bag. But, I mean, you can get it at half price, but if a cow won't eat it, what good is it?

FARMER, MCCRACKEN COUNTY: We went to politicians and they weren't your answer either. Because when we really got down to the nut cracking, and really brought the papers in and demanded our files from FHA and Federal Land Bank and got a court injunction to see them, guess where our letters we wrote to our Congressmen and to President Reagan and all of the people in Washington—guess where they really ended up—those letters came right back to FHA's office in Mayfield, to the Federal Land Bank. I doubt if they were ever even opened.

FARMER, CHRISTIAN COUNTY: Here we were all operating on this level in the mid-70's. Money was available. Not more than we needed but what we needed. Bankers were enthusiastic and supportive in these projects and in some cases helped to promote them. And then when they suddenly jerked out all the support. See, the farmer felt such a sense of betrayal that he doesn't know how to deal with that. It is almost foreign for a farmer to feel vindictive. You've got to go back . . . 'cause he nursed these little . . . he can't feel it's futile. He'll take the little ole pig that's not worth 15 cents, he'll fool with him, carry him and lay him down here by the stove. It's just second nature. It's that concept that won't allow you to become vindictive and revenge-minded and let you say what the heck and all that. You keep riding it along, putting your emotions, and then suddenly it won't get any better and you're at the end of the road and don't have any options. It'll eat you up.

The hardest thing though is purging yourself of this urge and this need to farm and this need to be associated with that. I mean, I'm out here since I was 20 years old and go and get on an assembly line and put Ford emblems on that pickup truck out there? I believe I would die. I really do. I believe I would really just die.

FARMER, CALDWELL COUNTY: Farmers are gentle people. In their eyes anger is wrong—they may feel it, but they will not express it. But there is enough fellows like me that have been pushed off the farm through public policy and monetary policy that, by God, we're going to get even. Now, it's just a matter of when. We're going to get even. I think I am too damn smart and too damn motivated not to get even. I don't know yet how I'm going to do it, but when I do, by God, they'll know about it.

FARMER, BUTLER COUNTY: There are some people that tend to blame financial institutions, or tend to blame the government—I don't. I made some mistakes and I am paying for them. I don't—nobody twisted my arm and made me buy the land that I bought. I made the decision. I think I am going to come out of this thing—but if I have to sell everything I've got—I didn't have nothing to start with—and I've had 23 good years.

FARM WOMAN, HENRY COUNTY: It's kind of like you have a disease or something when people first start finding out that you've filed bankruptcy—we filed Chapter 11—because when the bank got an official notice that we had done this, I mean, they just went crazy, like we had done something bad to them. See, Chapter 11 allows us to hold our creditors at arms' length. We had to have our land and our cattle and our machinery appraised. And when we did that, they set a value on it, then that is how much we owe—and the rest of it they have to forget. And they're not very excited about it. But then neither are we. So they get this notice. So our banker called us up and said:

BANKER: What's going on?

FARM WOMAN, HENRY COUNTY: I don't know.

BANKER: What does this mean? What's a Chapter 11?

FARM WOMAN, HENRY COUNTY: I don't know. Go look it up. You told us to go get a lawyer and we did.

RADIO STATION FARM REPORTER: I don't know how the farmer feels right now. But I worry about it, 'cause I hate to see it happen when we've had it real good. But when you try to get the farmer to see it, like I told you . . . getting the big machinery, buying land, getting too big, see, and you know what happens . . . you can't farm, wouldn't make no money at it. Better you get a job and go to work.

FARM WOMAN, CHRISTIAN COUNTY: About two weeks ago this realtor came in and said, "Would you be willing to work in my office just part-time—answer the phone and that." But that's all that's available for me. I can't even find anything else unless you go to Clarksville and go-go dance, and I think I'm a little too old for that. But, I mean, would you believe I've been told to do that? I have two children. I have self-respect, and they tell me "Would that be so bad? That's an option you've got to consider." A legislator told me that.

FARMER, MCCRACKEN COUNTY: Alright. I just got through telling you a few minutes ago that my place brought $94,000—they loaned me $600,000 on it. So they was either one heck of a stupid loan officer out there, or it was worth a lot, wasn't it.

You can't sell hogs in 1986 for 39 cents a pound when it costs 45 cents to produce them. My God, anybody knows that. And then I pick up the paper and it says 400 of the top corporations pay little or no income tax. The top 40 pay none, AT&T is refunded millions, and I am losing every cotton-picking thing that I have got. How do you think that makes me feel? But hey, they say, you run up these horrible debts, you should be ashamed of yourself. Let me tell you something—I paid my debt—I sold my hogs for 27 cents a pound and somebody was setting at a table eating them up—I wasn't making the money, but the packers, the grocers, and everybody else was making theirs. And I subsidized all of them to keep them going. When the farmer quits subsidizing this country, she is going down the tubes. She already is. So I paid my debt to society.

FARM WOMAN, HENRY COUNTY: My husband's not the same person that he was five years ago. Well, I'm not either. I'm real cold. Stronger. But I'm colder. I'm just real cold-hearted. I don't feel sorry for anybody anymore.

FARMER, CHRISTIAN COUNTY: Well, I'll just be glad when this damn country's importing everything. Everybody will be on welfare then. Well, that's what it's coming to. There's going to be a shortage of food is what some's been saying—I don't think so. I think there's always going to be enough food. You'll · be hungry because you can't afford it, not because it's not there.

FARM WOMAN, CHRISTIAN COUNTY: My husband had something the other farmers around here didn't have. He had cows that he could take it out on. He—one of them would act up, and she left dancing—her leg did not touch the floor, 'cause he'd get the old lead pipe out and work her leg over. He, since the cows are gone—that has been my fear, you know—who is going to get the lead pipe on the foot trick. The kids wait every day . . . what is going to break Daddy into finally punching somebody out?

FARMER, CHRISTIAN COUNTY: Got an ulcer. See that belly? That's not fat. This is an ulcer. It ain't bona fide 'cause I ain't got a doctor to go see, but I know what he's going to tell me. Stop smoking, stop eating, and no Pepsi. And we're living on Pepsi. Pepsi is the only thing that keeps the thing quiet.

FARM WOMAN, CHRISTIAN COUNTY: We woke up one time right after his Daddy died—he wasn't sleeping, and there was a chicken lot down there—I raised chickens, and there was something in with my chickens. So he had gotten up and gone down there with a gun and he was standing there, and he realized he could have done anything you know, he could have blown his brains out. It would have been so easy just to have gotten rid of it all.

FARMER, CALDWELL COUNTY: How are we going to get even? I don't know. I think that we have openly, we're going to have to develop some type of political mechanism—this is a political nation, we solve our problems politically. We haven't solved them with guns and bullets and blood. We haven't since the Civil War. But, . . . I don't know.

RADIO STATION FARM REPORTER: We're inclined to want to cut the farmer down, and yet we all love to eat. I enjoy it, and like I told you, I got more respect for the farmer than most folks have, anybody I can think of. I think it's great to be a farmer.

FARMER, CALDWELL COUNTY: The labor movement, of course, used blood. The civil rights movement used blood. As a matter of fact, Jesse Jackson threw up his hands at a meeting not long ago that I was present at, and he said, "My God, why haven't you people picked up guns and started shooting?" He said, "I do not understand how you people can be subjected to the forces that you have been subjected to and haven't responded."

BANKER: I think what happened to these guys is they had a couple of bad years, and who's gonna help 'em? These farmers'll come to the bank and say, "I need more money to bail out." Well, sure he does. But do you wanna throw that money in hope that he'll pay off your first loan? 'Cause now you may have jeopardized your second loan. Those are tough decisions 'cause these guys have got to understand how banks work. Banks are owned by shareholders, and the shareholders elect the directors and the directors appoint the officers and ultimately the directors are responsible. So they set up the various loan committees, and the loan committees are the loan officers and you look good to the board of directors and then to the stockholders if you got good loans. You look bad if you got bad loans. And when you get in a situation where you've got a farmer who's turning up on a bad loan and he wants a bunch more money and you know that the weather may be bad again next year, you may lose that too, and that's where you draw the line. You say, you've gone out one time and, uh, as much as you'd like to help him, as much as you sympathize with him, and as hard-working as he was, you got your shareholders. Or all of a sudden, you'll be out of a job.

FARMER, CALDWELL COUNTY: Well, if we can start electing people that are particularly knowledgeable of the needs of agriculture, that understand what it is to be a farmer—if we can elect enough of them nationwide, then maybe we will have a voice that can be heard.

FARMER, BUTLER COUNTY: I think that there is some people that I know that if they hadn't given up on themselves, they'd still be farming. But now they have gone the bankruptcy route because they simply threw their hands up and said I am not going to do this anymore. They just decided—well you know when you decide that you are a failure, you probably are.

I know I've give it all I've got for 25 years and I look back and I don't know many things that I've done that I thought was wrong when I done it. I know when I get up in the morning, I am going to get out there at 6:00 and I'm going to work till whatever I want to and I am going to do the best I can tomorrow. And the people that I deal with knows that I am going to, and I think I am going to be here when a lot of the rest of them are gone—just on that.

FARM WOMAN, CHRISTIAN COUNTY: The doctor says that one day he'll just not be able to stand it anymore—he'll get in the truck and he'll go away and we'll never see him again. I live every day thinking today might be the day. He'll finally maybe be at peace, though. I keep telling myself I'll be able to accept it, because he'll finally be at peace.

FARMER, CALDWELL COUNTY: What the point becomes is how do we as farmers—we don't have a Martin Luther King standing up giving a speech. We can't—you don't have a mass. You know, where are you going to get 2,000, 4,000, 5,000 farmers together for a rally to listen to one man talk? You can't do it. You can't get that mass movement going.

BANKER: I know it sounds like we are turning a deaf ear. Well, the magnitude of the problem—We can't do it. Of course, we've got to try to help as best we can. Do whatever we can to try and help him out, but eventually if the guy's operation isn't going to cash flow, well . . .

FARMER, MCCRACKEN COUNTY: And I go through all these Congress records like that and I come up with plenty of proof of what is happened to us. I look back to the Nixon Administration and I realize stuff doubled in 10 months, and I realize Carter's phony gas shortage, the grain embargo—I see the whole thing and I say—I say I see something that I can't control. But I'm gonna fight with every ounce of strength I got until they come out and say hit the road, or lead me down the road like they have been doing other people, then I'll walk away and I'll say I knew the truth and I stood up for it.

FARM WOMAN, CHRISTIAN COUNTY: It's so hard to live with. Everyday. 'Cause when I go to school at night—what if it happens when he is here with the kids—would he take the kids? My kids. I live and breathe my kids. If he left the kids, how long would they be here by themselves?

FARMER, CALDWELL COUNTY: I think we've got to become subversive, conspiratorial. We are going to have to drive the people back out into the farms where they can get food directly. There is only one way to do that and that is destroy the distribution system that they got now, and you . . . there is 116 warehouses and seven distribution centers in this country, and if they were shut down in the morning, it could be coordinated very easily.

FARM WOMAN, CHRISTIAN COUNTY: You think it's going to be different for your children. But they've lost as much as we have lost. They've hurt as much as we have hurt. Maybe they didn't understand about it, but it was just . . . it took something away we all loved.

FARMER, CALDWELL COUNTY: I don't know how I would physically shut them down. Maybe try to contaminate them. I personally am in favor of blowing the sons-of-bitches up.

FARM WOMAN, CHRISTIAN COUNTY: Tommy doesn't want to talk about what bad could happen next. He's seen his whole life—everything he has always grown up with—taken away and it hurts him, so we don't talk about it. My kids they just don't want anything else bad to happen. They want to get moved to wherever we got to move to and get started over again.

The next section is the coda and should be rapid fire and very staccato. Slide changes should punctuate, until the final image, which should fade slowly. Radio Station Farm

Reporter and Banker stay frozen in silhouette through this section. Very little physical movement. The idea is of paralysis; let the voices carry the emotion.

FARMER, CHRISTIAN COUNTY: I got bigger than I was aiming to and lost more money than I was aiming to.

FARMER, MCCRACKEN COUNTY: Went broke.

FARMER, BUTLER COUNTY: I could go down there and they would just want to give me money. Say, don't you need this to do some bulldozer work and set you up for $5,000 just like that.

FARMER, MCCRACKEN COUNTY: Done it lots.

FARM WOMAN, CHRISTIAN COUNTY: And also, when you would get behind on payments, they would loan you the money to pay them on money you already owed.

FARM WOMAN, HENRY COUNTY: They called it emergency loans. I'll say that they was so free with their money 'til—they would just give you money and give you money.

FARMER, MCCRACKEN COUNTY: Go down there and make a payment and they'd want you to take that money and do something else—put it back in your farm—and everything would be alright. Till they got it where they wanted it, and they started wanting their money right then, and they knowed that you didn't have no money.

FARMER, CALDWELL COUNTY: You've got to drive the people back to the farm. Literally.

FARMER, BUTLER COUNTY: I'd say they done a whole lot of people just like they done me.

FARMER, CHRISTIAN COUNTY: They'd want to just keep writing you money, knowing all the time that you had to pay that money back. A lot of times I knowed that I couldn't make that payment at the end of the year, but they would go ahead and insist on me taking it, and me telling them all the time I didn't want it.

FARM WOMAN, CHRISTIAN COUNTY: Well, we went ahead and took it. I thought they knew what they were talking about.

FARMER, CALDWELL COUNTY: Shut the whole damn distribution system down. Just blow 'em up.

FARMER, BUTLER COUNTY: They were putting the money out to everyone just like they was to me, and then they just cut everyone off.

FARMER, CALDWELL COUNTY: Personally, I don't see any other way to do it.

FARMER, MCCRACKEN COUNTY: The land is my life.

FARMER, CHRISTIAN COUNTY: I'd rather, if I had a choice of laying down and dying and keeping it for my sons and my wife, I could gladly do it.

FARMER, MCCRACKEN COUNTY: You know what I mean?

FARM WOMAN, HENRY COUNTY: There is no hole, there is no place you can go, there is no escape thing, there is nothing you can do.

FARM WOMAN, CHRISTIAN COUNTY: We are backed in the corner.

FARMER, CHRISTIAN COUNTY: There is nothing we can do.

FARMER, CALDWELL COUNTY: We're just going to have to blow the sons-of-bitches up.

FARMER, MCCRACKEN COUNTY: I lost a farm and I feel like I lost it, but I feel like I had some help in losing it.

All characters face forward, frozen. The two older farmers, still sitting to the side of the stage are frozen. There is a pause, and then the Young Boy stands and begins the Future Farmers Creed, as in the beginning of the play. The lights do a slow cross fade. By the end of the Creed the Young Boy is bathed in warm yellow light.

YOUNG BOY: I believe in the future of farming with a faith born not of words but of deeds—achievements won by the past and present generations of farmers. I believe that to live and work on a good farm is pleasant as well as challenging; for I know the joys and discomforts of farm life. I believe in leadership from ourselves and respect from others. I believe in my own ability to work efficiently and think clearly. I believe that rural America can and will hold true to the best traditions of our national life and that I can exert an influence in my home and community which will stand solid for my part in that inspiring trust.

THE END

Tent Meeting

LARRY LARSON, LEVI LEE, AND REBECCA WACKLER

 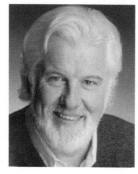 

LARRY LARSON, LEVI LEE, and REBECCA WACKLER are the co-authors of *Tent Meeting* and *Isle of Dogs,* both of which premiered at the Actors Theatre of Louisville, as did Wackler's one-act *Wild Streak* and Larson and Lee's *Some Things You Need to Know Before the World Ends: A Final Evening With The Illuminati.* Larson and Lee are also co-authors of *The Bloody Orgy Trilogy* and *The Salvation of Iggy Scrooge.* Larson currently writes and acts in Atlanta, Lee is the artistic director of *The Empty Space* in Seattle, and Wackler is pursuing an acting career in Los Angeles.

TENT MEETING

was first performed by Actors Theatre of Louisville on March 14, 1985.

CAST

REVEREND ED ....Levi Lee
DARRELL ....Larry Larson
BECKY ....Rebecca Alworth

Artistic Coordinator ....Patrick Tovatt
Set Design ....Paul Owen
Costume Design ....Marcia Dixcy
Light Design ....Jeff Hill
Sound Design ....James M. Bay
Properties Mistress ....Diann Fay
Fight Director ....Steve Rankin
Stage Manager ....Bob Hornung
Assistant Stage Manager ....Craig Weindling

CHARACTERS

THE REVEREND EDWARD O. TARBOX, an evangelist
DARRELL, his adult son
BECKY ANN, his adult daughter
VOICE ON RADIO
VOICE OF CUSTOMS MAN
VOICE OF DRIVER

TIME

1946

PLACE

Outside a laboratory at the University of Arkansas; in Moose Jaw, Saskatchewan;
and on the road in between.

PLAYWRIGHTS' NOTES

1. The primary setting for the play is in the interior of a makeshift house trailer, vintage 1930s–40s.

2. The voices in the blackouts should be on tape.

3. Whenever it is indicated that Becky Ann has the cotton in her ears, it should be assumed that she is humming, in various degrees of loudness and energy, according to how it affects the focus of the scene.

4. The baby, although seen only as a shapeless lump wrapped in a baby blanket, should be able to move and squirm. This is easily accomplished using a remote control airplane motor and operating it from offstage.

5. Darrell wears a Purple Heart at all times.

ACT I

Scene 1

Night. Outside a laboratory at the University of Arkansas. Dim light on a high balcony. Reverend Eddie and Darrell stand in front of the trailer, carrying large flashlights and a wicker basket. They look up at the balcony, and speak in hushed, urgent tones.

REV. ED: This is it!

DARRELL: How do you know?

REV. ED: Because God told me this is it.

DARRELL: Oh.

REV. ED: He has led our footsteps to this place. This is it. Up there. *(Shines his flashlight on the balcony.)*

DARRELL: Way up there?

REV. ED: It's not that high.

DARRELL: Not that high! If I had a good leg, I would go up, which I don't . . .

REV. ED: Darrell . . .

DARRELL: So I'll just stay here . . .

REV. ED: Darrell, you're going up.

DARRELL: Yes sir. *(Dog barks.)*

REV. ED: Hand me the rope?

DARRELL: What rope?

REV. ED: The rope to get up there with! You haven't got the rope?

DARRELL: No.

REV. ED: Then how do you aim to get up there?

DARRELL: Well, I don't have no rope.

REV. ED: I hear you saying that! I am simply asking you how you aim to get up to that window?

DARRELL: I'll go up the fire ladder.

REV. ED: And what about the rope?

DARRELL: What rope?

REV. ED: The rope, the rope, the rope! We gotta have a rope! How's the rope gonna get up there? It can't just climb up there magically by itself! *(A rope comes tumbling from the balcony. They are startled.)*

DARRELL: Jesus!

REV. ED: Shhhhhh! *(We hear humming from the balcony, the Rev. Ed shines his flashlight up on the balcony, illuminating the face of Becky Ann. She is leaning over the railing, with large wads of cotton stuck in her ears.)* Becky Ann!

DARRELL: Jesus!

REV. ED: Don't say Jesus.

DARRELL: You say Jesus.

REV. ED: I'm praying when I say it. *(Looks up at balcony.)* Becky Ann I thought I told you to wait in the car. Get down here!

DARRELL: Someone's gonna hear that hummin. We're all gonna go to jail for a hundred years . . .

REV. ED: Becky Ann!

DARRELL: She can't hear you. She's got that cotton in her ears.

REV. ED: I know she does. Becky Ann! Take that cotton out! Becky Ann!

REV. ED and DARRELL: *(Ad-libbing. Overlapping.)* Take the cotton out . . . take it out . . . etc. TAKE THE COTTON OUT!

Becky Ann removes the cotton from one ear.

BECKY ANN: Huh?

DARRELL: Jesus.

BECKY ANN: What?

REV. ED: Get down here!

BECKY ANN: Okay. *(She stuffs the cotton back in her ears and starts down, humming.)*

REV. ED: All right. You go up. I'll stay down here and tie the rope.

DARRELL: Daddy, I've got an idea. I've got a good idea. Here's my idea. See, Becky Ann is already up there, right? She's already up there. And I'm down here. See what I mean. Why don't Becky Ann just stay up there since she's already up there and I'll just stay down here, since I'm already down here. I'll just stay here and help you. Isn't that a good idea? I'll tell Becky Ann. *(He turns and comes face to face with Becky Ann.)*

BECKY ANN: Hi.

DARRELL: Hi. OK, I'm going up there now, at the risk of my own life.

REV. ED: Hold this flashlight on the knot, Becky Ann. Knot! *(He hands her the flashlight.)* Stop humming. Now hold your finger there . . . *finger*, Becky Ann. *(He puts her finger in the knot.)* Okay . . . stop humming . . . stop humming, Becky Ann. Someone will hear you . . . stop humming . . . *(He snatches the cotton out of one ear.)* Becky Ann!

BECKY ANN: Huh?

REV. ED: Stop humming.

BECKY ANN: Okay.

REV. ED: Darrell, are you up there? Darrell? *(Darrell appears at the edge of the balcony.)*

DARRELL: What?

REV. ED: Are you up there?

DARRELL: Yeah!

REV. ED: Are you ready for the basket?

DARRELL: I guess.

REV. ED: Pull it on up.

DARRELL: Yes sir. *(He begins to pull the basket up.)* Daddy! It's caught on something! *(The Reverend Eddie shines his flashlight on the basket. Becky Ann's finger is still in the knot.)*

REV. ED: Becky Ann! Take your finger out of the knot! Finger! Finger! *(She does so. Darrell pulls the basket up. Becky Ann disappears.)*

DARRELL: Okay, I got the basket up here. Now what?

REV. ED: Go get him.

DARRELL: Where is he?

REV. ED: Just look around. There ain't no two like him.

DARRELL: That's the truth. *(Pause.)* Wait. I think I see him.

REV. ED: Well fetch him and put him in the basket. *(Pause.)* What's takin' so long?

DARRELL: There's all kind of tubes and wires hooked up here . . . I got to pull them out . . .

REV. ED: Hurry!

DARRELL: Okay, I think I got 'im out.

REV. ED: Put him in the basket.

DARRELL: Yeccch! Yeccchhhh!

REV. ED: Hurry up! *(Darrell brings the basket to the edge of the balcony.)*

DARRELL: Okay! I got 'im in the basket. I'm gonna lower it down, now. You gonna catch it?

REV. ED: No, I'm gonna let it fall splat at my feet! Just lower it down! *(Darrell lowers the basket and the Reverend Eddie takes it, unties his end of the rope.)*

REV. ED: I got it. *(He walks away from the balcony, and kneels over the basket, praying.)*

DARRELL: Bombs away! We did it! We did it, didn't we Daddy? Where are you goin? Daddy what are we doin? Why don't you answer? *(He runs to the kneeling Reverend Ed.)* C'mon let's go.

REV. ED: . . . and John the Baptist. Thank you Lord. Thank you in Jesus' name. Amen.

DARRELL: We better get out of here.

REV. ED: Start the car.

DARRELL: What if it won't start?

REV. ED: Darrell start the car! The car ain't gonna start magically by itself! *(Sound of the car starting. They are startled.)*
DARRELL: Becky Ann. *(Loud car horn honking.)*
REV. ED: Jesus!
DARRELL: See, you said Jesus.
REV. ED: I was praying. *(They exit.)*

ACT I

Scene 2

In the darkness, we hear a radio: Old time programs from the 40's; the sound of someone switching the dial, moving from program to program. Lights up on the family in their trailer. Darrell is frantically switching stations. The Reverend Eddie is standing beside the baby basket, reading his Bible. Becky Ann is at the stove, the cotton in her ears, cooking and humming.

REV. ED: Turn off that radio.
DARRELL: Nothing. There's nothing about it on my radio. I've tried every station.
REV. ED: I told you God would look after us.
DARRELL: Yeah, well I just wish God could do the driving with his headlights off, in the middle of the night, pullin' this trailer in one thousand degree heat, and a carburetor that coughs like an ol' coal miner with black lung and TB . . .
REV. ED: Sit down and eat your breakfast. *(Becky Ann serves food and continues humming. Darrell sits at the table.)*
DARRELL: I don't like eatin' breakfast at ten o'clock at night. I don't see why we can't eat and sleep like normal people.
REV. ED: I told you. We sleep during the day and drive at night.
DARRELL: I wouldn't mind so much if I didn't have trouble sleepin' because of my war memories . . . *(By this time Becky Ann is seated at the table, Darrell is beginning to eat. Reverend Ed reaches up and places his hands on their shoulders. Silence. They bow their heads.)*
REV. ED: Amen. *(The humming resumes.)*
DARRELL: . . . which I do. I don't know this whole thing just seems kinda crazy.
REV. ED: Crazy? Crazy? I suppose you think Daniel was crazy. I suppose you think Job was crazy. I suppose you think God was crazy.
DARRELL: Here it comes. Here it comes.
REV. ED: Everybody at this table who thinks God is crazy, raise your hands. *(Pause.)* I suppose I was crazy when I had my affliction. I just imagined it. What caused the itching. The rash. The oozing sores. *(He rolls up his sleeves and shows his bare arms.)*
DARRELL: Poison ivy.
REV. ED: It was *not* poison ivy! I have never been allergic to poison ivy a single day in my life. The day we gave this baby away, blisters popped out under my

arms. Then the creeping plague of God spread to my legs and feet. My feet swole up so big I couldn't lace my shoes. Then it infested my eyes. I couldn't see nothing but dark and light. Then . . . then it spread into my mouth. My mouth filled with pus. My tongue blistered, and my lips swole so big that I couldn't speak God's name.

DARRELL: Poison ivy.

REV. ED: It was *not* poison ivy! It was a sign from God. He was telling me that we had to get the child back. That we all sinned, all of us, in giving away one of our own. The baby was a gift from God!

DARRELL: Yeah, well it was Becky Ann's gift, why didn't she get poison ivy?

REV. ED: You know, Darrell, I feel sorry for you. Because you're blind. Not in your eyes, but in your soul. The glory of God is in front of you in all its majesty and splendor and you're too blind to see it. If you weren't my own son, I would cast you out to wander the earth in darkness.

DARRELL: Why don't you just cast me out, then?

REV. ED: Because family is in the flesh and in the blood. And because I swore on your momma's Bible that I would bring you to Jesus. And by God I aim to do it. *(Hits Darrell with Bible several times, accenting the last sentence.)* "The Son of man goeth as it is written of him: But woe unto that man, by whom the Son of man is betrayed! It had been good for that man if he had not been born!" *(Reverend Eddie exits, after grabbing his plate and greasy bacon. Darrell sits for a moment, then rushes over to get his Bible.)*

DARRELL: I'll bet that's not even in there. He makes most of that stuff up! He thinks nobody will call him on it . . . He thinks just because he says a few "thees" and "thous" and stuff that nobody'll call him on it . . . well, I'll call him on it.

REV. ED: *(Yelling from offstage.)* Matthew 26:24 *(Darrell pauses for a moment, starts to throw the book down angrily, then places it softly on the table.)*

DARRELL: Well, he makes some of it up. Momma wouldn'a let 'im get away with this. *(Darrell puts on a baseball glove and smacks a ball into it. Becky Ann stacks dishes and hums. They go on like that for a while, smacking and humming, smacking and humming. Finally, Darrell stops and turns to Becky Ann, whose humming has built to a loud tuneless symphony.)* Becky Ann? *(No response.)* Becky Ann? *(No response.)* Becky Ann? *(He places himself in front of her face and waves. She looks up. He points to his ears. She takes the cotton out.)*

BECKY ANN: Huh?

DARRELL: You were hummin' again, Becky Ann. Did you know that? That you were hummin' again?

BECKY ANN: Was I?

DARRELL: Yes you were, Becky Ann. Hummin' up a storm, and not no tune that I ever heard, neither.

BECKY ANN: It weren't.

DARRELL: No, no tune at all. Now, Becky Ann, some people would get real bothered by that constant loud hummin' but not me, no sir, because you're my sister, and I know you've been under a lot of worry what with the . . . baby . . . and all. But maybe . . . and I would take this as a personal favor . . . if you could just stop that hummin'.

BECKY ANN: But I don't know I'm hummin'. How can I stop it if I don't know I'm doing it?

DARRELL: Maybe if you left the cotton out of your ears . . .

BECKY ANN: Oh, I'm sorry, Darrell, I can't do that. *(Picks up her knitting and the baby basket.)*

DARRELL: Why not?

BECKY ANN: Well . . .

DARRELL: What are you trying to keep out, Becky Ann?

BECKY ANN: *(Laughs.)* I ain't trying to keep nothing out. I'm just trying to keep it in.

DARRELL: What? What are you trying to keep in?

BECKY ANN: The music. I'm really sorry it don't sound to you the way it does to me. Maybe if I hum better. I'll try it for you again.

DARRELL: *(Protesting.)* No, no, that's allright . . . *(She puts the cotton back in her ears and hums loudly. She takes the cotton out of her ears.)*

BECKY ANN: How was that?

DARRELL: That wasn't no better, Becky Ann.

BECKY ANN: Oh, I know! You put the cotton in your ears.

DARRELL: No, I don't want no cotton!

BECKY ANN: But I want you to hear the music! *(Despite Darrell's protests, she stuffs the cotton in his ears. He resigns himself and sits for a moment, listening.)* Darrell? *(Darrell just sits with a blank look on his face.)* Darrell? *(No response.)* Darrell? *(No response. She takes the cotton out of his ears.)*

DARRELL: Huh?

BECKY ANN: Did you hear it?

DARRELL: What?

BECKY ANN: The music.

DARRELL: No, I can't hear nothing with cotton in my ears.

BECKY ANN: I know, you just need more cotton. *(She goes and opens a kitchen cabinet. The cabinet is stuffed to overflowing with cotton.)* I once tried putting corn silk in my ears, but it didn't work as good.

DARRELL: No, Becky Ann, no. I don't want no more cotton in my ears. I don't think I'm gonna hear it no matter how much cotton I put in my ears. 'Cause I don't think it's really there. *(She looks at him, hurt. Stuffs cotton back in her ears.)* I'm sorry, Becky Ann. I'm sorry. *(He takes the cotton from her ears.)* Sure, it's there. I know it's there. I think I heard it a little bit!

BECKY ANN: Really? What did it sound like?

DARRELL: Well . . . it was . . . real nice . . . kind of faint . . . but nice . . .

BECKY ANN: Then you understand.

DARRELL: Sure. Sure I understand. Tell me when did you first hear that music Becky Ann? Do you remember?

BECKY ANN: Oh, I remember. I remember the exact moment. *(Pause. Darrell waits expectantly.)*

DARRELL: When was that moment?

BECKY ANN: It was almost a year ago. We were still living at the farm, in that old house. I'd gone to bed early the night before. 'Cause it was rainin' real hard. And it was real dark outside and the wind was blowin' so hard like it would take the sides of the house off. I was all alone in the house. Daddy was off in Little Rock, and you was at the war . . . and the awful loudness of the wind kinda scared me. So I got in bed and crawled way down low under the quilt.

DARRELL: And that's when Daddy came home.

BECKY ANN: No, that's when I stuffed cotton in my ears, to keep out the beating of the rain and the roaring of the wind. I finally fell asleep. I don't know for how long, but when I woke up, it was daylight, and it was unearthly quiet. I'd forgot I had the cotton in my ears. Then I got up . . . and I felt dizzy . . . real good dizzy . . . purposeful dizzy . . . not Ferris wheel dizzy . . . and I knew right then and there that I had been filled. *(She pats her stomach.)* And that's when I heard the music.

DARRELL: Filled. Then, nine months later you had this little . . . rascal here, is that right?

BECKY ANN: That's right.

DARRELL: You know, Becky Ann, it don't look nothing like you. It must look more like . . . uh . . . what was the daddy's name again?

BECKY ANN: I didn't say.

DARRELL: Oh, I'm sure you did, Becky Ann. I'm sure I've heard you mention it.

BECKY ANN: I never.

DARRELL: Oh, you never . . . well, just for the record, what was the daddy's name? *(She puts the cotton back in her ears and begins to hum.)* Don't do that, Becky Ann. I'm talkin' to you! I'm askin' you a question! I'm your brother. I have a right to know! *(She puts up her knitting and moves away.)* Stop hummin'! Stop that! *(Her humming gets louder.)* You might as well tell me now, Becky Ann, because I'm gonna find out one way or another! Becky Ann! *(Pause.)* BECKY ANN! *(She washes the dishes. Darrell looks disgusted and finally sits at the radio. He turns it on. He turns the dial and gets static and music. Suddenly, we hear the sound of a newscaster.)*

RADIO: " . . . In his speech, he praised the integrity of General Douglas MacArthur and defended his own order to drop the atomic bomb on Japan last year. The President went on to say the effects of atomic power have not begun to be measured. In state news, authorities at the University of Arkansas are still baffled by the apparent kidnapping of a seriously deformed infant from the university laboratories . . .

DARRELL: *(Jumping up and running to the door.) Daddy! It's on! (He runs back and turns up the radio.)*

RADIO: "State Police working on the case say the infant was apparently abducted sometime during the night a few days ago from the laboratory where scientists were studying it. The window of the second-story lab showed signs of a break-in, police said." *(The Reverend Eddie enters, Darrell motions to the radio.)*

DARRELL: Jesus, the State Police!

RADIO: "Authorities pleaded with the abductors to return the birth-defective infant, saying that it could not live without special care. Elsewhere in the state, it looks like a good year for hog farmers. Barrows and gilts were up . . . *(Darrell turns the radio off.)*

DARRELL: There! You said God would look after us! You said God was watchin' us! Well, I wonder if God is goin' to jail for a hundred years, 'cause that's where we're going. God God God God God God that's all I hear around here. Sometimes I think you love God more than you do me! *(Reverend Eddie looks at him and laughs.)* Well, you heard the radio. That baby needs special care. If that baby had a chance of living, I would stay and help Becky Ann out, which it don't. *(He starts to throw his clothing into a duffel bag.)* You know what they do to kidnappers? They don't even bother puttin' 'em in jail. No sir. They *fry 'em!*

REV. ED: Darrell, this is not kidnapping.

DARRELL: What do you mean?

REV. ED: The baby is our own flesh and blood. We are simply reclaiming what is ours.

DARRELL: *(Intensely.)* Ours. What do you mean, ours? This baby is none of mine and I ain't gonna fry for this baby. I'll tell you who oughta fry. We oughta put this baby out of its misery. And then we oughta bury it alongside this Godforsaken road, then go somewhere and live like normal people!

REV. ED: You want this baby to fry, Darrell? *(The Reverend Eddie goes to the stove and grabs the skillet full of hot grease. He crosses to Darrell.)* Well, Darrell, do you think this is what's best for this family? Do you think this is what God wants? To kill our own flesh and blood? Just say the word, Darrell. *(Pause.)*

DARRELL: If I hadn't already seen so much death . . . it would've been easy . . . which I did . . .

REV. ED: *(Handing the skillet to Becky.)* Get your Bibles! We need to be going.

DARRELL: Where?

REV. ED: Get your Bibles. *(Darrell and Becky Ann fetch their Bibles. The three gather together. During the reading, Becky Ann alternately comforts the baby and stares daggers at Darrell.)* Open to Matthew 2:14. "When he arose, he took the young child and his mother by night and departed into Egypt. And was there

until the death of Herod; that it might be fulfilled which was spoken of the Lord by the prophet saying, out of Egypt have I called my son!" Amen?
BECKY ANN: Amen. *(Reverend Ed turns to Darrell.)*
DARRELL: Amen. *(Blackout. Sound of motor.)*

ACT I

Scene 3

Lights up on trailer. Darrell is alone in the trailer. He is lying on the bed, snoring loudly. It is several days later.
REV. ED: *(Offstage.)* Darrell! Becky! Becky! Darrell! *(He bursts though the door, still yelling. Glancing frantically around the trailer, he sees Darrell asleep.)* Darrell! *(Darrell continues snoring. Reverend Eddie goes to the sink and fills a glass of water. Striding to the bed, he throws the water in Darrell's face. Darrell starts awake sputtering.)*
DARRELL: I was coming back . . . I was coming back, sergeant . . . I got lost . . .
REV. ED: Darrell, rise and shine buddy!
DARRELL: Oh! I coulda drowned! You coulda killed me! Jesus!
REV. ED: Don't say Jesus.
DARRELL: Well, Daddy, you coulda drown me. If I could breathe underwater, I'd be all right, which I can't! Were you trying to drown me? Who woulda drove the trailer then . . . *(Reverend Eddie has retrieved a map from a drawer and spreads it on the table.)*
REV. ED: Darrell, you better take a look at this map. *(Darrell starts back to the bed.)*
DARRELL: I don't need to see no map. I got a perfect sense of direction.
REV. ED: We've got a long way to go to a place you've never been.
DARRELL: *(Crawls under the cover.)* I been most everywhere.
REV. ED: Am I to assume then that you've been to Canada?
DARRELL: *(Leaping up.)* Canada! I thought you said we was just going to hold up here across the state line! When did you get this idea?
REV. ED: It was not my idea. *(Pulls out letter.)* It was God's idea!
DARRELL: Another letter! *(He goes to brush his teeth at the sink.)*
REV. ED: That's right, Darrell, a letter . . . a sign from God! This time, He found me on the banks of the moving water. I had gone down by the creek to perform my morning ritual. As you know, for the past three days, my morning ritual has gone . . . unrewarded.
DARRELL: I know.
REV. ED: Well, this time, I was squatting amongst some rocks, gazing at my image in a crystal stream, when suddenly, the earth . . . and my bowels . . . moved! After three days! Then the miracle happened. I reached for the Sears

and Roebuck catalogue and it was gone! And this was in its place. I tore it open and read it. It tells us to get out of here as quick as we can and get up to Canada . . . the promised land!

DARRELL: The promised land! Daddy, if you think Canada is some kind of promised land, then this is dumber than I thought it was. There ain't nothing up in Canada but ice . . . and seals . . . and Eskimos.

REV. ED: Sounds to me like maybe you don't know the way.

DARRELL: Huh! Canada. That's easy. Lemme see . . . Canada . . . that's Arkansas . . . Missouri . . . Kansas . . . Nebraska . . . South Dakota . . . North Dakota . . . Canada! That's how you get to Canada. *(Reverend Eddie laughs and put his arm around Darrell's shoulder.)*

REV. ED: That's right, Darrell. That's good!

DARRELL: Yeah, I can get us to Canada and I don't need no map. *(Becky Ann enters sans cotton.)*

REV. ED: Becky Ann!

BECKY ANN: Hi.

REV. ED: Get everything packed. We're going to the promised land . . . *(Puts finger on the Map.)* Moose Jaw . . . Saskatchewan . . . Canada!

DARRELL: Moose Jaw! *(Blackout. Motor noises.)*

ACT I

Scene 4

In the black, we hear Becky Ann singing "Softly and Tenderly," Lights up on trailer. The Reverend Eddie is playing a ukulele. Becky Ann sings "Softly and Tenderly" sweetly and simply. There is no cotton in her ears. Before she can finish the song, the Reverend Eddie interrupts her.

REV. ED: That was very pretty, Becky Ann. But it's gonna have to be different if you're going to do it when the time comes in the tent, in front of all those people.

BECKY ANN: I don't want to do it in front of all those people.

REV. ED: You want to do it right for the baby, don't you?

BECKY ANN: Yeah.

REV. ED: Then let's do it again. Come here. *(She stands facing the audience. She begins to sing. Reverend Eddie interrupts her.)* You know, Becky Ann, that's better, but there's a certain way we sing hymns in church. Let's clasp our hands together. *(He illustrates, she imitates him.)* Smile. *(She smiles awkwardly.)* Look up. *(She looks straight up.)* No, not that far up, Becky Ann. About there. *(He adjusts her face.)* Like you're looking at God.

BECKY ANN: Why is God always up there?

REV. ED: Because He is. Because it's in the Bible.

BECKY ANN: Oh. *(She drops her hands each time he interrupts her.)*

REV. ED: Now, go ahead and sing. Clasp, smile and look up.

BECKY ANN: "Softly and tenderly Jesus is calling . . ."

REV. ED: That's so much better! Now let's add a little something. Maybe a little gesture on "calling." *(He punctuates the word "calling" with a sharp stab of his fingers.)* Shall we? Let's start again. Clasp, smile, look up . . . *(She sings. When she reaches the word "calling," she stabs the air sharply as he did. He hangs his head in frustration.)* I didn't mean that exact gesture, Becky Ann. I had in mind something like . . . "calling." *(He makes a gentler, Las Vegas singers gesture.)* Did you see that? Let's try it. Clasp, smile, look up. *(She sings. When she gets to "calling," she makes the same gesture, mechanically.)* There now. You see how natural that is? *(Blackout. Motor noises.)*

ACT I

Scene 5

Lights up on trailer. Except for the glow from Becky Ann's flashlight as she sits at the kitchen table studying the map, the interior is dark. The Reverend Eddie is asleep on the cot. Suddenly, there is a pounding on the door—three blows. Becky Ann starts, freezes. She runs to her sleeping father, but, as she reaches the bed, the knocks come again, as before. Becky Ann slowly approaches the door, debating whether or not to open it. The door opens slowly. There is the sound of loud rushing wind and eerie music. She looks fearfully into a blinding white light. It is as if the wind is talking to her.

BECKY ANN: Uh, yes, yes he does, but he's asleep. A what? It can't be! *(Clipboard drops magically into the doorway.)* He can't sign anything. He's asleep. *(Pause.)* Well, why do I have to sign? *(Pause.)* Oh. Okay. *(She signs and takes a letter from the clipboard. The clipboard ascends.)* Oh . . . thank you. Would you like something cold to drink? *(The door slams. Becky Ann looks at the letter, turning it over in her hands. She takes it to the table and looks at it in the light. Reverend Eddie begins to stir awake.)*

REV. ED: Becky Ann? *(Becky Ann thrusts the letter in her pocket and moves away from the table.)* Becky Ann?

BECKY ANN: What?

REV. ED: Who was that at the door?

BECKY ANN: A salesman.

REV. ED: A salesman. *(He gets up and goes to the door.)* What was he selling?

BECKY ANN: I'm not sure.

REV. ED: He must not have been a very good salesman.

BECKY ANN: You want breakfast?

REV. ED: No. I won't eat breakfast till ten o'clock. Where's Darrell?

BECKY ANN: He's out fixin' the generator.

REV. ED: That's good. It's good for him to keep busy. *(She searches for the cotton in her pocket and starts to put it in her ears.)* Don't do that, Becky Ann. You won't be needing that. *(She returns the cotton to her pocket.)* Tell me some more about the salesman, Becky Ann. What did he look like?

BECKY ANN: Well, he was *real* tall, and . . . he had a moustache.

REV. ED: A moustache.

BECKY ANN: Yes. And he had a real kind face and a leather suitcase. And he said he traveled everywhere all over the United States and even to Canada where we're going.

REV. ED: *(Angrily.)* You told him where we were going?

BECKY ANN: No, I didn't tell him. I just listened.

REV. ED: Good. That's good. *(He goes to the basin and washes up.)*

BECKY ANN: He said that he had a little baby at home just like mine. Well not *just* like mine . . . and . . . uh . . . his little baby likes to run and play and he reads stories to it and he takes it fishing with him and even though it's just a little bitty baby it knows everything that people are saying to it and everything that's happenin' around it . . . and it really loves its mommy and it wants to take care of its mommy and protect its mommy.

REV. ED: Sounds like you had quite a conversation.

BECKY ANN: I just listened.

REV. ED: That was a big mistake, Becky Ann. You should have just sent him on his way. You should have slammed the door in his face. Those fellows who travel from town to town are Godless. They leave their families behind and traipse around the country with no responsibilities or any thought for anybody but themselves. They only want one thing from someone like you, Becky Ann. First, they worm their way inside the door. They act sweet and charming and sugar wouldn't melt on their tongue. And they find a way to snake close to you and touch you. Maybe they touch your hair, or your dress, or they just happen to brush up against your breasts. And they say, oh I'm sorry, I didn't mean to, but all the time they are looking for another chance to press their flesh against your flesh. *(With growing anger.)* They want to wind themselves around you and get inside you and possess you. They want to turn flesh into filth. They make you unclean. The only thing they're selling is sin. Is that what he was selling, Becky Ann, with his kind face and his leather suitcase?

BECKY ANN: *(Almost crying.)* It weren't no salesman.

REV. ED: What? It weren't?

BECKY ANN: No.

REV. ED: You lied to me, Becky Ann?

BECKY ANN: I didn't mean to. *(Reverend Eddie falls to his knees.)*

REV. ED: God, give me strength. Help me, now, in my hour of need. How sharper than a serpent's tooth is a thankless child. I can't have you lying to me, Becky Ann.

BECKY ANN: I know.

REV. ED: Not now.

BECKY ANN: Daddy, I know.

REV. ED: There's no time for that now. *(He reaches into a cabinet and pulls out an old wooden box.)*

BECKY ANN: I know. I know there isn't. *(She sees the box.)* No, Daddy, no . . .

REV. ED: Pull down your dress, Becky Ann.

BECKY ANN: No, Daddy, Please. *(He opens the box and pulls out a crude wooden cross, to which are attached long leather thongs, and a crown of thorns.)*

REV. ED: Pull down your dress, Becky Ann. NOW!

BECKY ANN: *(Frantically.)* It was another letter! *(She hands the letter to him.)*

REV. ED: A letter? Why did you keep it?

BECKY ANN: Because there's no telling what might be in it.

REV. ED: It's another one of the letters. Look at it. Typed on the same machine as the other ones. It's another sign. Another instruction. Thank you, Jesus. Thank you, Jesus. *(He opens it and reads it silently. He looks puzzled.)*

BECKY ANN: *(Watching him intently.)* Daddy, what does it say?

REV. ED: What?

BECKY ANN: The letter, Daddy, what does it say?

REV. ED: Oh . . . never mind. Never mind what it says. It don't matter. *(There is the sound of a generator kicking in. The lights blink on.)* It's a sign. It's a sign. *(Darrell enters, covered with grease. He sees the box on the table. He looks at Reverend Eddie and Becky Ann suspiciously. Holding up letter.)* Darrell! So you fixed the generator, that's fine boy, that's fine. Look Darrell another letter. Found us in the wilderness. *(He puts the crown and cross back in the box.)* You can't say God isn't looking after us. You can't say that God isn't giving us a road map. *(Darrell goes to wash.)* God's on his highway and all is right with the world. We'll celebrate God's goodness. Tonight we'll drive two hours with the headlights on. You'd like that wouldn't you Darrell? *(Pause.)* I say you'd like that wouldn't you Darrell? *(Pause. He crosses to Darrell.)* Or maybe you're unhappy. *(He shoves Darrell's face down into the basin and holds it there. Darrell gurgles loudly.)* That would be odd. Becky's happy, I'm very happy, we're happy to be doing God's work. *(He releases Darrell.)* You know if you're unhappy Darrell I think you should just pack your bag and get out of here. *(He gets Darrell's duffel bag and throws it at him.)* I think you ought to, Darrell, hitch a ride . . . back to Fort Chaffee. Anybody would be happy to give a ride to a war hero. I'm sure they'd be real happy to see you back at Fort Chaffee. Why don't you just leave? *(Darrell sits. Becky Ann puts the cotton in her ears and begins to hum. Blackout. Motor sounds.)*

ACT I

Scene 6

Lights on the trailer. Becky Ann, Reverend Eddie and Darrell are at the table playing cards. Reverend Eddie is very cheerful. Becky Ann is leaning over the baby, humming, her cards dangling loosely from her hand.

REV. ED: Okay, Darrell give me all your . . . fives. *(Darrell angrily throws three cards on the table.)* Aha! Okay, got yer fives, got yer fives. Lemme see, lemme see, Becky Ann, give me all your . . . jacks. *(Becky Ann, of course, cannot hear. Reverend Eddie raps on the table. Becky Ann looks up. Reverend Eddie draws a large "J" in the air. Becky Ann looks through her cards.)*

BECKY ANN: Daddy, go fish. *(Reverend Eddie draws a card.)*

REV. ED: Okay, go fish, go fish. Wonder what I'm gonna get. *(He draws.)* Very interesting all right. Darrell, it's your turn.

DARRELL: *(Laughing with anticipation.)* Yessir, give me all your . . . jacks. *(Pause.)*

REV. ED: Well, I reckon you're just gonna have to go fish. *(Darrell looks confused.)* I hope you got your wadin' boots on! *(Laughs.)* Hope you got a good net, Darrell, hope they're bitin' today . . . what do you say, Darrell, I hope they're bitin' today, eh? *(He pokes Darrell in the ribs.)*

DARRELL: All right, all right. I get it. *(He draws a card.)*

REV. ED: Becky Ann, it's your turn. *(He raps on the table. She looks up. He points at her.)*

BECKY ANN: Daddy, give me all your queens. *(Resumes humming.)*

REV. ED: Well, Becky Ann, I guess I'm gonna have to tell you what I told Darrell. I hope they're bitin' today . . . I hope you got your wading boots on, right Darrell? *(Becky Ann looks at him blankly. He makes a rod-and-reel motion. She draws a card.)* Okay, I guess it's my turn. Guess the game's in my hands . . . okay . . . I hope I won't have to put on my . . . what?

DARRELL: Wading boots.

REV. ED: *(Laughs.)* That's right, wading boots. But something tells me I'm not gonna have to do that. Just one more card and I can go out, win all the matches. I wonder what that card could be? Maybe I'm gonna ask for a six. But no, Darrell laid down the sixes, that's the only book he's got. *(Darrell is in an agony of impatience.)* Well, that don't leave much. What do you think I'm gonna ask for, Darrell?

DARRELL: If my memory wasn't shot up, I could guess what you got, which it was.

REV. ED: Well, I'm gonna tell you, Darrell. Yes sir, here it comes. The big moment. Could we have a drumroll please? *(He lays his cards down and plays a drumroll on the table. Becky Ann looks up.)*

BECKY ANN: Is it my turn?

DARRELL: Jesus take me now.

REV. ED: For all the matches, and the Go Fish championship of the entire world . . . he asks for JACKS! *(Darrell, surely, takes a card out of his hand and starts to slam it down. He pauses.)* Could that be a Jack? Praise God! *(He takes the card, makes his book, and takes in the matches.)*

DARRELL: I asked for jacks last time it was my turn, and you said you didn't have any!

REV. ED: I must've drew one.

DARRELL: You got three jacks! How could you draw three jacks! That's impossible!

REV. ED: Nothing's impossible with the Lord.

DARRELL: You tellin' me the Lord lied about havin' three jacks?

REV. ED: Darrell, it's only a game. And I don't appreciate your yellin' durin' family time. *(Darrell throws his cards down angrily and crosses to the radio.)* Now I have something tremendously important. The flight from Egypt is almost over . . . *(Darrell switches on the radio.)* Darrell, turn off the radio.

DARRELL: I'm trying to find out if they're still lookin' for us.

REV. ED: We do not play the radio durin' family time.

DARRELL: To hell with family time. *(The Reverend Eddie looks at Darrell, who for a moment continues to turn the dial. Suddenly, in one swift movement, the reverend moves to the table, picks up the radio, and smashes it to the floor. Darrell looks at it, stunned.)*

REV. ED: There's where your hell is . . . right there. *(Darrell picks up the pieces and returns them to the shelf.)*

DARRELL: You broke it. That was *my* radio! And you broke it.

REV. ED: We don't need a radio. It has no information that we need. Now as I was saying that . . .

DARRELL: No, you'd rather play Go Fish! I don't see why we have to play the same dumb game every night! And you always win! Why can't we do something else during family time? *We're* family, too!

REV. ED: Son, come here.

DARRELL: No. *(Reverend Eddie reaches out a loving arm for Darrell. Darrell relents and comes closer. Suddenly, Reverend Eddie grips Darrell in a vicious hammerlock.)* Ow!

REV. ED: Darrell . . . when our Lord gathered Simon Peter and his brethren on the rocky shores of the Sea of Tiberias, they were so afraid that their simple way of life was over . . . that they would no longer cast their rough nets to reap the harvest of the salty sea. But our Lord took Simon Peter aside and sat him upon a rock. *(He sits Darrell down.)* He looked him in the eye . . . and what did our Lord say to Simon Peter?

DARRELL: Go fish. *(Reverend Eddie releases him.)*

REV. ED: That's right, Darrell. Go fish. Be ye fishers of men! That's why Go Fish is the only card game not considered sinful in the eyes of God.

DARRELL: Aw, come on. That's not in there! God never said anything in the Bible about Go Fish! Where did you read that? Did you read it in one of your letters? What's in 'em Daddy? How come you don't read 'em to us anymore? We used to have to sit and listen to 'em over and over again. Signs from God! Why don't you read 'em to us now! *(Snatches cotton out of Becky Ann's ears.)* Ask him Becky Ann! Ask him why he don't read us no more letters!

BECKY ANN: I hear the baby.

DARRELL: That's another thing. How can you hear the baby? It don't never make no sound. It *can't* make no sound. It ain't got no mouth.

BECKY ANN: The baby needs me.

DARRELL: What does it need? It don't ever seem to need nothing. It just lays there. *(She takes the baby from the basket.)*

BECKY ANN: Hi, baby.

DARRELL: It can't hear you. How can it hear you? It ain't got no ears.

REV. ED: Hold it! Just hold it a minute! Now, for this entire trip I have head this baby being called "it" and "baby." Don't nobody call him by name?

DARRELL: It ain't got no name.

REV. ED: Exactly. That's exactly my point. He don't have a name. And it's time. I've been waiting for the right time. And this is it. This is the time. The flight from Egypt is almost over. *(Darrell starts out.)* You stay and hear this. The flight from Egypt is almost over. The child is about to enter his father's temple. He baffles the elders.

DARRELL: He baffles me. *(Darrell sits.)*

REV. ED: In generations to come, all mankind will praise His name. Will glorify *His* name. Will exalt *His* name! Of course, in order for this destiny to be fulfilled, the child must actually have a name. Now I have a name in mind. But this will be a family decision. We will all make our suggestions. Darrell why don't you go first? What do you think the little baby's name should be?

DARRELL: What difference does it make? You're gonna decide anyway.

REV. ED: Darrell, I am giving you an opportunity to partake in a moment that mankind will long remember. Now what do you think the baby's name should be? *(Long pause.)*

DARRELL: Bubba.

REV. ED: Bubba?

DARRELL: Yeah, Bubba or what about squash or turnip or eggplant? 'Cause it ain't nothin' but a vegetable anyway.

REV. ED: Darrell, you, by your blasphemy, have forfeited your right to take part in this moment. Henceforth you are erased from the recorded history of this event. Now, Becky Ann, you are the child's mother. I am sure you have given this much thought. What do *you* think your little baby's name should be?

BECKY ANN: Arlene Marie. *(Pause. Darrell snorts. Reverend Eddie gives him a warning look.)*

REV. ED: Becky Ann . . . Arlene Marie is a very lovely name.

BECKY ANN: Thank you!

REV. ED: But it is a little girl's name.

BECKY ANN: It could be a girl.

REV. ED: It could *not* be a girl!

DARRELL: How can you tell, it ain't got no . . .

REV. ED: Shut up, Darrell! Becky Ann, I will ask you again for a suggestion and give you the opportunity to put forth an appropriate name.

BECKY ANN: Arlene Marie.

REV. ED: Becky Ann, don't do that! *(She jams cotton in her ears.)*

BECKY ANN: Arlene Marie! *(Reverend Eddie snatches the cotton out of her ears.)*

REV. ED: Becky Ann! *(She pulls more cotton from her pocket and stuffs it in her ears.)*

BECKY ANN: Arlene Marie! *(He snatches the cotton from her ears.)*

REV. ED: Becky Ann, stop it!

BECKY ANN: Arlene Marie.

REV. ED: It's a boy! *(She puts more cotton in her ears.)*

BECKY ANN: Arlene Marie Arlene Marie Arlene Marie . . . *(He snatches the cotton out. This happens a few more times, until suddenly she is out of cotton. She rummages around in her pockets. She is panicky. Suddenly, she claps her hands over her ears.)* Arlene Marie Arlene Marie Arlene Marie . . .

REV. ED: Becky Ann! Stop it! *(He grabs at her arms and tries to jerk them away from her ears, but she holds fast, repeating the name over and over. Suddenly, she bolts from him. He gives chase. She gets the table between them as he grabs at her. She runs from the trailer.)* Darrell! Help me! *(They run outside and around the trailer, Darrell close behind Reverend Eddie. Reverend Eddie stops and turns to Darrell.)* Don't get after me, get after her! *(Darrell runs after Becky Ann to head her off. He and Reverend Eddie chase her back into the trailer. They struggle around the room, knocking over furniture, Reverend Eddie and Darrell screaming and Becky Ann shouting "Arlene Marie!" over and over.)* Tie her to this chair! *(Darrell and Reverend Eddie tie her in an armchair and stuff a gag in her mouth. Reverend Eddie and Darrell catch their breath. Silence. Reverend Eddie walks to the basket.)* I have had a revelation. I have decided on a name for the child. He shall be called Prince of Peace, Wise Counselor, Blessed Redeemer, Savior Anointed. He shall be called as he was in his first incarnation, when he promised to all those who kept his covenant that he would return in glory. From henceforth, the child's holy name shall be linked with the distinguished name of our family. The child shall be called Jesus. *(Raises his arms.)* Jesus O. Tarbox. *(He takes out a pocket watch and looks at it.)* Well, family time is over. *(Blackout.)*

ACT I

Scene 7

Lights up on Reverend Eddie at the typewriter. Becky Ann and Darrell are asleep. Reverend Eddie looks to heaven.

REV. ED: God . . . I've done everything you've asked. I've followed all your instructions. I've never questioned you. But God . . . in a few days, we're gonna raise that tent, and cover ourselves in glory, and I've got to tell those people . . . *(He gestures to the typewriter.)* . . . something. Won't you please help me? See God, I'm confused. I'm talking about the letters. In the beginning, your voice was clear. *(He gets the old letters.)* In the beginning, you said . . . and I quote . . . *(Reads.)* "You should not have give the baby away. Shame on you, you should not have did it. Blood is thicker than water. Shame." Or this one . . . "This baby may not look like much, but it is family. Go get it as quick as you can, or you will burn in Hell." Or . . . "You are like a fly on the kitchen table. If you do not go get that child, you will surely . . . be swatted." I have listened to these letters, Lord, I have followed the signs. Fortunately, I was able to interpret them correctly. I saw your plan for my salvation . . . I saw my seat in glory. God . . . your son is in my hands. But now . . . I am bewildered. I don't understand what you're telling me with these *new* letters. *(He holds up a stack of new letters, and opens one.)* What does this mean? "We have come from the light, where the light originated through itself." *(Pause.)* That makes no sense to me. Or this . . . "Knock on yourself as upon a door . . . and walk on yourself as upon a straight road." *(Shrugs. He looks at the third letter for a few seconds.)* "Make no friendship with an elephant keeper . . . if you have no room to entertain . . . an elephant." God, I've never *seen* an elephant! These letters just don't fit! God, we're close, so close. Why do you abandon me now? I have endured hardship and persecution in your name. I've lost my church, I've lost my home, I have been accused of a horrendous crime against you . . . people have took up rocks against us, and now this! It's just not fair! Are you testing me, God? I can pass the test. Speak to me through this baby. I will use this baby. He will have his thirty-three years of glorious ministry. I will see that your prophecy is fulfilled, even unto death and resurrection. *(Holds up letters.)* But what do I do with these? I'm not thinking of myself, Lord. I'm thinking of you. I'm thinking of how you will look if I read these letters at the tent meeting . . . especially the one about the elephant! What do I do with these? What do I do? What do I do? *(Pause.)* What did you say, Lord? Yes, I hear you. I *hear* you! I think that is the right idea. *(He takes the new letters and throws them into a bucket. He strikes a match and holds it to the corner of an envelope.)* And the Lord said . . . "The fire next time . . ." *(He leaves the letters burning in a bucket. He watches them burn for a second then exits. There is a pause. We hear the crackling of the flames. Then the baby basket begins to glow. It gradually slides across the stage until it is in front of the table. A light comes up on the typewriter. By itself, it begins to type in rhythm with the pulsing light in the basket. The typing continues, picking up speed, as the lights fade.)*

END ACT I

ACT II

Scene 1

We hear a car idling. We hear the following conversation:

CUSTOMS MAN: What is your destination?

DARRELL: Who cares?

REV. ED: Saskatchewan. Moose Jaw, Saskatchewan.

CUSTOMS MAN: How many in the car?

DARRELL: Four, if you count the . . .

REV. ED: Three! There are three us, officer. Only three.

CUSTOMS MAN: Do you have any fruits or vegetables?

DARRELL: We're not sure.

REV. ED: No, officer, no fruits or vegetables.

CUSTOMS MAN: How long do you plan to stay in Canada?

REV. ED: Not long, officer. Two weeks from this very day, we will hold our tent meeting, then we will leave your lovely country, basking in the glory of that event. I hope you will be able to attend, officer, and hear my message.

CUSTOMS MAN: I'll try. *(Lights up. The trailer is empty. The basket is glowing. It moves to the radio. Then a light begins to glow inside the smashed radio. It begins to play—Fibber McGee and Molly. The dial begins to switch stations until it arrives at the news.)*

RADIO: " . . . have given up the search for the infant abducted from the University of Arkansas. Scientists at the university were experimenting with the child, who was born without vital organs. Doctors said that the infant needed special care, and must be presumed dead. In other news . . . a giant chicken . . ." *(The dial switches stations, arriving at a bouncy verse of "If I Knew You Were Coming, I'd Have Baked a Cake."—The baby's light bounces in rhythm to the music. Darrell bursts through the door, but the radio has stopped playing and the lights have ceased glowing. He walks over to the radio and shakes it suspiciously. Disgusted, he puts it down. He starts to go out, but turns and walks slowly to the basket. He has his ball and glove. He looks into the basket. Reaches in and moves the blanket slightly. He recoils from the sight.)*

DARRELL: Yecch! Boy you sure are ugly. Hell, we'd have to hang a pork chop around your neck to get the dog to play with you. If we had a dog and you had a neck which we don't and you don't. You hear me? Of course you can't hear me. You need ears to hear. Can't see me either can you? Wait a minute, maybe that's an ear. Yeah, that could be an ear. Or maybe it's a hand. Nah! I don't see what's so special about you anyway. Where were you during the war, Jesus O. Tarbox? I didn't see you out where I was on the front lines in France, Europe, where it was so freezin' cold out there in the field that we had to stuff newspapers in our uniforms to keep from freezing to death! I bet you are wondering about this medal. *(Fingers his Purple Heart.)* This is called the Purple Heart, and except for the Congressional Medal of Honor, it's the best medal a person in the armed forces can get. I could've got a lot of other medals, but I wanted this one. They gave it to me for valor, bravery, courage and getting stuck with a bayonet. Oh yeah?! You want to see my war scar? *(He raises his shirt.)* There it is, right there.

And that's why I'm not playing professional baseball to this day. If them krauts hadn't of stuck me, I'd still have my fastball. Which they did, and I don't. But I'm still better off than you. I got a good nickel curveball which is more than you've got. I got a spitball, which is more than you got. I got spit, which is more than you got. You couldn't throw a baseball if your life depended on it, which fortunately for you it don't. Hell, you can't even catch. You know, I bet if I was to take this baseball right here and throw it as hard as I can right in your . . . your . . . face, I'd probably kill you. I'd probably splatter you all over this trailer. End all this craziness forever. No more hearin' how special you are. So maybe that's what I ought to do. Put you out of your misery. End all this craziness. Course if you really was Jesus, like Daddy says, you could, stop me . . . you could stop this baseball in midair, or turn it into a rabbit or something. Is that what you're gonna do? Come on, Jesus O. Tarbox, what'll it be? The catcher, give me a sign. Curve or spitball? Just give me a sign. *(He raises his arm to throw. Pauses, lowers his arm and sits by the basket. Becky Ann enters carrying groceries.)*
BECKY ANN: Darrell! What are you doing?
DARRELL: I wasn't doing nothin'! I wasn't hurtin' your precious baby! I was just showing it my war scar.
BECKY ANN: Oh, she don't want to see any old scar from your hernia operation.
DARRELL: Hernia!
BECKY ANN: It's all right baby. I don't like no ugly old scars either.
DARRELL: Hernia, hell. What'd you get to eat? Eggplant? Becky Ann, I told you no more eggplant. What's this?
BECKY ANN: A letter.
DARRELL: Another letter. How many of these we git today?
BECKY ANN: Five or six since this mornin'.
DARRELL: Five or six? How are all these letters finding us? How did this one get here?
BECKY ANN: It was waitin' for me at the market.
DARRELL: At the market? How the hell did anyone know you was goin' to the market?
BECKY ANN: Well, Darrell we gotta eat.
DARRELL: No, no. How did anybody know you was going there today? *(She shrugs.)* Has he seen this yet?
BECKY ANN: No.
DARRELL: Where is he?
BECKY ANN: He stayed in town to nail up leaflets.
DARRELL: Leaflets! I wonder what it says.
BECKY ANN: It says, "Big Tent Meeting Sunday night at 8 o'clock."
DARRELL: No, Becky Ann, the letter, not the leaflets! I know what the leaflets say!

BECKY ANN: Oh.

DARRELL: *(Reads.)* "Reverend Edward O. Tarbox, c/o Scofield's Market, Moose Jaw, Saskatchewan, Canada." No stamp. No return address. No nothin'. Hmmmm. What's in it, Becky Ann?

BECKY ANN: I don't know.

DARRELL: Come on, Becky Ann. What's in it?

BECKY ANN: I don't know what's in it.

DARRELL: Let's open it.

BECKY ANN: Ain't addressed to you. It's addressed to Daddy.

DARRELL: He'll never miss it. He burns 'em all now anyway.

BECKY ANN: It's against the law.

DARRELL: The hell with the law. I'm gonna open it. *(He looks around as if the Reverend Eddie might be looking over his shoulder and rips the envelope. He reads. He looks puzzled.)*

BECKY ANN: Darrell, what does it say?

DARRELL: Oh, now you want to know what it says. I thought you said it was against the law.

BECKY ANN: Darrell . . .

DARRELL: All right! *(Reads.)* "We wrote a hundred letters, and you did not answer. That, too, is a reply." What the hell does that mean?

BECKY ANN: I don't know.

DARRELL: Aw, come on! What's it mean?

BECKY ANN: I don't *know* what it means!

DARRELL: Becky Ann, I ain't stupid! I didn't just fall off the damn turnip truck! I've seen you from the time you was a little girl! I know you'd do anything to get that baby back. You wrote the letters! You wrote all those letters and sent them to him so's he would think they was signs from God! You think I couldn't tell you wrote all that stuff about how sinful it was to give away the baby, and how it was our own flesh and blood. How he was gonna burn in hell. How he was like a fly going 'round the kitchen table and was surely gonna get swatted. What was it you rubbed on his skin so's he would have an "affliction" like Job?

BECKY ANN: Lye.

DARRELL: I knew it. Lye. I knew it. *(Laughs.)*

BECKY ANN: And Darrell, you know what?

DARRELL: What?

BECKY ANN: Sometimes, late at night, when he was asleep, I'd sneak into his room and whisper things in his ears, holy things like Bible verses, so's maybe he would think it was the blessed Virgin Mary come to him in his dreams . . . He must not have heard me though, or if he did, he didn't mention it.

DARRELL: He'd kill you, if he found out.

BECKY ANN: Well, he won't find out. Unless you tell him. *(Very frightened.)* You ain't gonna tell him, are you?

DARRELL: Aw, I wouldn't tell him. He wouldn't believe me, if I did. But he's gonna get wise if you keep sendin' him those letters! I don't understand why you keep doin' it.

BECKY ANN: I ain't doin' it, cross my heart and hope to die!

DARRELL: Aw . . . Becky Ann.

BECKY ANN: I swear!

DARRELL: You swear? On what?

BECKY ANN: On Jesus' Holy Name!

DARRELL: Which Jesus? The real Jesus or Daddy's Jesus?

BECKY ANN: On my own life.

DARRELL: Ain't good enough.

BECKY ANN: I'm tellin' the truth. I'll swear on anything you want!

DARRELL: If that's true, if that's really true, you swear right here on our Momma's Holy Bible. *(He gets Momma's Bible and holds it in front of her. She places her hand on it.)*

BECKY ANN: I swear on Momma's Holy Bible that I ain't wrote any of the letters since we got Arlene Marie back. Oh, except for the one about Moosejaw. Sorry Momma. *(Darrell takes his Momma's lock of hair from the Bible and holds it out to Becky Ann. She kisses it. She then holds it for him to kiss. He lovingly returns it to the Bible, and returns the Bible to its place.)*

DARRELL: Then who the hell is writin' these letters?

BECKY ANN: I don't know!

DARRELL: Wait . . . maybe he's writin' 'em himself.

BECKY ANN: Why?

DARRELL: I don't know. So he'll keep gettin' signs from God!

BECKY ANN: Then why would he burn them?

DARRELL: Because he's *crazy!* He thinks he's God. Don't you see how this whole thing's backfired on you?

BECKY ANN: What are you talking about?

DARRELL: Ain't you heard him? Don't you know what his plans are? Don't you know what he thinks God has prophesied for that baby?

BECKY ANN: Darrell, ain't nothing bad gonna happen to this baby! *(She begins to knit.)* This baby makes Daddy real happy and she makes *me* real happy! Can't you just leave it alone?

DARRELL: You think that baby is yours, Becky Ann? That baby ain't yours. He thinks that baby is the second coming of Christ! *(She stuffs cotton in her ears and begins to hum.)* He's gonna fulfill the prophecy. That's what this tent meeting is for, don't you know that? Little Jesus O. Tarbox is gonna be baptized under the big top next Sunday night! . . . And then you know what's gonna happen? He said it, Becky Ann! Even to death and resurrection! He ain't talkin' about his own death. He's talking about your precious baby! *(Gets right down in front of Becky Ann's face.)* Is that what you want, Becky Ann? IS IT? IS IT? *(He snatches the cotton out of her ears.)* Is it?

BECKY ANN: Did you say something, Darrell?

DARRELL: Becky Ann . . . we gotta get outta here. You and me and . . . Arlene Marie.

BECKY ANN: But what would happen to Daddy?

DARRELL: Who cares? He don't care about us!

BECKY ANN: He needs us.

DARRELL: Sure he needs us! Who else would drive his car without no headlights? Who else would cook his breakfast at ten o'clock at night? Who else would take care of that baby! Who else would go along with a lunatic that thinks that God is talking to him by way of the U.S. Mail?

BECKY ANN: Where would we go?

DARRELL: Back home.

BECKY ANN: Darrell, I can't go there . . . they would take her away from me again.

DARRELL: Maybe that's for the best.

BECKY ANN: No!

DARRELL: Maybe they wouldn't. Maybe we could talk to them.

BECKY ANN: No!

DARRELL: Maybe they'd let us take care of the baby together.

BECKY ANN: NO!

DARRELL: Becky Ann, we got to get out of here! That maniac is gonna kill us all! We're all gonna fry! *(He starts to pack his duffel bag.)* I ain't gonna let him do that. I'm going whether you go with me or not, I'm going. If he was right here now, I'd tell him right to his face . . . *(The door bursts open. It is the Reverend Eddie. He is dressed up, in a seedy kind of way. He carries an armful of leaflets.)*

REV. ED: This . . . has been . . . a very interesting day.

BECKY ANN: What's wrong, Daddy?

REV. ED: Nothing's wrong. God is still with us. He can do no wrong.

BECKY ANN: That's good.

REV. ED: I'll tell you what's wrong. Satan has arrived in the town of Moose Jaw. He has taken control of this town.

BECKY ANN: What did he do, Daddy?

REV. ED: He got a law passed that nobody can put up advertising without a license. I went to the city hall to get a license. They asked to see my ministerial credentials. Credentials! When Jesus spoke to his disciples, he told them to go out and preach the word. He did not tell them to go out and get six years of college and preach the word!

BECKY ANN: Well Daddy, did you show them your Bible?

REV. ED: They spit upon the Bible!

BECKY ANN: Well I'll wipe if off for ya. *(She takes it and starts to wipe it off.)*

REV. ED: They spit on it *spiritually!* *(He snatches it from her.)*

BECKY ANN: Oh. *(She resumes knitting.)*

DARRELL: What about the permit to set up the tent?

REV. ED: Do you think I'd soil my purpose by continuing in conversation with agents of the devil?

DARRELL: So you didn't get the permit.

REV. ED: Permit! Permit! Who gives God a permit. Who tells God what to do and what not to do? Who gives God leave to conduct his business? Who dares to do that?

DARRELL: You ain't God.

REV. ED: *IT'S THE SAME THING!*

DARRELL: Well, Daddy, whatcha you gonna do? You know if we set up that tent without a permit, they're gonna arrest us. They're gonna put us in jail . . . they're gonna try to find out if we got any other kind of record. Probably gonna get on the phone to them authorities back in El Dorado, them authorities are gonna get out our permanent records and find them "black marks" on our permanent records—mine and yours. Then, them authorities back in Arkansas, they're gonna expedite us back to Arkansas. And we're gonna stand trial, and that judge is gonna bang down his gavel and say "I find you guilty as sin and I sentence you all to fry." Of course, if we was to fry because that's what God wanted, it would be one thing . . . but maybe God is trying to tell us that he don't want us to fry. Maybe he's tryin' to tell us to get our butts out of Moose Jaw. Maybe he's trying to tell us to give the baby back. It's still alive as far as anyone can tell. We ain't hurt it any. They'll probably take the baby back and just forget the whole thing.

REV. ED: Maybe . . . maybe . . .

DARRELL: Maybe that's the right answer . . . the right reply!

REV. ED: What? *(Darrell pulls out the letter.)*

DARRELL: God says that He ain't heard no reply. You ain't answered his letters. Maybe the reply He wants is for us to get our butts . . .

REV. ED: *(Interrupting.)* What's that?

DARRELL: *(Stunned pause.)* What?

REV. ED: Is that a letter?

DARRELL: This? I don't think so . . . I . . . uh . . .

REV. ED: Give me that!

DARRELL: Oh, you don't want to see this . . .

REV. ED: *Give me that! (Darrell reluctantly hands him the letter. He takes it out of its envelope and reads it. He puts it back in the envelope.)* You opened my letter. You read it.

DARRELL: No! No I didn't. I swear I didn't. It was open when it got here. It kinda just fell out of the envelope . . . I couldn't help but see what it said . . . it was just laying there open . . . I didn't open it. I swear to you I didn't. Becky

Ann, tell him. *(Pause.)* Tell him, Becky Ann!

BECKY ANN: You did. You did, Darrell. You opened Daddy's letter and you read it.

DARRELL: Becky Ann . . .

BECKY ANN: And then you tried to get me and the baby to run away with you.

REV. ED: Is that right, Darrell? Is that what you did?

DARRELL: I was only kiddin'.

REV. ED: Is that right, Judas? You were only kidding were you? What else did he say, Becky Ann?

BECKY ANN: That you was crazy.

DARRELL: I never said that.

BECKY ANN: And you thought you was God and he wanted to give my baby away and he didn't fall off the damn turnip truck.

DARRELL: Becky Ann . . .

REV. ED: *(Picks Darrell up and throws him across the room.)* Satan! You are erased. I have erased you. Your name is dust. Your body is ashes. God will no longer recognize your face. Get out of my house.

DARRELL: No Daddy, no.

REV. ED: Get out!

DARRELL: I'll do anything!

REV. ED: Get out of my house and go back to your father in hell! *(Reverend Eddie throws Darrell out the door. He throws some of Darrell's things after him.)*

DARRELL: *(Offstage.)* I could tell you something about your precious letters, but you wouldn't believe me. And I know what you did! I know what both of you did! And I ain't gonna be the one who's gonna burn in hell!

BECKY ANN: We've upset the baby. It's all right, baby. *(Reverend Ed paces about angrily. Suddenly, he falls to his knees.)*

REV. ED: Becky Ann.

BECKY ANN: What?

REV. ED: The Holy Ghost is in this trailer.

BECKY ANN: Where?

REV. ED: The moment I drove Satan out that door, the Holy Ghost came in and my mind cleared. I can see everything like it was crystal.

BECKY ANN: What do you see, Daddy?

REV. ED: I see a vision. I'm in the vision. And you're in the vision.

BECKY ANN: *(Fearful.)* Is the baby in the vision?

REV. ED: Yes, Becky Ann. The baby *is* the vision! In my vision he stands tall and straight and he has limbs of ivory and his eyes are as bright as brass and his mouth speaks with a tongue of fire. And all mankind bow down to him and worship his name. And he wants us to help him.

BECKY ANN: How?

REV. ED: Here's what I'm going to do. I'm going to find a way to get this tent up!

I am going to go to the house of every farmer in this Godforsaken territory. I will ask them for permission to put our tent up on their property. I will ask them in God's name and explain to them that we are doing God's work. I will get down on my knees and beg them if I have to. After dark, I will return. Then, you will take the leaflets and spread them all over town. And then, together, we will bask in God's glory.

BECKY ANN: Is that what you see in your vision?

REV. ED: Among other things.

BECKY ANN: And am I the mother in the vision?

REV. ED: Yes, Becky. You are the blessed Virgin.

BECKY ANN: Will I always be the mother?

REV. ED: Yes, Becky Ann. You will be revered through all eternity. You are the vessel of glory. And you will be there as God's plan is fulfilled, even unto death and resurrection. *(Becky Ann looks down at the baby.)*

BECKY ANN: Oh. *(Blackout.)*

ACT II

Scene 2

In the blackout, we hear Becky Ann singing, to the tune of "Jesus Loves Me."

BECKY ANN:

Happy birthday, baby girl.
I love you more than all the world
You are sweet and you are purty
You don't even get things dirty.

Yes, Arlene's one month old
It's the happiest story ever told
Yes, Arlene's one month old
One month old today.

(Lights up on the trailer. Becky Ann, wearing a party hat, is sitting at the table holding the baby, who is squirming. She lights the lone candle on the birthday cake. She looks at the cake.) Make a wish. Blow it out. *(Pause.)* Oh, that's all right. *(She blows out the candle.)* Ain't it a pretty cake? I didn't have no food colorin' for the icin', so I had to write your name in grape jelly. *(She puts baby in basket.)* Look at this birthday girl! She's so purty. *(She stands and bats the balloon that's tied to the edge of the basket. She bats it again.)* Ain't birthdays fun? Oh! You want your present? I made it just for you. *(She goes to her knitting bag and pulls out a lop-sided rectangular piece of knitting. She shows it to the baby.)* I hope it fits. *(She lays it on the baby.)* There. That fits perfect. *(She picks the baby up.)* Oh my, I love you, Arlene Marie. They always said I couldn't take care of a baby, but you ain't no trouble at all. You never wet, or cry, or nothin'! You are such a good baby.

(She talks to the right end of the baby.) Ol' Darrell, he makes fun of you all the time, *(She talks to the left end of the baby.)* but he's just jealous because he wants to be special. Always remember, Arlene Marie, no matter how hard life gets, you are special. And your daddy was special. I'm gonna tell you something, Arlene Marie, that I ain't ever told nobody. It's about your daddy. I didn't know at first that it was happenin'. I thought it was a dream. It happened so sudden and so forceful that I got really scared. But I guess it was good . . . cause I got you. And I was filled with this music . . . an unearthly kind of music that I never even heard before. I can't even sing it for you. I wrote you a song, though! Yeah, for your birthday! *(She fetches the ukulele and plants her foot on the chair. She plays and sings.)*

I'm gonna tell you 'bout your daddy and me
How you was born, how you came to be
You're a big baby now, old enough to know
Wasn't like they tell you in the picture show
Lots of fear
It was his idear
Raped by God.

You know it's kinda hard for even me to understand
I guess you know your daddy's not an ordinary man
I wanted to scream but I didn't have a voice
I wanted to run but I didn't have a choice
I guess you could say
he had to have his way
Raped by God.

(She moves the chair away.) And now this part I learned at the picture show. You ready, here I go. *(She begins to hum, play the ukulele, and do a very bad soft-shoe to the tune of the song she has written. During this the baby basket begins to spin to the verse. She stops and looks at the baby.)* Arlene Marie! That was really good! How'd you learn to do that? *(She begins to dance again.)* Doodle li doodle li doo, Hi! Doodle li doodle li doo, Boo! I'm just gonna have to teach you all the songs and dances I know. I wish I could remember everything to tell you exact but there was all this wind and fire and fog and stuff. He whispered to me though. He said, "I'm gonna give to you what the eye has not seen, what the ear has not heard, what the hand has not touched, and what has not yet risen up in the heart of man" and "ye who are near to me are near to the fire," and then he said something about an elephant. And then the wind and the fire and the fog was gone. I'm really sorry no one else remembered your birthday. Happy birthday, Arlene Marie. *(She begins to sing and dance with the baby. Reverend Eddie bursts through the door. She freezes.)*

REV. ED: Hallelujah! God has opened the door. What are you doing?

BECKY ANN: It's the baby's birthday . . .

REV. ED: Never mind. *(He rips the party hat off her head and throws it on the floor.)* I have something important for you to do. Get your coat on.

BECKY ANN: Why?

REV. ED: Because God's wheels are in motion, His train is pulling into the station. I have been through this Godforsaken territory from one end to the other, hoping I could convince God to spare this barren Sodom by helping me find one good man. Well, I found him, not two miles from where we speak. He will allow us to raise our tents in his pasture for only a modest fee. God's plan is working! It is inevitable!

BECKY ANN: What does He want me to do?

REV. ED: *(Hands her the pamphlets.)* He wants you to spread them so far and as wide as you can before daylight.

BECKY ANN: What if someone tries to stop me?

REV. ED: Tell them you are doin' God's work. Anyway, they will be loath to detain a woman. Go, do God's will, and hurry back. *(He ushers her out the door. Reverend Eddie joyfully whoops and claps his hands. In his exuberance, he suddenly pops the baby's balloon. Becky Ann bursts back through the door.)*

BECKY ANN: I think I'll take the baby . . .

REV. ED: No, leave the baby where it is. You will have your hands full enough.

BECKY ANN: *(Trying to get to the baby, but blocked by Reverend Eddie.)* I think the baby needs fresh air . . .

REV. ED: Fresh air could be the worst thing in the world for that child. He might get the croup.

BECKY ANN: *(Struggling.)* I'll dress it real warm . . .

REV. ED: No! Leave the baby here. I will look after the baby! *(He grabs her roughly by the arm and pushes her roughly out the door. Pause. He hangs his jacket up, then notices the cake. Casting the single candle aside, he scoops up some icing with his finger and licks it. He looks into the basket. He begins to croon, "The Old Rugged Cross." As he sings, he picks the baby up from the basket and cradles it awkwardly. He sits.)*

"On the Old Rugged Cross, stained with blood so divine

A wondrous beauty I see . . .

For 'twas on that old cross, Jesus suffered and died

To pardon and sanctify me . . .

(As he reaches the end of the verse, the door behind him opens with a squeak. He freezes. Darrell appears in the doorway, wearing army fatigues and a helmet. He carries a bayonet. He lets the door slam. Reverend Eddie turns.) Darrell! You scared the hell out of me . . .

DARRELL: I hope so, Daddy . . . I hope so. *(He plunges the bayonet into the countertop.)*

REV. ED: I was just singin' the baby to sleep.

DARRELL: I know you were.

REV. ED: That's a mighty sharp bayonet you got there. Is that the one they stabbed you with during the war?

DARRELL: What do you think, I'm crazy. I got it at the army surplus. *(He pulls the bayonet from the counter.)* I know where I got it.

REV. ED: Of course you do, Darrell. The same place you got your war medal. *(With a swift movement, Darrell cuts Reverend Eddie on the neck.)*

DARRELL: We weren't talkin' about my war medal.

REV. ED: You cut me.

DARRELL: Well, you better wash it off. Cuts can get infested. *(Silence. Reverend Eddie does not move. Darrell lowers the bayonet. He laughs maniacally.)* What did you think I was gonna do with this bayonet, Daddy? What did you think? I was gonna kill you?

REV. ED: No, Darrell, I know you're not gonna kill your father.

DARRELL: Well, you're wrong. I was gonna kill you. And I still am. *(He suddenly grabs his father by the hair and puts the bayonet to his throat. Pause.)*

REV. ED: Some fun huh Darrell? Look . . . we can talk about this. Just let me put this baby down.

DARRELL: Why do you want to put the baby down? I thought that baby was Jesus. I thought that baby was your salvation. Well, let's see him save you now. Come on, Jesus, save my daddy. *(Pause.)* We're waitin'. *(Pause.)* Well Daddy, it looks like that baby ain't gonna save you. *(He releases his father.)* I wonder who's gonna save you now. Anybody in this trailer who can save my daddy, raise your hand.

REV. ED: I just don't understand what I've done that's so wrong that would make you want to kill me. Was it beatin' you at cards?

DARRELL: You cheated!

REV. ED: Well, Darrell, if it makes you feel better to think that I cheated, then . . . yes, I cheated, and I beg your forgiveness . . .

DARRELL: You broke my radio.

REV. ED: Son, I'll fix your radio. We'll take it into town. I'll buy . . .

DARRELL: I don't care about no radio!

REV. ED: Was it because I cast you out?

DARRELL: You erased me!

REV. ED: I'd have taken you back with open arms . . .

DARRELL: I'm erased!

REV. ED: All you'd have to do is come back and apologize . . .

DARRELL: Oh, all I'd have to do is come crawlin' back on my hands and knees! You'd really like that, wouldn't you?

REV. ED: You're wrong, Darrell. I don't like it when you crawl. *(Starts to rise.)*

DARRELL: Sit down! You know what you did. To that poor simple girl, who didn't have mind enough to know what was happenin'. And I want to hear you say it.

REV. ED: What?

DARRELL: That that baby ain't from God, and this whole thing is crazy!

REV. ED: So that's what you think . . . that I fathered this child . . .

DARRELL: I'm gonna kill you whether you say it or not, so you might as well say it.

REV. ED: Then after you've killed your father, what'll you do?

DARRELL: Then I'm gonna take Becky Ann and that baby and we're gonna get out of here.

REV. ED: Where will you go?

DARRELL: Somewhere. While you're rotting in your grave, we're gonna go somewhere and live like normal people.

REV. ED: Listen!

DARRELL: What?

REV. ED: Hear that?

DARRELL: What?

REV. ED: The devil! Satan is laughin' and dancin' on your soul.

DARRELL: Stop it! I know what you're doin'.

REV. ED: Darrell, it doesn't matter what the truth is. It only matters what you believe.

DARRELL: Say it.

REV. ED: Alright Darrell, the truth. *(He stands.)* Hand me your mother's Bible.

DARRELL: Why?

REV. ED: Shall I get it myself?

DARRELL: No.

REV. ED: I thought you wanted to hear the truth. Darrell, I'm putting the baby down. And now, I'm going to get your Momma's Bible. *(He picks up Momma's Bible, moves away from Darrell, and kneels.)* Jesus, to manifest the truth, and to bind the devil I swear on this Holy Bible that I have only wanted for this family.

DARRELL: That's a lie.

REV. ED: I swear I have repented for all my sins!

DARRELL: Lie.

REV. ED: And I swear . . . on this Bible . . . and in Jesus' holy name . . . that I did not father that child . . . *(Darrell drops the bayonet and falls on his knees, grabbing the Bible.)*

DARRELL: Don't swear that! Don't swear on my Momma's Bible! *(The Reverend Ed closes his hands over Darrell's.)*

REV. ED: And I swear Darrell, on this Holy Bible . . . with Jesus and your Momma looking down from heaven . . . that this child is Christ come again . . . and that every word I speak is the gospel truth. *(Pause. He looks to Heaven.)* Jesus, give me my son back. What is loosed on earth shall be loosed in Heaven. Jesus I bind the devil! *(He strikes Darrell on the head with his palm.)* I bind the devil and cast him out in Jesus' name. I cast him out in Jesus' name. Get out Devil! Get out! *(He slaps Darrell on the forehead and sends him sprawling.)*

DARRELL: What do I do?

REV. ED: What you do Darrell is you think upon your sins.

DARRELL: I don't know what to think . . . cause I always thought . . .

REV. ED: Judge not that you be not judged.

DARRELL: I'm sorry.

REV. ED: Don't say you're sorry to me, Darrell. It was God who you offended.

DARRELL: I'm so sorry.

REV. ED: You beg forgiveness?

DARRELL: Yes . . .

REV. ED: From who?

DARRELL: *(Reaches for Reverend Eddie.)* From you . . .

REV. ED: *(Slaps his hand away.)* From God . . .

DARRELL: From God . . .

REV. ED: From his mercy . . .

DARRELL: From his mercy . . .

REV. ED: From his grace . . .

DARRELL: From his grace . . .

REV. ED: I have sinned . . .

DARRELL: I have sinned . . .

REV. ED: I have sinned against God . . .

DARRELL: I have sinned against God . . .

REV. ED: I have sinned against man . . .

DARRELL: I have sinned against man . . .

REV. ED: I am a coward . . .

DARRELL: No!

REV. ED: Say it! *(Pause. Darrell weeps.)*

DARRELL: I am a coward . . .

REV. ED: I am a traitor . . .

DARRELL: I am a traitor . . .

REV. ED: I am a deserter . . .

DARRELL: I am a deserter . . . *(Reverend Ed picks up the fallen bayonet and walks up slowly behind the kneeling Darrell.)*

REV. ED: I am empty . . .

DARRELL: I am *so* empty . . .

REV. ED: Unworthy of life . . .

DARRELL: Unworthy of life . . .

REV. ED: I do not deserve to live . . .

DARRELL: I do not deserve to live . . .

REV. ED: I deserve to die . . .

DARRELL: I deserve to die . . . *(Suddenly Reverend Eddie grabs Darrell, throws him down on the table and holds the bayonet to his throat. Darrell screams.)*

REV. ED: Oh, God, thy servant Abraham laid his lamb upon the altar. God make manifest thy will. God's will be done! *(Jerks Darrell's hair.)* God's will be done!

DARRELL: God's will be done . . .

REV. ED: I am the lamb . . .

DARRELL: I am the lamb . . . *(Reverend looks to the Heavens and raises the bayonet. He pauses.)*

REV. ED: What God? What? I hear you. Yes . . .

DARRELL: No . . .

REV. ED: Yes . . .

DARRELL: No . . .

REV. ED: Darrell, you know what God has told me?

DARRELL: No, what?

REV. ED: Your life . . . has been spared! *(Reverend Eddie throws the bayonet aside. Darrell flings himself to the floor.)*

DARRELL: Oh God . . . thank you, thank you.

REV. ED: Thank you, Jesus . . .

DARRELL: Thank you, Jesus . . .

REV. ED: Thank you Lord . . .

DARRELL: Thank you Lord . . .

REV. ED: Thank you, Jesus . . .

DARRELL: Thank you, Jesus . . .

REV. ED: Jesus, I am empty . . .

DARRELL: Jesus, I am empty . . .

REV. ED: But I want to be filled!

DARRELL: I want to be filled!

REV. ED: With the Holy Ghost . . .

DARRELL: With the Holy Ghost!

REV. ED: Come in to me, Holy Ghost!

DARRELL: Come in to me, Holy Ghost!

REV. ED: Come in to me, now!

DARRELL: Come in to me, now!

REV. ED: Now!

DARRELL: Now! *(Darrell falls to the ground ranting in tongues and twitching spasmodically. Gradually, he comes out of it and lies on the ground, exhausted, with a beautiful smile on his face. Reverend Eddie kneels beside him.)*

REV. ED: Pray with me, Darrell. Pray with me. *(Darrell repeats the prayer after him.)* God . . . you have seen my only son become lost and turn away from God. And you have seen fit to return him to me in glory. Now, together we can go forth and do your will, and glorify thy Son. In the name of Jesus. Amen.

DARRELL: Amen. Is it all true?

REV. ED: Yes, Darrell.

DARRELL: Is it really in there?

REV. ED: What?

DARRELL: Go fish. *(Pause.)*

REV. ED: Yes it is, Darrell!

DARRELL: Amen . . .

REV. ED: *(Reaches in the basket and picks up the baby.)* Darrell, do you know why God has saved your life?

DARRELL: No, Daddy. *(Becky Ann enters the trailer as Reverend Eddie puts the baby in Darrell's arms.)*

REV. ED: Because God has sent another lamb to die in your place. And now, God wants you to help to glorify and bless that lamb even unto death and resurrection.

DARRELL: I know, Daddy. *(Pause.)* I know. *(Becky Ann takes in the scene. Blackout.)*

ACT II

Scene 3

The scene changes to the tent meeting. Becky Ann rolls in the podium, then the baptismal pool. Over the loudspeakers we hear the congregation singing the hymn "Washed in the Blood of the Lamb." After the first verse, we hear the Reverend Eddie exhorting, "Come on, everybody, you all know this one . . . sing along!" Hopefully, by the time the scene is set up, the audience will be singing along. When the lights come up, Reverend Eddie is in the audience singing and shaking hands. Becky Ann is leading the singing. They are both dressed in white. After the hymn is over, the Reverend Eddie shouts.

REV. ED: Are you washed in the blood of the lamb! I hope you are. I wish there was thousands more of you here tonight to be washed in the blood, but those of you who *are* here tonight, are in fine, fine voice, and GOD . . . is blessing us all here tonight! Can I hear an amen? *(Response.)* It's wonderful to be with you here in this glorious country full of so many holy, God-fearing people. I have never felt so welcome. I would especially like to thank you wonderful city officials of Moose Jaw for their marvelous cooperation. I am so . . . HAPPY . . . tonight! Why? Because tonight is a very special night. More special than you can possibly imagine! What could be so special? What could be so monumental? Well, I'm not gonna tell you. You know, this meeting kinda reminds me of something that happened a few years ago back in a little town where I come from, in Arkansas. In this little town, one day a sign went up in the town square . . . and all it said was, "It's comin'." Well folks didn't pay much attention to it. Well, the next day, that sign was gone, and another was in its place. It said, "It's comin' soon." Well, now people was beginnin' to get a little curious . . . so every day, a new sign showed up. "It's comin', don't miss it." "It's comin' . . . Thursday." Then, the night before the big event, there was a huge sign and it said, "It's coming' tomorrow . . . two dollars." Well the next day there was a tent in the town square an people was lined up for miles. There was now another sign that said "It's Here." They all plunked down their two dollars, and crowded into that tent. Hundreds of 'em. An after they was all in there the lights went down, went up . . . and there was a sign. And it said . . . "It's Gone" . . . I want you to think about that while we listen to that lovely old hymn, "Softly and Tenderly." It will be sung by that vestal flower that has been blessed by God's Holy spirit, my lovely daughter, Becky Ann. *(Becky Ann looking frightened, does not budge.)* Becky Ann! "Softly and Tenderly." *(Sotto voce.)* Clasp, smile, look up. *(Becky Ann comes forward and sings "Softly and Tenderly." She carries Reverend Eddie's idea of "gestures" to a literal, and "comic," extreme.)* Thank you, Becky Ann. You know, you're a wonderful group of people, a special group. I'd like to share something with you. Becky Ann, will you come forward? *(Becky Ann hesitates.)* Becky Ann! *(She comes forward, tentatively.)* Some months ago, Becky Ann had a child. A son.

BECKY ANN: No, it was a . . .

REV. ED: Now! . . . Ordinarily, the birth of a son is a happy event in the life of any family. But this was no ordinary child. Becky Ann, would you tell these people about the birth of your baby?

BECKY ANN: Daddy!

REV. ED: Go on!

BECKY ANN: Well . . . uh . . . there was a lot of wind and fog and fire and stuff . . .

REV. ED: No, Becky Ann, we want to hear about your reaction after the baby was born.

BECKY ANN: Oh. Well, I was laying in the bed at our house near El Dorado, Arkansas. And the doctor came in the door with a little bundle and laid it on my chest. I pulled back the blanket and I looked at it. And I went *(Bloodcurdling scream. Reverend Eddie starts, dropping his Bible.)* And the doctor took the baby away . . .

REV. ED: Becky Ann screamed because she had seen a hideous sight. Her son was deformed, defective, and misshapen. I was in despair. I said, "Father, I have always been your loyal servant, how could this have happened to me? To my family?" And then, in a moment of shame and guilt, I told the doctor to take the baby, to take it out of our sight. And so he did. I did not know then what I know now. I did not know what you are going to know in the space of a few minutes. I doubted God. And I was punished. I was visited by an affliction that looked like poison ivy, but was certainly *not* poison ivy because I have never been allergic to poison ivy a day in my life! My daughter refused to eat or speak for a number of weeks. Satan visited my home in the body of my own son, Darrell. But then a miracle happened. And I'm gonna tell you about it. But first, let's join together in song. Becky Ann *(Becky Ann looks puzzled.)* "Shall We Gather at the River," *(She leads the audience in singing "Shall We Gather at the River." During the song, the Reverend Eddie removes his coat and rolls up his sleeves.*

He gestures toward the back of the auditorium. A white light reveals Darrell, dressed in a white baptismal robe and beaming, holding the basket, which has been painted for the occasion, and has festive ribbons on the handles. In time with the music, Darrell marches down the aisle, transported. He joins Reverend Eddie and Becky Ann on the stage. Reverend Eddie puts his arm around Darrell's shoulder.) Well . . . who is this handsome young man? This is my son Darrell. Darrell, as I told you was filled with Satan. But now, Hallelujah, he is filled with the spirit of the Holy Ghost! He has come back to God's bosom, and he has been born again. Born again! Hallelujah, praise God! It's like in the words of the old hymn, "When the pain and grief would start, Jesus pardoned me! He took the evil from my heart . . . Jesus pardoned me!" Say amen, somebody! *(Response. He is almost crying.)* Darrell! *(Darrell steps forward.)* I think Darrell has something he wants to say to all of you. Darrell, step forward.

DARRELL: Before I was born again, when the devil was still inside me, I committed sins against my father . . . and my family . . . and God . . . and the United States of America. Then I took Jesus Christ as my personal saviour. *(Reverend Eddie applauds.)*

REV. ED: Praise God, Darrell?

DARRELL: Praise God.

REV. ED: Thank you, Jesus?

DARRELL: Thank you, Jesus.

REV. ED: And *this* wasn't the only miracle. My daughter . . . is at peace. And all of my oozing sores are gone. And who caused these miracles? *(He takes the basket from Darrell and brings it forward.)* Jesus. Now, I know what you're thinkin'. Is this what he's been leadin' up to? Is this what all of this is about? Is he sayin' that Jesus Christ is here in the flesh? Yes. That is *exactly* what I'm sayin'. In a moment of horrible despair, we gave Jesus away, and pestilence come upon us, and the sky darkened. We got Jesus back, our bodies and our souls were healed and light poured down on us from the sky like honey . . . He was gone. But now he's here. And tonight, Jesus begins his new ministry. How lucky . . . how lucky you people are. For someday it will be written that you were present at the baptism of Jesus Christ at his second comin'. You were there when God came down like a dove to say, "This is my beloved son, in whom I am well pleased." Darrell. *(Darrell steps forward.)* Darrell, will you take the infant to the river of his baptism? *(Darrell takes the basket.)*

DARRELL: I will. *(They wait for a moment.)*

REV. ED: Will you perhaps do it now?

DARRELL: Yes sir. *(Darrell walks to the edge of the baptismal pool. Reverend Eddie steps forward.*

REV. ED: Now, before this wonderous moment of consecration and baptism takes place, let's bow our heads in prayer. *(He kneels and holds up the letters.)* Father, we thank you for your signs. We thank you that you have given your prophet the wisdom to interpret them correctly . . . And we thank you, almighty God, for the gift of water. Because the Holy Ghost is in it. Just as it was in the Jordan River in which John the Baptist baptized your son as the Messiah who led us all to everlasting life through his death and resurrection. And now, Father, I will baptize your son in his second comin' and he will lead a new age to everlasting life through *his* death and resurrection! *(Suddenly, Darrell plunges the baby beneath the water.)* Father, let the blood of his lamb wash away our sins and our iniquities, and make our souls as clean and pure as the crystal stream and let the Holy Ghost descend upon us. *(Darrell is still holding the basket underwater. There is a determined, transported look on his face. Darrell raises the basket and plunges it in again.)* Bring us into glory, bring us unto the mountain. Bring us unto the throne. Let us look upon the throne like a jasper, or a sardine stone, and a rainbow be in sight around the throne unto an emerald, and around the throne let there be crowns of gold! *(Darrell plunges the basket in a third time.)* Let there be lightning, and thunderbolts, and voices! And let those voices say, this is my Prophet! This is my Prophet, without sin! Bathed in Glory! Came to the throne! Followed the signs! This is my Prophet! This is my Prophet. He who has ears! Let him hear! Let him hear! *(He begins to speak in tongues.)* Thank you God. *(He rises.)* And now, the moment has arrived. According to his commandment, we will baptize the infant Jesus.

DARRELL: I did it. I did it, Daddy. *(Reverend Eddie turns and sees him.)*

REV. ED: You did what?

DARRELL: Even unto death and resurrection . . .

REV. ED: NOOOO! *(He pushes Darrell away from the basket. He grabs Darrell by the neck and begins to choke him.)* What did you do! What! What! WHAT! *(He drops Darrell, and takes the basket from the water, whimpering.)* No . . . no . . .

DARRELL: Even unto death and resurrection, like you said . . . *(Slowly, the Reverend Eddie looks up. They notice the audience. Silence. Reverend Eddie allows Darrell to take the basket from him. Darrell slowly opens the basket and looks inside, dread on his face. He reaches into the basket and removes a bundle, wrapped in a soggy baby blanket. He slowly unwraps it. With surprise and awe, he holds up . . . an eggplant.)* Daddy . . . it's an . . . I thought it was the baby . . . *(The Reverend Eddie stares into space.)* Daddy, what happened to the baby? *(The Reverend continues to stare.)* Daddy, what happened to the baby? Daddy? *(Pause.)* Daddy? Daddy . . . what do we do now? *(Reverend Eddie does not respond. Darrell looks at the eggplant, then at the baptismal pool, and at the eggplant again. He makes his decision. He cradles the eggplant in his arms, walks to the edge of the stage, and faces the audience. As he speaks, the Reverend Eddie begins to sing, very quietly, a few lines of "The Old Rugged Cross." He trails off under Darrell's speech.)* Sweet Jesus . . . you have shown us that . . . even in death . . . there is resurrection. And let it be known . . . that . . . in the second coming of our Lord . . . sweet Jesus became a man . . . and was baptized in the Holy Ghost . . . died . . . and on that very same day . . . he arose again . . . and was resurrected . . . *(Pause.)* . . . as an eggplant. Praise God! Thank you, Jesus! And now . . . let us join together in our final hymn . . . "Faith of Our Fathers" . . . *(A pool of light on Darrell, holding the eggplant aloft. We hear the taped voice of the male driver.)*

DRIVER: Well, ma'am, this is as far as I go. *(Sound of car stopping.)*

BECKY ANN: *(Live.)* This'll be fine.

DRIVER: That's a real pretty baby.

BECKY ANN: Thank you.

DRIVER: What's its name?

BECKY ANN: Arlene Marie.

DRIVER: I hope you get another ride. *(Lights up on Becky Ann, carrying an old suitcase, her ukulele slung over her shoulder.)*

BECKY ANN: Oh, we won't have no trouble. *(Looks at the bundle.)* See there, Arlene Marie? He liked you. He saw how special you are. *(Sits. We see the sign on the suitcase. "We'd appreciate a ride.")* Whew! I feel a lot better now. *(Pause.)* This is fun, ain't it? *(She begins to play her ukulele. Her song is punctuated by the baby glowing.)*

Doodle li doodle li doo, Hi!

Doodle li doodle li doo, Boo!

Doo doo dooo . . .

As the lights fade, we see the baby glowing, illuminating the face of Becky Ann.

THE END

2

ROMULUS LINNEY

ROMULUS LINNEY is the author of three novels as well as thirteen long and twenty-two short plays, which have been seen over the past twenty-five years in resident theaters across America as well as in New York, Los Angeles, London, and Vienna. His plays include *The Sorrows of Frederick, Holy Ghosts, Childe Byron, 2,* and *Shotgun.* Six of his one-acts have been selected for Best Short Plays, and his adaptation of his 1962 novel *Heathen Valley* won the National Critics Award in 1988, as did *"2"* in 1990. He is the recipient of two fellowships from the NEA, as well as Guggenheim, Rockefeller, and National Foundation for the Arts grants, a 1980 Obie Award, three Drama-Logue Awards, the Mishima Prize for Fiction, the 1984 Award in Literature from the American Academy and Institute of Arts and Letters, and a 1992 Obie Award for Sustained Excellence in Playwriting.

was first performed by Actors Theatre of Louisville on March 23, 1990.

CAST

CAPTAIN	Scott Sowers
SERGEANT	Percy Metcalf
COMMANDANT	Bob Burrus
COUNSEL	Ray Fry
HERMANN GOERING	William Duff-Griffin
PSYCHOLOGIST	David A. Kimball
JUSTICE ROBERT JACKSON	Fred Major
PRESIDENT OF THE TRIBUNAL	Steve Wise
BRITISH PROSECUTOR	Christopher Fields
GOERING'S WIFE	Ellen McLaughlin
GOERING'S DAUGHTER	Ashley Mueller

Director	Thomas Allan Bullard
Stage Manager	Lori M. Doyle
Assistant Stage Manager	Sue Fenty
Dramaturg	Tom Szentgyorgyi
Scenic Designer	Paul Owen
Costume Designer	Lewis D. Rampino
Lighting Designer	Ralph Dressler
Sound Designer	Mark Hendren
Properties Master	Ron Riall
Casting—NYC	Jay Binder

PLACE

Palace of Justice, Nuremberg, Germany

TIME

May 1945–October 1946
The play may be performed in two acts as indicated here or without intermission.

SCENE

A large room, partitioned down the middle. A wire fence is suggested above its center, without actually splitting the room as was done at Nuremberg. The walls are roughly plastered and newly painted off-white.

Upstage, two doors, right and left of the wire fence. On one side of the stage left door, an American flag draped on a stand, on the other side, another flag, with a curious device: against an azure background, a large key suspended above a scales, below them, a German eagle fallen into a pit.

At center, a sturdy mahogany table, with a wooden chair on each side. The wire fence hangs above this table, as if it continued down and cut the table in two, separating anyone there.

On each downstage side of the room, a sink and mirror, and a small washstand table, with soap and towels.

Two double windows, high on the stage left wall, through which light falls.

From the outside come various sounds from time to time, muted, coming and going, etc.: Soldiers marching, cadences being counted, military bands playing American marches, airplanes flying over Germany, and sounds of a basketball game from a gym.

On the table, lit by a spotlight, is a thick black book.

ACT I

The spotlight on the black book fades.

Lights come up quickly. The room is empty. Stage left door opens suddenly. Pause.

The Counsel, a German in his late sixties, small, thin and rather frail, enters the room. The door closes behind him. He waits.

Stage right door opens. Enter a black Infantry Sergeant and a white Infantry Captain. Both have pistols in holsters, carry white billy clubs, and wear the white belts and helmets of American Army Guards at Nuremberg. The Sergeant chews gum. They stand at ease. Pause.

Enter Commandant, a Colonel in the American Cavalry. He is very spit and polish, in a perfectly pressed and creased uniform. He carries a swagger stick, and he wears a gleaming black helmet, on which, as on his shoulder patches, are a key and a scales.

The door closes swiftly behind him. The Captain and the Sergeant snap to attention.

SERGEANT: Ten-shun!!

COMMANDANT: *(To Guards.)* At ease. *(To Counsel.)* Good morning.

COUNSEL: Good morning, sir.

COMMANDANT: You will represent the prisoner?

COUNSEL: I will, sir.

COMMANDANT: You will confer with him here. This wire fence will separate you at all times. You are never to touch him. Never. Understood?

COUNSEL: Yes, sir.

COMMANDANT: When papers are exchanged between you, a Sergeant in the Army of the United States will inspect each transaction, himself overseen by a Captain in the Army of the United States. Nothing, say again, nothing, but paper is to pass between you. Understood?

COUNSEL: Absolutely.

COMMANDANT: If you need assistance, you inform the guards.

COUNSEL: Thank you, sir. When do I see the prisoner?

COMMANDANT: When I have finished talking to you.

COUNSEL: Yes, sir.

COMMANDANT: The Military Tribunal has instructed me, as Commandant of the prison within the Palace of Justice at Nuremberg, to give defense counsel free access to the prisoner, and ample time to prepare a defense. Here is a complete and official copy of the Indictment. *(He points to the black book.)*

COUNSEL: Thank you.

COMMANDANT: Your notes will be in hand only, no briefcase. You will be searched before and after every meeting. Understood?

COUNSEL: Yes, sir.

COMMANDANT: Any questions?

COUNSEL: No, sir.

COMMANDANT: Bring in the prisoner.

CAPTAIN: Yes, sir. *(The Sergeant opens the right door and exits after the Captain, closing the door behind them.)*

COMMANDANT: You may sit down.

COUNSEL: Thank you. *(He sits in his wooden chair.)*

COMMANDANT: I understand you never met him.

COUNSEL: No, sir.

COMMANDANT: Ever seen him, in person?

COUNSEL: Everyone did.

COMMANDANT: When was the last time *you* did?

COUNSEL: A year ago. He gave a speech here.

COMMANDANT: What was he like then?

COUNSEL: He wore a great white and green uniform, with many medals, as usual. He was—ah—overweight, as usual.

COMMANDANT: A great white pig.

COUNSEL: Ah, yes.

COMMANDANT: What did he say?

COUNSEL: He told us the war would be won. And laughed.

COMMANDANT: When he walks in that door, you won't recognize him. The day I got here, he weighed almost three hundred pounds. Can you believe that?

COUNSEL: Ah—yes, I can.

COMMANDANT: He was eating forty morphine pills a day. I cut them out one at a time. "I'll kill myself!" he said. No suicide with me. His pill was a little cylinder of glass—this big—inside a cartridge case. Prussic acid. Turns a man green in thirty seconds. I found it, in his storage room gear. I gave him three months of G.I. rations, healthy exercise, and shaped him up. He's a model prisoner now. *(Enter Sergeant, holding the door open. Enter Hermann Goering. It is startling to recognize in him the familiar, obese, often cartooned figure. Goering weighs a hundred pounds less than he did at the end of the war. He still wears his pearl gray Luftwaffe uniform, which, though altered for him, is now too large. It hangs on him loosely but does not, oddly, look bad. He has kept his high military boots, of the finest leather. His skin is clear. His eyes are bright. He has indeed been restored to health. The Captain enters, closes the door, takes up his position with the Sergeant.)* Good morning, Goering.

GOERING: Good morning, my Colonel.

COMMANDANT: Here is the counsel you requested.

GOERING: A million thanks.

COMMANDANT: Under the rules we have discussed, you are now free to consult with him. Gentlemen. *(The Sergeant opens the door. Exit Commandant. The Sergeant goes to parade rest again.)*

GOERING: Good morning.

COUNSEL: Good morning. *(Goering smiles, looks at the Sergeant.)*

GOERING: I knew I was in trouble when I saw soldiers standing around me, chewing gum. *(Goering laughs.)* You don't recognize me?

COUNSEL: You've—lost weight.

GOERING: It is a first class health resort, this place. Seventy-one pounds, gone! I'm fit! Are you wondering why I picked you?

COUNSEL: Yes.

GOERING: That Swagger Stick Colonel handed me a list of Nuremberg lawyers. I said I didn't know any lawyers. I never needed one. He said, shut up, you need one now. I closed my eyes and picked you. How old are you?

COUNSEL: Sixty eight.

GOERING: Do you want to defend me?

COUNSEL: Yes.

GOERING: Why?

COUNSEL: I do not like the charges.

GOERING: *(Laughing.)* Neither do I!

COUNSEL: You are being tried for breaking laws that did not exist when you broke them. Ex post facto.

GOERING: What did you do during the war?

COUNSEL: I was a civil court judge. Appeals, mostly.

GOERING: Can I trust you?

COUNSEL: I will defend you to the best of my ability.

GOERING: I don't mean that. What I mean is, do you love Germany?

COUNSEL: I do love Germany. Can I trust you?

GOERING: How?

COUNSEL: Will you tell me the truth?

GOERING: Always.

COUNSEL: Then I will do my best for you. But—

GOERING: What's the matter?

COUNSEL: *(Smiling.)* What do I call you?

GOERING: Anything! Hey, you! Whist, *hey Buddy!* Fats!! *(Laughs.)* While chewing gum! *(Goering smiles, regains his composure.)* I thought the Reichsmarshall of Germany would make peace with the Supreme Commander of Europe, man to man. But no. General Eisenhower throws me in prison and calls me a war criminal. Is that what you call me?

COUNSEL: No.

GOERING: So what am I? Just another client?

COUNSEL: No.

GOERING: *Hermann?*

COUNSEL: I was fifty-six-years-old when you came to power. I watched my country—led by Hitler and by you—become one with itself, strong and vigorous. When you stood up—in those childish uniforms, with all those gleaming medals, dancing over a belly getting bigger and bigger every day—you made no bones about any of it. We were dazzled by Hitler, but we loved you. You were human, sometimes harsh but good at heart. A mirror for Germans. Then, with our cities in flames, we still loved you. I don't know why, but we did. I do now. I will defend you with all my heart but—I will never know what to call you.

GOERING: Good old man! I couldn't have made a better choice. I will be simply what you defend. Man to man.

COUNSEL: Defendant.

GOERING: Counsel. So.

COUNSEL: So.

GOERING: Begin!

COUNSEL: The indictment. You and twenty-one associates are specifically charged with Crimes Against Peace, War Crimes, and Crimes Against Humanity. The Tribunal will be composed of two judges each from France, Russia, Great Britain and the United States.

GOERING: They're wrong already. That's not a tribunal.
COUNSEL: It will function as one.
GOERING: Who prosecutes?
COUNSEL: A representative of each country, in turn.
GOERING: Four to one. Who is leading all this?
COUNSEL: The Chief Prosecutor is an American. Robert Jackson, a Supreme Court Justice of the United States. Very eloquent man. He has declared this trial an opportunity to outlaw all future wars.
GOERING: Has he, really?
COUNSEL: The Tribunal claims it will convict on hard evidence alone. But it will use the records kept by us.
GOERING: That cooks me, does it?
COUNSEL: Not completely. You were so far up in the structure of command, I do not think it will be so easy to pin you to individual events so far down.
GOERING: Can I call witnesses?
COUNSEL: Yes.
GOERING: Shift responsibility down to subordinates?
COUNSEL: Yes.
GOERING: And up to the top?
COUNSEL: We can shift a great deal of the blame.
GOERING: We shift nothing! Not a word against Hitler.
COUNSEL: What? But we must!
GOERING: Not one word!
COUNSEL: The other prisoners will do exactly that!
GOERING: No, they won't. I won't let them.
COUNSEL: This will make things very difficult! Please understand—
GOERING: I *do understand!* I will not deny! I will debate! I will *challenge!* I know more about what happened in Germany than any man alive! I am not TWO now! I am ONE!!
COUNSEL: Very well. *(Pause.)* One! *(They smile. Change of light. Sounds of an American military band, playing a Sousa march, "El Capitan." Counsel's door opens. Exit Counsel. Goering walks around the room. Door opens. Enter Psychiatrist. He is a Jewish Army Major, in his thirties, intelligent and formidable.)*
PSYCHIATRIST: Good morning, Goering.
GOERING: Doctor Freud? Is that right?
PSYCHIATRIST: That's right. How did you know?
GOERING: It's time for you. You are my sixth Doctor Freud. You have that quietly receptive look about you. *(The Psychiatrist puts his briefcase down on his side of the table, takes out some notes and a pad.)* What happened to the Irishman?
PSYCHIATRIST: He went home.

GOERING: Why?

PSYCHIATRIST: His tour of duty was over.

GOERING: Please, Doctor Freud.

PSYCHIATRIST: OK. I'll be honest with you, if you will be honest with me.

GOERING: With all my heart, now and forever. What happened to him?

PSYCHIATRIST: The Irish psychologist you liked, liked you, too. In fact, he hated the British so much, he ended up loving you. Ever read Shakespeare?

GOERING: In English, thank you. I love the theatre. My wife was an actress.

PSYCHIATRIST: Then maybe you saw *Richard III.*

GOERING: Several times.

PSYCHIATRIST: He was powerful because the people around him wanted to be corrupted.

GOERING: Richard III being me, corrupting Irish psychologists?

PSYCHIATRIST: Yes.

GOERING: So they send him home and replace him with—what? A Jew? My lawyer said you were. Are you? *(The Psychiatrist makes notes.)*

PSYCHIATRIST: Yes.

GOERING: Congratulations.

PSYCHIATRIST: *What?*

GOERING: *(Smiling.)* You won. *(Deadly pause. The Psychiatrist takes a deep breath.)*

PSYCHIATRIST: At a price. *(Goering shrugs.)*

GOERING: We all paid a price. What's the matter? *(With a great effort the Psychiatrist controls himself.)*

PSYCHIATRIST: *(Briskly.)* There are tests to give you. I must ask about your psychological background. I must consult with you about your interpersonal relations with the other prisoners. I must be of help to you in a situation that will be difficult for both of us. But first, I've brought you this. *(He holds up a packet of letters and starts to hand them to Goering.)*

CAPTAIN: Sergeant.

SERGEANT: Hold it! *(The Sergeant moves swiftly to Goering's side.)* Hand 'em over.

CAPTAIN: Sir.

SERGEANT: Sir. *(The Psychiatrist hands the packet of letters to the Sergeant, who flips through them roughly. Goering, closing his eyes, looks away.)*

GOERING: Who from?

PSYCHIATRIST: Your wife. And your child.

GOERING: Oh, my God. *(He looks at the Sergeant, ruffling through the letters. Pause.)* Where are they?

PSYCHIATRIST: Safe.

GOERING: WHERE?

PSYCHIATRIST: In an Army prison. Just for interrogation. *The Sergeant hands the letters to Goering.)*

SERGEANT: OK. Here. *(Goering takes them. He closes his eyes. The Sergeant goes back to his place. Pause.)*
PSYCHIATRIST: Aren't you going to read them?
GOERING: I will read—these letters—in my cell alone or not at all.
PSYCHIATRIST: Being observed reading your family mail is intolerable?
GOERING: Yes!
PSYCHIATRIST: I want you to know that I am in favor of your communication with your wife and daughter.
GOERING: Why should you care?
PSYCHIATRIST: I think it is a key to my understanding of you and your understanding of yourself. I will make sure your letters are sent and theirs received. Just be reasonable and talk to me. OK?
GOERING: OK! *(He puts the letters in a pocket.)* Shall I tell you about my childhood? My father and mother?
PSYCHIATRIST: Good.
GOERING: Fine. My first memory of my mother's face. Age four. I was bashing it in with my little fists.
PSYCHIATRIST: Why did you do that?
GOERING: I didn't like her. What does that mean, Doctor?
PSYCHIATRIST: Let me explain something to you. I am an officer in the American Medical Corps. My orders are One: gather psychological information about Hermann Goering, and Two, when I can, relieve his psychological distress. I am a Jew and I am a Pole and I am a citizen of the United States! Unlike the Irishman, I don't like you now and never will. But on duty, I am your friend! So don't try to get my goat.
GOERING: Get your what?
PSYCHIATRIST: Goat. American expression, meaning make me mad.
GOERING: Good, thank you. I don't get your goat. You relieve my distress. I do beg your pardon, and bang my head upon the floor.
PSYCHIATRIST: Will you take some tests?
GOERING: What kind of tests?
PSYCHIATRIST: Standard I.Q. Army Intelligence.
GOERING: I want to be as helpful to you as you do to me. *(Goering laughs.)* Which means I want to live, you want me to die and we hate each other to death. Doctor. You aren't the war criminal. I am. If I can joke a little, why can't you?
PSYCHIATRIST: You aren't funny. And I saw *Richard III.* "I can smile and smile, and murder whilst I smile."
GOERING: You are a hard case, but you're right. The Irishman was fudge. All I had to do was be a good fellow—man to man to man—and he'd believe anything I said. You won't.
PSYCHIATRIST: You are god damn right I won't.

GOERING: Fine. Give me your tests, and ask me your questions—my family excepted—and I will answer. And I will try to get a smile out of you somehow! Dr. Freud? Agreed?

PSYCHIATRIST: OK.

GOERING: OK. *(Change of light. Sounds of GIs marching. Psychiatrist's door opens. He exits. The door closes. The Captain whispers to the Sergeant, opens the door and the Sergeant exits. Goering sits in his chair, watched by the Captain. Outside, GIs are being marched in cadence.)*

GIs *(V.O.)*.

    HUP, TOOP, THREEP, FOUR!

    HUP, TOOP, THREEP, FOUR!

CADRE *(V.O.)*

    AIN'T NO USE IN WRITING HOME—

GIs

    AIN'T NO USE IN WRITING HOME—

CADRE.

    JODY'S GOT YOUR GAL AND GONE.

GIs.

    JODY'S GOT YOUR GAL AND GONE,

    HUP, TOOP, THREEP, FOUR!

    HUP, TOOP, THREEP, FOUR!

CADRE.

    AIN'T NO USE IN FEELING BLUE—

GIs.

    AIN'T NO USE IN FEELING BLUE—

CADRE

    JODY'S GOT YOUR SISTER, TOO!

GIs.

    JODY'S GOT YOUR SISTER, TOO!

    HUP, TOOP, THREEP, FOUR!

CADRE & GIs. *(Fading away.)*

    LEFT, YOUR LEFT, YOUR LEFT, RIGHT, LEFT!

    HUP, TOOP, THREEP, FOUR!

    YOUR LEFT, YOUR LEFT, YOUR LEFT, RIGHT, LEFT!

    HUP, TOOP, THREEP, FOUR! *(Goering listens, trying to understand them. The counting and the marching fade away.)*

GOERING: So, who was Joe-dee?

CAPTAIN: Shut up. You're not supposed to talk to me.

GOERING: The Commandant said if I had a question, ask. You are a Hauptmann, is that right. Ah, Captain?

CAPTAIN: That's right.

GOERING: You see I pay attention to your rank. Hauptmann, who is Joe-dee? You must answer, no? Orders from the Commandant?

CAPTAIN: Well, all right. Just don't expect me to call you sir.

GOERING: Man to man to man.

CAPTAIN: Jody's a guy who 4-fs. That means he don't get drafted, put in the Army. Has flat feet or knows some Senator or something. So he stays home, and screws my girl. That's all, now shut up.

GOERING: Screw? *(He gets it.)* Ah! Joe-*dee!* Bang, bang.

CAPTAIN: *(Nodding.)* Bang, bang. Like everywhere else.

GOERING: Not in Germany. No Hans-ee or Fritz-ee in Germany.

CAPTAIN: How come?

GOERING: Nobody stayed home. I saw to that.

CAPTAIN: That's what you say. Reckon I'll believe whatever you say?

GOERING: Reckon?

CAPTAIN: Means guess, suppose.

GOERING: Ah. Slang. Brooklyn?

CAPTAIN: God, you're dumb. No, the South.

GOERING: Oh. Red neck?

CAPTAIN: Me? Do I look like a redneck?

GOERING: Of course not. But where?

CAPTAIN: God's country!

GOERING: Ah! Great Smoky Mountains? I know. "Daniel Boom kill'd a bear." Carved on a Smoky Mountain tree by the great hunter Daniel Boom. No?

CAPTAIN: Sort of.

GOERING: You see!

CAPTAIN: He was Daniel B-o-o-n-e, Boone. From Kentucky.

GOERING: Ah! Kentucky! Deadly shots! Blood feuds! The uh —um—

CAPTAIN: Hatfields and the McCoys.

GOERING: Tough men, hard! Shoot on sight!

CAPTAIN: Sometimes.

GOERING: I had once a rifle like Daniel Boone's. Hessian Grenadier musket. You know them, ah, here, the lock, the—

CAPTAIN: Flintlock. Had to put your powder in every shot.

GOERING: *(Miming.)* Like this!

CAPTAIN: Like this, yep. Bang!

GOERING: Bang!

CAPTAIN: Then reload.

GOERING: One shot. I like that. Turkey, deer?

CAPTAIN: One shot.

GOERING: Bear man?

CAPTAIN: One shot!

GOERING: Ho-ho! Don't miss!

CAPTAIN: Deadeye.

GOERING: You a deadeye?

CAPTAIN: My great granddaddy could hit a pheasant with a flintlock. In the *air.*

GOERING: Americans are best with rifles. The British with shotguns. Germans bang-bang firepower. No aim. What is the best hunting rifle you ever saw?

CAPTAIN: A 460 Weatherly Magnum. I'll tell you—*(Right door opens. Enter the Sergeant and takes up his place. The Captain looks stiffly ahead. The Sergeant glances at him, looks at Goering. Goering smiles at the Sergeant, man to man. Change of light. Sounds of airplanes flying over Nuremberg. Enter Counsel, sits in his chair.)*

COUNSEL: The Tribunal is doing something never done before. It is holding individuals responsible for the acts of nations. Each prisoner will be tried separately, in turn, and judged individually, at the end of the trial.

GOERING: Can we call friendly witnesses?

COUNSEL: Yes.

GOERING: Bodenchatz, Milch, Dahlerus?

COUNSEL: Yes, men like that, who respected you.

GOERING: They will tell the truth. I didn't want to invade Poland! I didn't want to invade Russia!

COUNSEL: Did you tell Hitler that?

GOERING: I did! He saw my point, listened to Ribbentrop, and we lost the war! If I'd had my way, there wouldn't have *been* a war!

COUNSEL: So you say, Defendant. But we must answer the indictment, without self-serving testimony. *(He picks up the black book.)* Allow me to prepare a defense.

GOERING: I beg your pardon.

COUNSEL: Basically, there are three indictments.

GOERING: All right! One, two, three!

COUNSEL: One. Crimes Against Peace. Conspiring to wage war in violation of international treaties.

GOERING: *(Laughs.)* What treaties? *Versailles?*

COUNSEL: Among others.

GOERING: That wasn't a treaty. That was a death sentence. Two!

COUNSEL: Two. War Crimes. Violations of the laws or customs of war.

GOERING: What crimes?

COUNSEL: Murder, slave labor, plunder, hostages, reprisals, wanton destruction.

GOERING: *(Laughs.)* What every soldier does! Or be shot himself! Three!

COUNSEL: Three. Crimes Against Humanity.

GOERING: *(Laughs.)* Against *all* humanity? What?

COUNSEL: They mean extermination on racial or political grounds.

GOERING: Extermination?

COUNSEL: Races. Slavs, gypsies—and—well—

GOERING: Well?

COUNSEL: Jews.

GOERING: Me? Exterminate Jews?

COUNSEL: I think they may accuse you of that, yes.

GOERING: What could be more grotesque, or untrue? I did everything I could for the Jews. So did my wife. Actor after actor from her old theatre days we got out. And many others. Let me tell you—

COUNSEL: None of that matters.

GOERING: I WAS SPEAKING TO YOU!!

COUNSEL: And talking nonsense! You wrote the Nuremberg Laws, that stripped them of their citizenship. *You* were what the Jews ran away from! *(Pause.)*

GOERING: My dear man, I beg your pardon. Please proceed, as you think best.

COUNSEL: One. Crimes Against Peace. Here you can defend yourself. You simply restored a country to prosperity, under the legal orders of a Chancellor. Just don't brag about it.

GOERING: But of course I am going to brag about it. I am proud of what I did.

COUNSEL: I wouldn't put it quite like that, if I were you. You will be asked if you created the Gestapo.

GOERING: What does that have to do with crimes against peace?

COUNSEL: Hostages, reprisals, conspiracies, infiltration of other countries, murder.

GOERING: Every country has a Gestapo. I established ours, then did more important work. It ran itself, until Himmler got it in 1934.

COUNSEL: You will be asked if you created the Air Force.

GOERING: As Germany's greatest flier, who else?

COUNSEL: Bombing civilians, machine gunning evacuees, and so on. Wanton destruction.

GOERING: Wanton destruction? Me?

COUNSEL: Yes, Defendant, you!

GOERING: Britain's Dresden? America's atom bomb? The Russians?

COUNSEL: No accusations against Great Britain, the United States or Russia are to be admitted as testimony.

GOERING: *What?*

COUNSEL: Yes!! Two. War Crimes.

GOERING: Absolutely not guilty! Never!

COUNSEL: Prisoners of war?

GOERING: Yes, some prisoners were shot, I know it happened, but I did not do it, and no genuine document will say I did!

COUNSEL: So war crimes, none?

GOERING: None. Now, Himmler, Heydrich, I don't know.

COUNSEL: I thought we weren't shifting blame.

GOERING: To subordinates. Himmler was no subordinate of mine, no matter what it looked like. Listen. When Adolf Hitler gave somebody something to do, he gave somebody else the same thing to do, so they would fight each other for his approval. That is the way he kept control of his staff. So I hated Goebbels and he hated me and we both hated Himmler and everybody hated Bormann and so on.

COUNSEL: It was really that simple for Hitler to control the leaders of the Reich?

GOERING: He did it in other ways, too. He had a photographic memory. Purely mechanical. He could recall how many ball bearings were packed to a crate twenty years ago in May. Not June! May! He ridiculed everyone that way. Generals, Ministers, me, everyone. He knew. You didn't.

COUNSEL: Tell the Tribunal that!

GOERING: Never. That's all about Hitler. I will not hide behind him. The truth is, I was his war hero, who stood up to Hindenburg for him. I made him Chancellor. But whenever he looked at me, my heart jumped out of my chest. If he scolded me, I became a little boy. I stood up when I talked to him on the telephone. I was his, get used to it. Any order I signed I am responsible for, no matter what. Period.

COUNSEL: Very well. Plunder?

GOERING: Of course I plundered. I stripped Europe of everything we needed to win the war!

COUNSEL: Paintings? Statues? Altarpieces? Tapestries? To win the war?

GOERING: All right, art collections. Everything was bought. Bills of sale exist for each transaction. I paid a fortune for a collection of art that would bear my name and be left to the German people! Hitler did the same!

COUNSEL: Legitimate purchases?

GOERING: Absolutely. Hitler, lucky for me, bought naked women with snakes around their navels, sleeping monks and perfect children, for God's sakes! I left him all that and found my Cranach Adam and Eve! I bought Rubens and my Van Dycks, the best! Bargains, but legal! Next!

COUNSEL: Three. Crimes Against Humanity.

GOERING: None! Never! None! I was hard, yes! I did my duty twice over! But humanity I love!

COUNSEL: You will be asked if you created the concentration camps.

GOERING: Using as models the British enclaves in South Africa and the Indian Reservations of the United States, yes I created concentration camps.

COUNSEL: And if you put Jews in them.

GOERING: Along with others, when they threatened us, yes.

COUNSEL: What do you think happened to them there?

GOERING: They worked hard. To death, sometimes, yes I understand that, and regret it, and always did what I could to stop it.

COUNSEL: As the creator of those camps, you can say that was all that was done in them?

GOERING: In the beginning, some camps presumed to disobey my humane directives. I made short work of them, and closed them down. Later, Himmler and Heydrich, and a Major—ah—Eichmann, who became very competent, took them over. *(Pause.)*

COUNSEL: Defendant. You asked me if I loved Germany. I said yes. I asked you if you were going to tell me the truth. You said yes.

GOERING: I *am* telling you the truth!

COUNSEL: You can't be. Everyone knew terrible things happened in those camps. First in Germany, then in Poland, and the east. No one said a word, since we could all be in one the next day.

GOERING: So where did you hear such things? Gossip?

COUNSEL: Yes, gossip, and the radio! It was everywhere! How can I tell the Tribunal that the second most powerful man in Germany knew nothing about the camps? You knew!

GOERING: Before 1934! After that, I was busy rebuilding the German economy, and creating the Air Force. What Himmler did then was none of my business.

COUNSEL: You expect me to say that in court?

GOERING: If you won't, I will! *(Pause.)* I only ask you to believe in me!

COUNSEL: I will try.

GOERING: Thank you. *(Right door opens. Enter Commandant, Psychiatrist. Captain and Sergeant snap to attention.)*

SERGEANT: Ten-shun!!

COMMANDANT: At ease. Gentlemen, morning session convenes in fifteen minutes. We will wait here for exactly five, then proceed, arriving in place one minute before nine. *(Exit Captain.)*

COUNSEL: But, my God, we've hardly begun!

GOERING: My Colonel is a Prussian! Exact! So! So!

COMMANDANT: No, I'm not. I'm a Swagger Stick. Right?

GOERING: How did you know I call you that? Very clever!

COMMANDANT: You will sit at the head of the dock.

GOERING: Number One?

COMMANDANT: Number One.

GOERING: Who's next to me?

COMMANDANT: Hess, then Ribbentrop.

GOERING: The madman and the fool. Then?

COMMANDANT: Keitel.

GOERING: A lackey. Doenitz?

COMMANDANT: On the back row.

GOERING: Bravo. Where is Speer?

COMMANDANT: In the back.

GOERING: Where he belongs! Perfect, my Colonel!

COMMANDANT: I'm glad you're happy.

GOERING: *(To Counsel.)* What happens first?

COMMANDANT: *(Looking at his watch.)* Tell him.

COUNSEL: Aides will read the Indictment. The prisoners will declare themselves guilty or not guilty. Lunch, probably. This afternoon, the American prosecutor will make his opening speech and I think there is a film.

GOERING: Movies! Good! And I will see the great Robert Jackson, of the Supreme American Court, at work?

COUNSEL: He will no doubt make a devastating speech.

GOERING: Speeches. Yes, I remember speeches. I listened to too many of them. You know what we should say? Two words. With that eloquent gesture taught me by GIs.

COUNSEL: What is that?

GOERING: Military Tribunal says, "What is your defense?" One. Prisoners stand up. *(He does.)* Two. Prisoners hold out their right arms. *(He does.)* Three, prisoners say "UP YOURS!" *(Goering hits his right arm at the elbow, sending his fist up into the air in the American "up yours" gesture, then roars with laughter. The Sergeant chews his gum. The Commandant, Captain and Counsel stare at him.)* Don't you think that would be funny? *(Enter Captain, with a red on white, polka-dotted aviator's scarf.)*

CAPTAIN: Got it. *(The Captain holds out the scarf to the Commandant.)* Sir. He asked for this.

COMMANDANT: Where'd you get it?

CAPTAIN: Through Quartermaster. In his gear. *(The Commandant looks at it a moment.)*

COMMANDANT: OK. *(The Captain gives Goering his aviator's scarf.)*

GOERING: Ah, Great American Hunter! *(With great pleasure, he puts on the scarf and tucks it under his collar. To Commandant.)* I thank you for allowing me this small decoration, as I go to battle. Wonderful. There. *(Goering goes to the wash basin, throws some water on his face, runs his hands through his hair.)* Wash my face! Look my best! *(He rubs his face and hands with a towel.)* Staring at me, aren't you. Well, guards look through a hole in my cell door every minute of the day and night. The only time they can't see me is when I take a shit. Which is the only time I wish they *could* see me! *(He sits again, his towel draped over one shoulder and looks about at everybody waiting.)* Very well! The great Inter-Galaxy Armies of Venus and Mars are packed into gigantic Space Ships. The Universe itself is to be invaded and conquered by these invincible forces, and the first planet to be conquered is Earth. The Supreme Leader of this overwhelming Air Force has studied the situation thoroughly. He sends his Ambassador, a great Martian soldier, to issue an Ultimatum, to the first man on Earth he sees. The Ambassador lands—at a filling station in Cleveland, Ohio, by a large gas pump. "Well," says the Supreme Leader, when he returns, "did you find an Earth-man?" "I did," says the Ambassador. "Did you issue our ultimatum?" "I did," says the Ambassador. "What did he say?" says the Supreme Leader. "Nothing," says the Ambassador. "He just stood there, with his dick in his ear." *(Goering roars with laughter. The others stare at him. Goering jumps up.)* Oh, come on, gentlemen. Laugh! Why not? Scarf! Uniform! Boots! I'm ready! Once Hermann Goering was known and loved all over Germany! And by God, years from now, he will be again! All right, not loved maybe, but known, and admired!! *(He hands the towel to the Sergeant.)* Thank you, nigger. *(The Sergeant starts to hit him. Lieutenant holds him.)* I beg your pardon! That *is* what they call you? You'll end up in a camp, too! Just watch!

COMMANDANT: Goering!

GOERING: Yes, sir!! My Colonel, sir! Tell me, my Colonel, sir, where are all the Generals? Eisenhower and Patton? Montgomery and Zhukov and De Gaulle? As far away from this travesty as they can get, where *they* would be on trial if they'd lost, and so would you. Doctor Freud, make a study! Who thought up this monkey trial!

COMMANDANT: Time!

GOERING: Time, Gentlemen! Let's go to the movies! *(Exeunt all. Blackout. Band music ends. All move to the back wall and stand in shadow. Downlight on Goering's chair, which becomes his place in the dock at the trial. Goering walks down and sits proudly in his chair. A flickering of light plays on him: it is a film being shown. Its horrible and familiar huge images wash behind Goering on the white back wall. They are images of the concentration camps. Piles of wasted, naked bodies being dumped out of carts. Faces whose teeth have been torn out. Great rows of people being shot and falling into ditches. Crematoria with burning smokestacks. Human skin, a shrunken head. Mothers and children. The dreadful sights of the Holocaust wash over Goering, and are magnified behind him on the white wall and on the pearl gray Luftwaffe uniform he is wearing. He stares at them, bolt upright, in mounting anger. Blackout. Lights come back up on the interrogation room. It is empty. Enter the Psychiatrist slowly, a handkerchief over his mouth. Then the Counsel, stunned. Enter Goering, the Captain and the Sergeant. Goering sits. There is a very long, shocked pause when no one can speak. Then Goering breaks the silence.)* Well *that* was a bad movie! *(Long pause.)*

COUNSEL: Is that all you can say about it? *(The Commandant appears at the door.)*

COMMANDANT: *(Grim.)* You have an hour. And this dreadful day is over. *(Exit Commandant.)*

PSYCHIATRIST: You never blinked.

GOERING: No.

PSYCHIATRIST: People wept, turned away, hid their faces. I almost got sick.

GOERING: I can't blame you for that. Saw your family, did you?

PSYCHIATRIST: I could have! Don't you understand what you saw?

GOERING: One, I don't believe those films tell the truth. Two, even if they do, I had nothing to do with it!

PSYCHIATRIST: That isn't the point! It happened! For God's sake, didn't you see what we saw?

GOERING: I saw it. I had nothing to do with it.

PSYCHIATRIST: We'll see about that, you bastard. I leave you to your counsel. *(Exit Psychiatrist.)*

GOERING: You sick, too?

COUNSEL: And you aren't?

GOERING: I've been a soldier since 1914. I have seen it all before.

COUNSEL: Not what we just saw, you haven't.

GOERING: It was a film! Propaganda!

COUNSEL: And the teeth? The eyeglasses? The hair? The *shoes?* Propaganda?

GOERING: Oh, really! I had bigger things to do than worry about mattress stuffings or little gold fillings or old shoes!

COUNSEL: There'll be more.

GOERING: Of what?

COUNSEL: Films. Testimony. They have the Commandant of Auschwitz. What will he say? Please tell me now!

GOERING: He'll say Himmler and Heydrich and Heydrich and Himmler! Which is true!

COUNSEL: You didn't know? *Hitler* didn't know?

GOERING: NO! Hitler would never have tolerated such atrocities. Never! If I thought he had, I would—be—very—very—

COUNSEL: WHAT would you be?

GOERING: Very upset!

COUNSEL: Oh, you would, would you? *(Pause.)* I don't think I can do this anymore.

GOERING: Can you believe Hermann Goering had anything to do with such horrors? I was never cruel! I had men shot, yes, that was military duty! Women? Children? Never! Hitler? Never! You will *never* find my name or his on anything like that!!! You do believe me! I can see it in your eyes! You want to, and you can!! *(Pause.)* Innocent life is sacred! Like animals! You know if a fox or even a rabbit got caught in a steel trap under my game laws, or cut open for some experiment, the guilty man went to a camp! Boom, like that!!

COUNSEL: And got cut open instead? I will see you tomorrow morning, before trial.

GOERING: Wait. All right, yes. The film will make a difference. I can admit that. Prison, maybe. What do you think?

COUNSEL: *(Weary.)* Good afternoon, Defendant.

GOERING: What am I to *do* until tomorrow? Twiddle my fingers? Think about my *soul?*

COUNSEL: Right now, I don't care what you do. *(Exit Counsel.)*

CAPTAIN: Chow time, Goering. *(A sound of airplanes, flying over Nuremberg. Goering looks up at them. Change of light. Exit Captain. Sound of airplanes. Pause.*

Goering waits in his chair, drumming his fingers on the table. Only the Sergeant stands guard. Pause.)

GOERING: Getting any? *(He laughs.)* That's what all soldiers say. American, German. No? Well, I understand, from the waiters in the mess, German woman have an especial penchant for black gentlemen from the States. Not, I understand, because you are demon lovers, so much. You are kinder to them, gentler, more understanding. You both know what it means, being niggers. I hope you enjoy them and are good to them. Do the Americans still have your women, and hang you from trees with crosses burning? *(Enter Psychiatrist.)*

SERGEANT: Ten-shun!

PSYCHIATRIST: At ease. Mail call, Goering. *(He holds out the letters. The Sergeant steps forward and the ritual examination is repeated, smoothly this time. Goering pockets his letters without reading them.)* The psychiatrists of Nuremberg have all come to the same conclusion. Your intelligence level is very *very* high.

GOERING: Higher than Speer?

PSYCHIATRIST: Much.

GOERING: Ha-ha! I knew it! Speer's a dummy! I win!

PSYCHIATRIST: But tell me something. Purely factual.

GOERING: I'll do my best.

PSYCHIATRIST: When Hitler became Chancellor, one of the first things to happen was the restoration of a medieval custom of execution. Decapitation, by the blade.

GOERING: Yes.

PSYCHIATRIST: *Beheading*, with a *sword*?

GOERING: Yes. Often a messy business, since it is very hard to cut through the neck at one blow. Many times, there was hacking. Like this. *(He hits a palm with the edge of a hand.)*

PSYCHIATRIST: Did you do that, or did Hitler?

GOERING: Ah, *that*, Hitler did.

PSYCHIATRIST: And the family of the dead man, or *woman*, I understand, was billed about fifty dollars for the beheading and a hundred for the burial?

GOERING: That part of it might have been my idea. Why do you ask?

PSYCHIATRIST: I should think that a man with your great intelligence could see something wrong when the first thing Germany's new Leader did was—literally—start cutting off heads. Then euthanasia executions. Then death squads shooting a thousand people a day. Then, what we saw in that horrible film.

GOERING: I wasn't interested in any of that!! No! All I wanted to do was fight, win what we needed and then stop. Hitler hated the Jews. All right, I didn't, but—

PSYCHIATRIST: Oh, come *on*!

GOERING: I wanted them somewhere else, out of Germany, so they wouldn't be standing there in your job somehow every time you turned around. Everyday anti-Semitism, yes, hatred, no! Hitler felt otherwise, so I did my duty. In my place you would have done yours, you to Germans as we to Jews.

PSYCHIATRIST: I would not! I would die first!

GOERING: Oh, now *you* come on!

PSYCHIATRIST: Can't you even imagine it? Just stopping something that is dragging you down to hell? Can't you?

GOERING: I imagined losing the war. The last two years, as much as I could, I stayed with my family, paintings and morphine. But what I didn't do was betray Germans, just as you wouldn't betray Jews and don't tell me you would.

PSYCHIATRIST: I certainly will tell you I would! I am a human being first and a Jew second.

GOERING: Horse shit. You are a pack animal first, a human being second, just like everybody else.

PSYCHIATRIST: No. Not everybody. Some see heads cut off and do their best to end it. *(Pause.)*

GOERING: But not quite yet. I'm not going to prison, am I? You're going to shoot us, aren't you?

PSYCHIATRIST: I don't know.

GOERING: Yes, you do. Your orders are to relieve my distress. Tell me the truth, Dr. Freud. Man to man.

PSYCHIATRIST: I think we will. *(Pause.)* I hope we do. *(Pause.)* You wanted the truth.

GOERING: Thank you. I'll be shot first of course. Well, I can pull in my stomach now. I'll look very good. Put my head under the tap, comb my hair, march right out to it. No blindfold. When you shoot, I'll say, "Heil Hitler!" OK with you?

PSYCHIATRIST: OK with me! *(Door opens. Enter Commandant. The Captain and the Sergeant snap to attention.)*

SERGEANT: Ten-shun!!

COMMANDANT: Goering!

GOERING: My Colonel!

COMMANDANT: Now hear this! *(Goering salutes, American Army style.)*

GOERING: Yes, my Colonel!

COMMANDANT: You will *not,* say *again, not,* bully the other prisoners further. It is one thing for you to assume command as their ranking superior, and since they seem to accept that, all right, but when they don't, you leave them alone!

GOERING: My Colonel, please understand. That pig-dog Albert Speer wants to blame everything on Hitler! We were all seduced by him!

COMMANDANT: Let them say what they please!

GOERING: I won't have it!!

COMMANDANT: Yes, you will—

GOERING: It's wrong!

COMMANDANT: If *I* say you will!

GOERING: But can't you see—

COMMANDANT: And don't you forget it!

GOERING: *(Quickly.)* I beg your pardon, my Colonel! Whatever you say.

COMMANDANT: And another thing! Sitting on the end of that dock, you keep turning in and talking to the others during the trial. No more. Shake your head, bounce up and down, but not a whisper, not a sound! You leave everybody alone!

GOERING: Yes, *sir*!!

COMMANDANT: And if you call me, "Swagger Stick" again, I'll have you on your knees cleaning grease pits.

GOERING: Joking! Kidding!

COMMANDANT: You'll turn green without that suicide pill, understand? *(Goering claps his hands to his mouth.)*

GOERING: Never again!

COMMANDANT: *(To Captain.)* Carry on. *(Exit Commandant.)*

PSYCHIATRIST: Does it turn you green, that pill?

GOERING: Oh, yes. Potassium cyanide. Makes your skin look like a cucumber.

PSYCHIATRIST: Green, eh?

GOERING: You are thinking what a wonderful cucumber I would make.

PSYCHIATRIST: You would have been a good psychiatrist. If you need me, let me know. *(Exit Psychiatrist. Exit Captain. Goering sits and thinks. The Sergeant watches him.)*

SERGEANT: Cranach.

GOERING: What?

SERGEANT: The painter. Cranach.

GOERING: What about him?

SERGEANT: Never mind.

GOERING: Go ahead, talk. We are alone. I give you my word, no one will know what you say to me.

SERGEANT: You bought his pictures?

GOERING: I did.

SERGEANT: Had 'em in your house?

GOERING: Yes. How do you know about the paintings of Cranach, if you don't mind my asking?

SERGEANT: My daddy's a preacher. He showed me.

GOERING: In a museum?

SERGEANT: In a book. Did you buy his picture about Mary, Jesus and Joseph?

GOERING: Which one?

SERGEANT: I don't know.

GOERING: There were many.

SERGEANT: It looked like this. Mary and Joseph were on a road, under some pine trees. Joseph had that worried look an old man'd get with a wife real young, like Mary was. Baby Jesus was reaching out to a lot of little angels, mess-ing around like any bunch of kids. One caught a bird and, see, had that bird fluttering by the wings and didn't know how to get it to Jesus. Me and my Daddy liked that.

GOERING: The Flight into Egypt. You have good taste. So does your father. *(Pause.)*

SERGEANT: There's something you ought to know.

GOERING: My dear man, what is it?

SERGEANT: They're not going to shoot you.

GOERING: Oh?

SERGEANT: I was at personnel, and I saw orders cut. Dated two months ahead but cut. For a Master Sergeant, the U.S. Army executioner. They already know. They going to hang your ass. *(Doors open. Enter Counsel, with a copy of Stars and Stripes.)*

COUNSEL: Great news! *(Goering whirls about. He stares at his Counsel.)* It's in the Army newspaper! Senator Taft, in the Congress of the United States, has condemned the trial. Justice Black of the Supreme Court, calls it Jackson's lynching party. And Churchill has begun making speeches against the Russians! It's all falling apart! *(He hands the newspaper to Goering, who glances at it calmly and then looks at the Sergeant. Goering smiles at the Counsel.)*

GOERING: Perhaps. *(Overhead, heavy airplanes fly over Nuremberg. Goering listens, looks up. End of Act One.)*

ACT II

The Captain and the Sergeant on guard. Goering and the Counsel are sitting down at the table to confer. The Counsel is wearing his black court robe.

COUNSEL: Your wife is very calm, very possessed. You would be proud of her, and of your daughter. They are staying with me now.

GOERING: That is very good of you.

COUNSEL: It has finally been decided when families may visit prisoners.

GOERING: For God's sake, when?

COUNSEL: Before the verdict, but after the trial.

GOERING: Allright. So. The trial.

COUNSEL: You may carry notes, but only as cues. After our witnesses testify in your favor, I will lead you through your life and career.

GOERING: Then Justice Jackson cross examines me?

COUNSEL: Yes. He's dangerous.

GOERING: I don't think so. His mind isn't on what he's doing. Why?

COUNSEL: He expects to be the next Chief Justice of the American Supreme Court.

GOERING: Politics. All right, good.

COUNSEL: He will insist on yes and no answers. Which you must give, but then, whenever you can, insert the statements we have worked out. And whatever else you want. Remember, you are still a famous man. The judges are human. They will be curious.

GOERING: So speak to Jackson but aim at them. And the whole world will hear what Hermann Goering has to say. Good! *(Drumbeat. Downlight on Goering, as if now in a witness chair. Softer downlight on the Counsel, standing by him. The rest of the stage is dark.)*

COUNSEL: And finally, when did you first meet Adolf Hitler?

GOERING: November, 1922, Munich. Everything he said was spoken word for word as if from my own soul. I bound myself to him, with my sacred oath, which I have kept.

COUNSEL: And what was the last you heard from him?

GOERING: A telegram in April of this year, ordering my execution as a traitor.

COUNSEL: And the execution of your wife and child?

GOERING: Yes.

COUNSEL: And you still maintain that loyalty to Adolf Hitler? Now?

GOERING: You swear an oath in good times so you will keep it in bad. Otherwise, why swear an oath at all?

COUNSEL: Which brings us to the last questions. Under Hitler, Germany was run by the Leader principle. How would you define that?

GOERING: Authority moving from above downward, while responsibility moves from below upwards. It was the only choice for us. As it still is, I might add, for the Union of Soviet Socialist Republics, the Empire of China, the Roman Catholic Church and the nations of Islam. Western Democracy is not for everyone. I do not think it ever will be.

COUNSEL: May it please the Tribunal, this concludes my defense of this witness. *Drums. Light intensifies on Goering alone.*

VOICE OF THE PRESIDENT OF THE TRIBUNAL: *(British.)* Mr. Justice Robert Jackson, of the United States, may now cross examine. *(Jackson's Voice is very confident.)*

VOICE OF ROBERT JACKSON: You are perhaps aware that you are the only man alive who can tell us the whole truth of the Nazi Party?

GOERING: *(Smiling.)* Not perhaps, absolutely.

JACKSON: *(V.O.)* You fully intended to overthrow a democracy and establish a dictatorship?

GOERING: *(Pleased.)* And did so.

JACKSON: *(V.O.)* To abolish parliamentary procedure and rule by the Leader Principle?

GOERING: Germany was a sovereign nation. What we did with our government was nobody's business but ours.

JACKSON: *(V.O.)* So you did not permit government by the consent of the governed?

GOERING: That is not entirely correct. From time to time we called upon the people to express themselves with votes of confidence.

JACKSON: *(V.O.)* But you never permitted the election of anyone who could act with authority?

GOERING: Quite right. Elected officials simply acknowledged the authority of the Leader.

JACKSON: *(V.O.)* Now, was this Leader Principle adopted because you believed no people are capable of self-government, or because you believe some may be but not the German people, or even if some of us can use a democratic system, it should not be allowed in Germany? Briefly, please.

GOERING: I beg your pardon, but may I untangle your rhetoric so I can understand your question? *(Drums. Light change, time passes.)*

JACKSON: *(V.O.)* Now, in order to suppress opposing parties and individuals, you created a secret police to detect opposition.

GOERING: I said that in my opening testimony. It was on a bigger and stronger scale than ever before.

JACKSON: *(V.O.)* You created the concentration camps as well?

GOERING: I said that, too. We had many enemies. Camps are necessary. You are going to have to put all the people you can't handle somewhere. We had to do it. You will, too. It's obvious.

JACKSON: *(V.O.)* Not so obvious to us. You are explaining a system to men who do not understand it very well and want to know what was necessary and what was not.

GOERING: You are asking me if I considered it necessary to establish concentration camps to eliminate the opposition. Is that what you are trying to get me to say?

JACKSON: *(V.O.)* Yes or no!

GOERING: Yes. For my Leader I eliminated his opposition. Yes.

JACKSON: *(V.O.)* Were there no public trials? The Gestapo was subject to no court review?

GOERING: You must differentiate between two categories of enforcement. I was both Prussian Prime Minister and Reich Minister of the Interior—

JACKSON: *(V.O.)* Let's omit that. I have not asked for that. Just answer my questions. Your Counsel can go into details for you later.

GOERING: I have answered your questions, but I want to make an explanation in connection with my answer.

PRESIDENT OF THE TRIBUNAL: *(V.O. British.)* Mr. Justice Jackson, the Tribunal thinks the witness ought to be allowed to make what explanation he thinks right in answer to this question. *(Pause.)*

JACKSON: *(V.O.)* I bow to the Court. Explain then. *(Goering smiles a brief smile, and launches into a huge digression.)*

GOERING: In connection with your question—*(Drums. Light, time.)*

JACKSON: *(V.O.)* You were opposed to the invasion of Russia?

GOERING: I was.

JACKSON: *(V.O.)* And said nothing against it.

GOERING: I said a great deal against it.

JACKSON: *(V.O.)* And nothing happened. You were a "yes man" to Hitler.

GOERING: I would be interested to meet a "no man" to Hitler.

JACKSON: *(V.O.)* What I mean is, you gave no warning to the German people about this grave danger, you brought no pressure to bear to prevent this step, and you did not even resign to protect your own place in history.

GOERING: These are not only not questions, they are statements all at once and I would like to try and separate them.

PRESIDENT OF THE TRIBUNAL: *(V.O.)* The Tribunal will hear the answer to each.

JACKSON: *(V.O.)* May it please this Court, the witness is using the same tactic over and over. He says the question is not clear, then rephrases it to suit himself, and answers as he pleases!

GOERING: *(On his feet.)* I am not an echo! I cannot answer statements! Or vague questions with exact responses!

COUNSEL: I apologize for the witness's outburst, but I submit he has a point, and I beg the Tribunal to consider it.

PRESIDENT OF THE TRIBUNAL: *(V.O.)* Mr. Justice Jackson, I must say I find your cross examination unusual. Simply turning statements into questions and expecting yes or no answers does not do justice to the complexity of these situations. Continue, please! *(Goering smiles and sits back down.)*

JACKSON: *(V.O.)* Very well. *(To Goering.)* Separate my questions. *(Drums, Light. Time. The Captain hands Goering a sheet of paper.)*

GOERING: This document has just been handed to us.

COUNSEL: I repeat my objection to the prosecution introducing documents in evidence that we have not yet seen.

PRESIDENT OF THE TRIBUNAL: *(V.O.)* Your objection is noted. Proceed.

GOERING: This contains alternating statements of various individuals.

JACKSON: *(V.O.)* Third paragraph from the end.

GOERING: Yes.

JACKSON: *(V.O.)* "These plans must be kept in the strictest secrecy." Do you see that?

GOERING: Yes.

JACKSON: *(V.O.)* "They include: A: The liberation of the Rhine."

GOERING: Wrong. The word is not liberation. It is preparation. Of the Rhine River. Technically that means clearing it. Of *tugboats*.

JACKSON: *(V.O.)* These preparations were not military preparations?

GOERING: To develop the country generally, yes, but to occupy the Rhineland, no.

JACKSON: *(V.O.)* But it *was* military action you were keeping secret from foreign powers? Yes or no!

GOERING: I do not recall ever seeing publicized the mobilization plans of the United States. Do you? *(Pause.)*

JACKSON: *(V.O. Explosion.)* I submit to the Tribunal! This witness is not being responsive—

GOERING: *(Up, simultaneous.)* I certainly *am* being responsive, as well as I *can*—

JACKSON: *(V.O.)*—it is futile to waste our time if the witness—

GOERING: *(Simultaneous.)*—in the face of such inept and confusing questions *nobody* can answer—

JACKSON: *(V.O.)*—will not answer the questions!

GOERING: *(Simultaneous.)*—in any reasonable cross-examination!

PRESIDENT OF THE TRIBUNAL: *(V.O.)* Mr. Justice Jackson, you are making too much of a small point. Every country keeps certain things secret. Proceed.

JACKSON: *(V.O. Furious.)* I protest! We are losing control of a crucial situation in the history of law!

PRESIDENT OF THE TRIBUNAL: *(V.O.)* You may speak for yourself, sir, about losing control of a situation. *Continue, please! (Goering, smiling broadly, sits back down.)*

JACKSON: *(V.O.)* Is this Tribunal unaware that outside this Courtroom lies the great social question of the revival of Nazism? What defendant Goering is trying to do—as I think he'd be the first to admit—is to create propaganda here that will revive it!

COUNSEL: I object! *(Goering gleefully nods.)*

PRESIDENT OF THE TRIBUNAL: *(V.O.)* Counsel for the Defense.

COUNSEL: My client is hardly in a position to attack the United States with propaganda. Mr. Justice Jackson is possibly confusing him with Goebbels, who has been dead since April. Hermann Goering is fighting for his life, and should be allowed not only to answer "yes" and "no," but if a question is confusing, clarify it!!

GOERING: Bravo!

PRESIDENT OF THE TRIBUNAL: *(V.O.)* Quite so. Mr. Justice Jackson, the defendant's reference to the United States is a matter you might well henceforth ignore. We have won the war, sir, and are hardly threatened now. Let us adjourn, and compose ourselves! *(Drums. Lights change back to the interrogation room. Goering, Captain, Psychiatrist, Sergeant. Goering swings about in his chair, clapping his hands in delight.)*

GOERING: Got *his* damned goat, by God! In front of the whole world! *(Claps his hands.)* I don't think he'll be Chief Justice of anything now, do you?

PSYCHIATRIST: You did very well.

GOERING: With my little flock watching it all! They were proud of me! I saw it! I put some fight back in them!

PSYCHIATRIST: All but Speer. He says what you're doing is terrible.

GOERING: Oh, yes Speer! He doesn't want me making Americans look stupid. He wants me to fall on my face, and say Hitler did it! Well, I'll take care of him. After what I did to Jackson, we'll be all right!

PSYCHIATRIST: The Commandant of Auschwitz testifies tomorrow.

GOERING: I'm on the stand! He can't!

PSYCHIATRIST: The Tribunal has voted to suspend your testimony, and interrupt it for his.

GOERING: More films?

PSYCHIATRIST: More films. You are a formidable witness, but those cameras say you tried to exterminate whole races of human beings. That won't go away.

Goering laughs.

GOERING: Oh, won't it?

PSYCHIATRIST: No, it won't!

GOERING: Well, why should it? When the devil is right, he is more right than all the sanctimonious angels in the world. Hitler was wrong about the war, but right about people. You, me, *everybody* lives despising others. The Americans and the British, unfortunately for us, get along, sort of, because one country came out of the other, but the rest? You'll see, or your children will. There won't be countries anymore, just races, all hating each other. Hitler knew. We all hate our rivals, and the first chance one of us has to dominate them, boom! Tell me it isn't so!

PSYCHIATRIST: That is the past. How can I make you understand it is the purpose of this trial to change exactly that!

GOERING: Because it won't. People are what they are, no better.

PSYCHIATRIST: Then we will make them better.

GOERING: Oh, Doctor Freud. Is that your insipid answer to the struggle of life?

PSYCHIATRIST: I don't know what the answer to the struggle of life is! But I know it isn't *you*! I don't care if you love your family! I don't care if you tried to stop the invasion of Poland! I care about the blood you shed, which would drown Nuremberg! Your grand cosmic pessimism is an excuse for murder! The hell with you! You're done for, over with, a dinosaur, gone! After this terrible war, the world must come together, and give up its racial stereotypes.

GOERING: Oh, Doctor Freud! Tell that to the rabbis!

PSYCHIATRIST: Rabbis don't murder children, you son of a bitch! *(Exit Psychiatrist, opening the door himself and slamming it shut. Goering chuckles.)*

GOERING: Got his goat, too. Hauptmann? What am I to do now?

CAPTAIN: I don't know. I'll find out.

SERGEANT: You want me to go?

CAPTAIN: If'n I'd a-wanted you to go, I'd a said so, boy!

SERGEANT: Yes, sir!

CAPTAIN: Carry on. *(Exit Captain. The Sergeant stands at ease, but he is very upset. Goering smiles at him.)*

GOERING: He insulted you, didn't he?

SERGEANT: Yeah.

GOERING: Calling you a boy?

SERGEANT: Way he did it, means nigger.

GOERING: Ah. I see. *(Pause.)* All my fliers respected each other.

SERGEANT: Glad to hear it.

GOERING: I taught them that. Would you like to know how?

SERGEANT: Just leave me alone!

GOERING: Shhhh. My dear sir. Not another word.

SERGEANT: Don't need you to tell me about it. *(Pause. Goering goes to the wash basin and puts some water on his hair.)* What did you say to your men?

GOERING: Do you really want to know?

SERGEANT: I wouldn't mind.

GOERING: Don't say I'm just being nice to you.

SERGEANT: I said I wouldn't mind.

GOERING: In the first war, officers looked down on enlisted men. We broke up that caste system and made everyone equal as a man. I told my fliers this. "You are young and you will pay for it. Go have your fun. I want you to. But when you get into that plane, you will be comrades, each respecting the next, so that in battle you will be warriors, destroying all resistance, and if it must be, dying for each other." *(The Sergeant nods.)* No man in my command called another man "boy." *(Pause. Goering sits back down in his chair.)*

SERGEANT: How many Cranachs did you have?

GOERING: Fourteen.

SERGEANT: Lord. Think of that.

GOERING: They will say I stole paintings just for plunder. Well, some, yes. But not Cranach. He gave me—a great freedom.

SERGEANT: Me, too.

GOERING: Would you like me to describe them for you? The Cranachs I owned? I remember every inch of every one.

SERGEANT: Yeah, I would.

GOERING: Let's start with the Madonna and Child.

SERGEANT: All right. *(The Sergeant leans forward. Lights change. Sounds of a basketball game: shouts, thud of the ball, squeaking of sneakers in a gym. Passage of time. Lights up. Enter Commandant, on Goering's side of the partition, the Psychiatrist and the Counsel on the other.)*

SERGEANT: Ten-shun! *(Sergeant and Captain come to attention. Goering stands up, smiling.)*

COMMANDANT: At ease.

GOERING: Good morning, my Colonel!

COMMANDANT: Good morning. Gentlemen, we have something to get straight right now! Coercion, in my prison!

GOERING: Oh, my Colonel! How can that be?

COMMANDANT: Goering, you're not a damned Reichsmarshall anymore. *(To Counsel.)* During his exercise and at meals. Get it straight with him.

COUNSEL: The Commandant is concerned—

COMMANDANT: Not concerned, god damned furious!

COUNSEL: God damned furious, over his perception of a—slight manipulation—

COMMANDANT: Bullying!

COUNSEL: Bullying—

PSYCHIATRIST: Sir, it's best not to put words in their mouths.

COMMANDANT: *What* did you say, Major?

PSYCHIATRIST: I beg your pardon, sir. It weakens your own position.

COMMANDANT: When I need your advice, I'll ask for it!

PSYCHIATRIST: I beg your pardon, sir! *(To Counsel.)* Sorry!

COUNSEL: Bullying—the other prisoners. They have complained.

GOERING: About me, complained? Who?

COMMANDANT: That's not the point.

GOERING: Speer! Speer!

COMMANDANT: That's not the point!

GOERING: Speer, the bastard!

COUNSEL: Actually, it is Ribbentrop who is most concerned.

GOERING: Ribbentrop! Who told Hitler, go! Poland, everywhere! No one will do anything! Now he's sniveling on his knees! God, you can shoot me fifty times over before I'll do that!

PSYCHIATRIST: No one's asking you do do that. What's being asked—

COMMANDANT: God damn it, Major!

PSYCHIATRIST: I beg your pardon!

COUNSEL: What is being asked, as I understand it, is that you refrain from further influencing the opinions of the other accused.

COMMANDANT: You're going to leave them alone, you understand?

GOERING: How *can* I leave them alone? They are my responsibility! I am the leader of Germany now, and I refuse to let other Germans disgrace their country! They are Germans and they are mine, and I will lead them!!

COMMANDANT: No, you won't! You're in solitary, Mister. From now on, you eat by yourself!

GOERING: I protest!

COMMANDANT: To who? Me?

GOERING: Not to you, *SWAGGER STICK!* To the Tribunal! Counsel!

COUNSEL: I do feel this prisoner's rights are being abused!

COMMANDANT: The Tribunal has no jurisdiction over me! *I* run this prison!

GOERING: In the eyes of the world, Colonel! And the world will call you what you are, you ridiculous little, *petty* little, *pig-dog bastard! (Goering, in a rage, moves toward the Commandant. The Captain and the Sergeant strike down his arms with their billy clubs, seize him and force him face-down to the floor. Pause.)* I beg your pardon! I apologize!

COMMANDANT: *(Shaken.)* Do that again and I'll lock you in a cage! Let him go. *(They do. Goering backs away, swallowing his rage.)*

PSYCHIATRIST: Sir, this is an issue here.

COMMANDANT: Major, you're out of line!

PSYCHIATRIST: No, sir, I'm not!

COMMANDANT: Jesus Christ!

PSYCHIATRIST: You've got the most thankless job any officer in the Army ever had. I know that! But this man is world famous! And you aren't!

COMMANDANT: I'll court martial you, by God!

PSYCHIATRIST: All right, do that! But that's Hermann Goering! He's hateful and he's hideous and I have more right to despise him than you do, but if you are unfair to him, you'll get hurt! Don't underestimate him!

COMMANDANT: I've given my orders. Consult all you want. Then carry them out, Major, or you're on charges. That's all. *(Exit Commandant.)*

PSYCHIATRIST: Congratulations, Goering. You've got us fighting among ourselves.

GOERING: Don't let him do this to me. I must not be separated from—Germany.

PSYCHIATRIST: Breakfast, lunch and dinner in your cell. That's it. I did my best. Here, I brought your glasses. *(He holds up a pair of dark eyeglasses, for the Captain to see. The Captain nods. The Psychiatrist sets them down on the table. Goering picks them up, looks them over.)*

GOERING: Well, German lenses. Good. *(He puts them on.)* Now I look like an old woman in Florida.

PSYCHIATRIST: Right.

GOERING: No laugh? Not even a smile?

PSYCHIATRIST: No.

GOERING: I understand. It would violate your high moral position. I must be a monster. Gas pump creature, with my dick in my ear. You think you can march me into a courtroom, find me guilty, kill me, and change the course of human nature. But I am a man just like you. You are a man just like me. Pretending otherwise is a great mistake.

PSYCHIATRIST: Nuts. Just give me back the glasses. You'll get them going into court.

GOERING: I can't keep them?

PSYCHIATRIST: You could cut your throat with good German lenses.

GOERING: So I could. OK. *(He takes off the glasses, hands them back.)* Thank you. *(Exit Psychiatrist. To Counsel.)* If I can't eat with them, I can't talk to them. You must negotiate for me.

COUNSEL: How can I?

GOERING: Through their lawyers! They'll listen to you!

COUNSEL: Perhaps.

GOERING: Tell them I will not implicate anyone, not Ribbentrop, not even Speer, if they will stand fast, and not break ranks! Germans together, or else! Understand!

COUNSEL: Or else what?

GOERING: I know enough to send them all to hell a hundred times over.

COUNSEL: *(Quietly.)* Oh, do you? And how much of that do I know? Nothing?

GOERING: Yes. Do you want to quit? *(Pause.)*

COUNSEL: No. You want me to—threaten other prisoners—with exposure of crimes known only to you. Is that it?

GOERING: That will do. It is your duty as a lawyer.

COUNSEL: I have three duties. To my client, to the law, and to Germany. But not evidently, to myself.

GOERING: Thank you.

COUNSEL: The British cross-examine tomorrow. Only a staff lawyer, but be careful.

GOERING: I beat Jackson, didn't I?

COUNSEL: Yes, you did.

GOERING: So. You do your duty and I'll do mine. Until tomorrow.

COUNSEL: Good afternoon. *(Exit Counsel. Pause. Goering sags, wipes his face with his hands.)*

CAPTAIN: *(To Sergeant.)* You got a break.

SERGEANT: What?

CAPTAIN: I said you got a break. Take ten. Move out!!

SERGEANT: Sir. *(Exit Sergeant. Pause. Goering becomes aware that he and the Captain are alone in the room. He regroups his forces.)*

GOERING: I am sorry to see a Hauptmann standing guard with a black man. They aren't quite human, are they? No wonder you call him boy.

CAPTAIN: Yeah, well never mind that.

GOERING: None of my business.

CAPTAIN: Right. *(Pause.)* So what was the best rifle you ever had?

GOERING: Ah, well! My old bolt-action Dryse! It had a birch stock to it, fit my chin like a woman's hand. Fifty years old but lead a stag, and it fired itself! Bang! Clean through the heart!

CAPTAIN: I shot a 460 Weatherly Magnum once.

GOERING: And it kicked!

CAPTAIN: Nearly tore off my shoulder!

GOERING: High power, short range. Not my old Dryse. With it, easy, follow, lead—*(He mimes hefting a rifle to his shoulder and mimes leading a stag. The Captain does the same.)*

GOERING and CAPTAIN: *(Softly.)* Bang. *(Pause.)*

CAPTAIN: People say you raised lions. I mean, had them at home, in the house.

GOERING: Oh, yes.

CAPTAIN: *Lions?*

GOERING: Delightful creatures. Full of love and trust.

CAPTAIN: What do you do when a lion, all full of love and trust, jumps on your lap?

GOERING: You keep still.

CAPTAIN: I reckon. *(Pause.)* I hear you shot down thirty planes in the first war.

GOERING: Twenty-two.

CAPTAIN: One time, in this dogfight, you got this plane dead to rights. You saluted the man, and flew away. Really?

GOERING: His guns had jammed. He was helpless.

CAPTAIN: Oh.

GOERING: Hauptmann, why are you disobeying orders talking to me?

CAPTAIN: I'm proud to know you.

GOERING: And I you, American Hauptmann. Salute. *(Goering salutes, with the American Army salute. The Captain returns it.)*

CAPTAIN: Sir. *(Drums. Downlight on Goering again. Accent light on the Counsel.)*

PRESIDENT OF THE TRIBUNAL: The Prosecutor for Great Britain may now cross examine.

VOICE OF BRITISH PROSECUTOR: *(Dry and deceptive.)* A few minor questions. In 1944, fifty British Air Force Prisoners of War, upon their escape from Stalag Luft III, were captured and shot. Upon your orders?

GOERING: Absolutely not. I was on leave.

PROSECUTOR: *(V.O.)* It was Hitler's decision?

GOERING: We had a very bitter argument about it.

PROSECUTOR: *(V.O.)* As Minister of the Air Force, you had jurisdiction over medical experiments on captured aviators?

GOERING: I knew nothing of this.

PROSECUTOR: *(V.O.)* Then let me tell you about it. Men were frozen on the ground at sky altitude temperatures. Then they were put in a bed with naked women. They were allowed to come alive if they could, and if they could, have sexual relations. Then they were gassed. Air Force experiments!

GOERING: I never heard of anything like that in all my life!

PROSECUTOR: *(V.O.)* Do you consider it serious?

GOERING: It is an atrocity, whether in the name of aviation *or* science! I consider *nothing* more serious!!

PROSECUTOR: *(V.O.)* Atrocities upset you?

GOERING: Yes!

PROSECUTOR: *(V.O.)* Let us see about that. This document, numbered 786–QS. A letter addressed to Obergruppenfuhrer-SS Reinhard Heydrich. Would you read the last paragraph? *(The Captain gives Goering a paper.)*

COUNSEL: I have not seen this document before. I object.

PROSECUTOR: *(V.O.)* Last paragraph, or I will read it.

COUNSEL: I appeal to the Tribunal!

VOICE OF THE PRESIDENT OF THE TRIBUNAL: Letter addressed to Obergruppenfuhrer-SS Reinhard Heydrich. Last paragraph. *(The Counsel gives a sheet of paper to Goering.)*

GOERING: *(Reading.)* "I further instruct you to present to me at once all logistical preparations for the Final Solution of the Jewish Problem."

PROSECUTOR: *(V.O.)* That is your signature?

GOERING: It's only a formality, an enabling act. Drafted by Himmler, or Heydrich.

PROSECUTOR: *(V.O.)* Not Hitler?

GOERING: Never!

PROSECUTOR: *(V.O.)* Not you?

GOERING: No!

PROSECUTOR: *(V.O.)* You have boasted and boasted to this Tribunal that you are responsible for whatever you signed! Well? Who signed it?

GOERING: Signed, Goering, Reichsmarshall! But translated wrong. Final solution should read complete solution.

PROSECUTOR: *(V.O.)* Oh, please! What is the difference?

GOERING: Emigration, not liquidation! That's the difference!

PROSECUTOR: *(V.O.)* I don't believe you. I believe Number One gave Number Two a verbal order to murder eleven million Jews and Number Two put it in writing for him. Then Number One left Number Two holding the baby. How could you be so stupid? Of all the Germans, you were the only man with the power to oppose Hitler and his inhuman policies, and you can't even do it now, while he is putting the rope around your neck! Never mind your sacred oaths and heroic poses! Why didn't Number Two *ever* say no to Number One?

GOERING: To him?

PROSECUTOR: *(V.O.)* To him. *(A long pause. Then Goering holds up both hands, shakes his head, and smiles. Drums. Lights change. The interrogation room. Goering sits at the table, handcuffed to the Sergeant who stands by him. Across the table sits his wife, a handsome woman in her forties, dressed in stylishly made-to-do threadbare clothes.)*

WIFE: But I must ask you.

GOERING: No, please!

WIFE: Even now! I must! For God's sake, he was going to shoot me! Kill your child! The whole world knows he was the devil! He brought all Germany, and us, to ruin! Say so!!

GOERING: Never.

WIFE: Why not? It's the only chance you have!

GOERING: I have no chance at all.

WIFE: You don't know that!

GOERING: Of course I do. Don't fool yourself. Tell our child that I am going to die. Is she afraid they'll kill you, too?

WIFE: Always.

GOERING: Tell her I will die, but not you. Maybe it will help.

WIFE: Please.

GOERING: What?

WIFE: Hitler! Hitler!

GOERING: My dearest, Hitler is not to blame for what I did. I am. *(Pause.)*

WIFE: All right.

GOERING: Thank you. *(Pause.)*

WIFE: We would have been very happy, in the theatre.

GOERING: Do you think so?

WIFE: You would have been a marvelous actor.

GOERING: Yes, I would. Falstaff!

WIFE: You could have worn your costumes and been bigger than life. After performances, in the evening, we would drink, with the other actors, and then go home.

GOERING: But I wasn't acting. Unfortunately for me.

WIFE: You are the best husband any wife ever had. We have the most beautiful child in the world. Whatever happens, I am content.

CAPTAIN: Time's up. *(The Sergeant moves back, forcing Goering up by the handcuffs. The Wife rises, too. Goering reaches out for his wife and she moves toward him, as if they would kiss through a screen. The Sergeant jerks Goering's arms down roughly.)*

GOERING: Please. *(He waves a goodbye to his wife. She to him. Exit Wife, the Counsel opening the door and closing it after her. Then he moves down to her place. The Sergeant unlocks the handcuffs and joins the Captain on guard. Goering sits very still. Then he sees the Counsel staring at him.)* You will help her?

COUNSEL: All I can.

GOERING: In spite of what you think of me.

COUNSEL: Yes, in spite of that.

GOERING: What you think of me is very important to me.

COUNSEL: Some will admire you.

GOERING: But not you! *(The Counsel goes to the wash basin on his side of the room, to wash and dry his hands and face.)*

COUNSEL: At first, I thought the Tribunal unjust. Then the horrible realities of those camps wiped out everything. The trial is no longer about guilt as we ever knew it. It is about the absolute worst in human nature, and it looks squarely at you. I don't know how guilty you are anymore, or how guilty I am, for that matter. You awed me, charmed me, in spite of everything, made me admire you. I blackmailed men on trial for their lives. Right here, in this prison. For you!

GOERING: You were right to do so. They broke their vows.

COUNSEL: I had no right to do so. Men can change their minds.

GOERING: If that is what you think duty is, you know nothing of men and never will.

COUNSEL: At 68, I'm learning. And one of the things I am learning is that of all the ideas men have ever had, duty is the worst! *(He throws the towel into the basin.)*

GOERING: So, verdict tomorrow. What do you think?

COUNSEL: No one believes anything good about you now.

GOERING: Not even you?

COUNSEL: You are courageous. Everyone says that. You dominate the court-room, and everyone says that, too.

GOERING: What do you say?

COUNSEL: You *still* don't think anything wrong was done!!! *(Pause.)* Your wife was right. You should have bullied and pillaged and murdered in the theatre, where you belong.

GOERING: Well, you did your best.

COUNSEL: Thank you.

GOERING: I have one more thing to say to the Tribunal.

COUNSEL: Yes?

GOERING: Shooting I will accept. Hanging I will not.

COUNSEL: You hardly have that choice.

GOERING: I must have that choice. Think. What will be best for Germany? For its Reichsmarshall to be hanged, like a dog, or shot, like a man?

COUNSEL: To be shot like a man.

GOERING: You said you loved Germany.

COUNSEL: I do!

GOERING: Then you must do *your* duty as I must do mine.

COUNSEL: What duty now? *(Drums up. Lights change. Spots on Goering and the Captain.)*

GOERING: You alone will know. Only a great hunter, wise and cunning, can do it. Are you that man?

CAPTAIN: I could be.

GOERING: Will you do it?

CAPTAIN: I might.

GOERING: They don't search the guards, do they?

CAPTAIN: No, they don't. *(Drums. Spots on Goering and the Sergeant.)*

GOERING: The mother of Jesus holds him firmly. His infant hand lingers on her cheek. It can be yours.

SERGEANT: Nobody'd believe me.

GOERING: With my signature, they would legally have to. *(Pause.)* You might keep it. Or sell it for a fortune.

SERGEANT: What you want me to do?

GOERING: A few steps, a moment alone with my gear, slip something in your pocket, and give it to me. They don't search the guards, do they?

SERGEANT: No, they don't. *(Drums. Lights change. Spot on Goering. The drums continue, muffled.)*

VOICE OF THE PRESIDENT OF THE TRIBUNAL: You were the second only to Hitler in the Nazi movement—

GOERING: I did not want a war, nor did I bring it about—

PRESIDENT OF THE TRIBUNAL: *(V.O.)* You created the Gestapo and the concentration camps—

GOERING: Except as a military duty, I never ordered the execution of anyone—

PRESIDENT OF THE TRIBUNAL: *(V.O.)* You designed the German Air Force, and began the bombing of cities instead of military targets—

GOERING: Compared with Dresden and Hiroshima, my air force was a model of restraint.

PRESIDENT OF THE TRIBUNAL: *(V.O.)* You looted Europe of its cultural treasures as no other man in history—

GOERING: I paid for everything—

PRESIDENT OF THE TRIBUNAL: *(V.O.)* You persecuted the Jews, first by devastating economic laws—

GOERING: When my duty allowed, I was always a friend to the Jews—

PRESIDENT OF THE TRIBUNAL: *(V.O.)* You then issued orders to Himmler and Heydrich—

GOERING: I utterly condemn these terrible mass murders!

PRESIDENT OF THE TRIBUNAL: *(V.O.)* To exterminate the entire Jewish population of Europe! *(Drums are silent.)* Six million died. *(Pause.)* There are no excuses for you. The Tribunal finds you guilty, on all counts. You may address the Court before sentence is pronounced. *(Goering stands.)*

GOERING: I speak to the German people. The winner will always be innocent. The loser will always be guilty. This trial changes nothing.

PRESIDENT OF THE TRIBUNAL: *(V.O.)* Defendant, on the counts by which you have been indicted, this Tribunal sentences you to death by hanging. *(Burst of drums. Blackout. A young girl's voice is heard in the darkness.)*

DAUGHTER: *(V.O.)* "A Lady Stood," by Dietmar von Aist. *(Lights up slowly. Goering is standing by his chair. He is handcuffed to the Sergeant again. His eight-*

year-old daughter is standing across the wire fence in front of her mother, whose hands are on her shoulders, reciting a poem. The Counsel and the Psychiatrist stand in the background, as does the Captain. Speaking.)
"A Lady stood on a turret stone
Looking away o'er the moorlands lone,
To see her love come riding there.

"She saw a falcon in the air:
Oh, happy falcon, flying free,
Flying where your heart would be!

My eyes have singled out a knight.
What though his arms have lost their might?
For him I cry.

Though all my prayers be answered never,
My love for him will live forever."

Do you like it?
GOERING: It is perfect. So are you. *(Pause. The Wife presses the Daughter's shoulders.)*
DAUGHTER: I am to say goodbye now.
GOERING: I know.
DAUGHTER: God bless you.
GOERING: God bless you.
DAUGHTER: Goodbye, Daddy.
GOERING: Goodbye. *(She turns and walks out, followed by the Wife and the Counsel. The Sergeant unlocks the handcuffs, steps away. Goering wheels away, hiding his feelings, which are intense and genuine. He turns back, to face the Psychiatrist.)*
PSYCHIATRIST: You killed her. *Her.* A million times. Can't you understand that? *(A terrible pause. Goering struggles with himself.)*
GOERING: *UNDERSTAND IT? YES!! I UNDERSTAND IT!* (Pause.) And it makes no difference whether we understand it or not.
PSYCHIATRIST: Why?
GOERING: Because we are men, and men will do what men will do.
PSYCHIATRIST: My God! That's all you have to say?
GOERING: What do you want me to say? I am a fool? Yes! I would do it all again? Yes? That there is nothing worse than a man? ABSOLUTELY!!! *Why* did it happen? I don't know! *You* can tell everybody that, Doctor! What will you put in your book?
PSYCHIATRIST: The truth about the war, as I saw it!

GOERING: Authoritarian regression, psychological sadism, the household origins of global treachery, and that explains everything. So much for psychologists. What else do we have to say to each other?

PSYCHIATRIST: One more thing.

GOERING: What's that?

PSYCHIATRIST: You asked me to find out whose work this trial was. I did.

GOERING: Churchill, Roosevelt, Stalin?

PSYCHIATRIST: It came out of Roosevelt's cabinet. The man who gave it its form was a Colonel Murray C. Bernays.

GOERING: Bernays?

PSYCHIATRIST: That was the maiden name of a great man's wife. Freud's.

GOERING: The man who created the tribunal was related to Freud?

PSYCHIATRIST: By marriage, yes.

GOERING: Hung by a Jew? *(Goering laughs. The Psychiatrist smiles. Goering laughing.)* So! Now you smile! Doctor, how much do you hate me?

PSYCHIATRIST: *(Smiling.)* Beyond description.

GOERING: Then how you would like to kill me? *(Light change. Echoing sounds of GIs playing basketball. Exit Psychiatrist. Enter Counsel.)* Well.

COUNSEL: Well.

GOERING: Did you find out?

COUNSEL: It will be at night. You'll be awakened, quickly, and rushed to a gymnasium, where the playing of basketball games mask the building of the gallows. They will hang you then.

GOERING: You can save me from that. *(Lights change. Sounds of basketball, dim. Exit Counsel and with him, the Sergeant. Goering is alone on stage. He walks slowly to the washbasin, quietly washes his hands and face and dries them with a towel, then moves to the center of the stage. The basketball game stops. Sound montage, with echoes and vibrations.)*

VOICES:

They get to sleep!

They don't expect anything!

We get them out fast!

Colonel!

Goering first, then the others!

Colonel, get the colonel!

We hang them before they know what's happening!

Colonel! Colonel!

VOICE OF COMMANDANT: What?

VOICES:

Goering!

He's on the floor in his cell!

He's in convulsions!

He's bitten something!

My God, he's turning green!

He's dead!

VOICE OF COMMANDANT: He can't be! Oh, my God! He can't be!!

VOICES:

What'll we do!

How did he do it?

This will wreck the trial!

Who did it?

Who got that stuff to him?

VOICE OF COMMANDANT:. Somebody *helped* that bastard! WHO??

VOICES: Who did it? Why??? *(The voices echo and vibrate into silence. Goering stands at center. A greenish, ghastly light falls on him. Muffled drum roll.)*

GOERING: Dear Swagger Stick. You will find a letter telling you I had the pill with me all the time. You know that's not possible. Somebody gave it to me. The Army can quote my letter, clear itself, and then, I hope, court martial you. *(Drum roll ends. Goering smiling, speaks to the audience.)* I am at peace with what I have done. I know you all very well. You always liked me, and saw yourselves in me. You will find other Hitlers, and other ways to go to war. When you do, he will need me, and he will call me back. I will bind myself to him again, laughing, a good number two. *(Goering's smiles vanishes. He stares out coldly.)* After all, what do you think men are? *(The green light fades on him.)*

THE END

Loving Daniel Boone

MARSHA NORMAN

MARSHA NORMAN won the 1983 Pulitzer and Susan Smith Blackburn Prizes for her play 'Night Mother. Her first play, Getting Out, which premiered at Actors Theatre of Louisville, received the John Gassner Playwriting Medallion, the Newsday Oppenheimer Award and a special citation from the American Theatre Critics Association. Other plays premiered at Actors Theatre of Louisville, including Third and Oak: The Laundromat and The Pool Hall, Sarah and Abraham, Loving Daniel Boone, and Trudy Blue. She also wrote the book and lyrics for the Broadway musical The Secret Garden, for which she received both Tony and Drama Desk Awards. Her first novel, The Fortune Teller, was published in 1987.

Copyright © 1992 Marsha Norman. Reprinted by permission of the Author and the Author's Agent, The Tantleff Office, 375 Greenwich Street, Suite 700, New York, NY 10013. Commissioned by ATL in recognition of Kentucky's Bicentennial with a grant from the Honorable Order of Kentucky Colonels.

LOVING DANIEL BOONE

was first presented by Actors Theatre of Louisville on February 26, 1992.

CAST

DANIEL BOONE ....Gladden Schrock
RUSSELL ....Rod McLachlan
FLO ....Catherine Christianson
HILLY ....Dave Florek
BLACKFISH ....Chekotah Miskenack
INDIAN ....Steve Willis*
MR. WILSON ....Mark Shannon
RICK ....Skipp Sudduth
JEMIMA BOONE ....Kathryn Velvel*
SQUIRE BOONE ....Eddie Levi Lee

Director ....Gloria Muzio
Scenic Designer ....Paul Owen
Costume Designer ....Pamela Scofield
Lighting Designer ....Karl E. Haas
Sound Designer ....Darron West
Properties Master ....Ron Riall
Stage Manager ....Mark D. Leslie
Fight Director ....Susan Eviston
Assistant to the Fight Director ....Whitney Wilcoxson
Production Dramaturg ....Julie Crutcher
Casting arranged by Susan Shaw, C.S.A.

*members of the ATL Apprentice Company

CHARACTERS

(In order of appearance)
DANIEL BOONE, the frontier hero
RUSSELL, a settler
FLO, a cleaning woman in a history museum
HILLY, the new night cleaning man
BLACKFISH, Chief of the Shawnee
MR. WILSON, a curator at the museum
RICK, a mechanic
JEMIMA, Boone's daughter
SQUIRE BOONE, Boone's brother
(Other Indians and Settlers may be used, but are not essential.)

The action takes place both in the museum where Flo has been working, and in the frontier Kentucky of 1778 to which she has gained access. Care should be taken so the set does not suggest we are doing an outdoor drama. Representations of the frontier life should rather be bold and mysterious, helping to indicate that this is the world that Flo prefers. Further, there will be no barriers to Flo's movement between the worlds. Frontier costumes should be vivid and sensuous. Present day costumes should be as simple as possible.

All actors will speak with a Kentucky accent, but should be careful not to lower the perceived intelligence of Kentuckians by doing so.

IN THE FOREST
In dim light, we see two men in buckskins holding long rifles, one leaning comfortably against a tree, the other squatting nervously beside him. Owls hoot in the darkness. Or it could be Indians signaling each other. Russell, the nervous one, drinks from his canteen.
RUSSELL: You got any opinion about this?
BOONE: No. I don't.
RUSSELL: But you *are* thinkin' about it, right?
BOONE: No. I don't think I am.
RUSSELL: Why not?
BOONE: It don't concern me, Russell.
RUSSELL: It does too concern you, and you know it.
BOONE: All right, maybe it does. That still don't mean I have to think about it.
RUSSELL: You know damn well what you think about this. You just don't want to say it.
BOONE: Well. Maybe I don't.
RUSSELL: So *why* don't you want to say it?
BOONE: Do you want to say what *you* think?
RUSSELL: Yes, I do. I think they're gonna kill us.
BOONE: Well, maybe they will. I'd just relax, if I were you.

RUSSELL: How do you think they'll kill us, exactly?

BOONE: Rush in, knife us. Hide in the bushes and shoot us. It's hard to say.

RUSSELL: Both at the same time, or me first?

BOONE: You first.

RUSSELL: Be just my luck, they'll kill me first, and then you'll talk your way out of it.

BOONE: I'd have to try, Russell.

RUSSELL: 'Fore you know it, the whole gang of 'em would be walkin' you back to their camp. "Hey, Blackfish, look what we got here. It's Daniel Boone."

BOONE: Yeah. I could see somethin' like that.

RUSSELL: Course you'd eventually escape.

BOONE: Maybe I would.

RUSSELL: Of course you would. Get home, get paraded around the fort. Get elected to the legislature, for God's sake.

BOONE: No, I know.

RUSSELL: Well why not? I'd vote for you. If I were still alive, I mean.

BOONE: If you want to try sneakin' out of here right now, let's go.

RUSSELL: You think we could get past 'em?

BOONE: Probably not.

RUSSELL: But if we head back to the salt lick, they'll just get the whole party.

BOONE: I was thinkin' if the Shawnee had all of us for the winter, they might not attack Boonesborough 'til the spring.

RUSSELL: I think about 'em sometimes, back at the fort, dryin' tobacco, diggin' wells. Wonderin' where the hell we are.

BOONE: Course now . . .

RUSSELL: Yeah.

BOONE: They could all be dead.

RUSSELL: I know.

Daniel hears something, smiles and comes up to a squatting position.

BOONE: Well, Russell. Maybe our red brothers are gonna forget about us for the night.

RUSSELL: *(A deep sigh of relief.)* Oh Lord. Really?

BOONE: Nope. Here they come.

And to the sound of a loud war cry, shrieking Indians come onstage in the darkness and attack them. A furious struggle begins. Boone and Russell are outnumbered, outfought, and finally, dragged offstage.

IN THE MUSEUM

And then, an overhead light switches on, and we find we are not in the forest at all, but rather in a museum, with painted backdrops of pioneer struggles, large cases of rifles and household equipment, huge stuffed birds and animal skins, etc. In the center of the room is a tree stump, on which is carved D. BOONE KILL A BAR. 1803. ZOIS.

The person who turned on the lights is Flo, the night cleaning woman. She is in her mid-30s, and almost pretty, with long dark hair. She wears a long skirt and moccasins. Following her is Hilly, a young man wearing faded jeans and a black T-shirt. Flo pushes the cleaning cart into the room. Hilly carries the mop and pail and the feather duster.

FLO: So. In this room, you start with the birds. 'Cause if you do the floor first and then do the birds, the dust from the birds will fall on the floor and you'll have to do the floor all over again.

HILLY: Whatever you say, Flo.

FLO: I guess starting tomorrow night you can do it however you want. But tonight, you do it like I say, so I can know it's done right.

HILLY: O.K.

FLO: What's your name again?

HILLY: Hilly.

FLO: And you be real careful around this tree stump. Daniel Boone himself carved his name right there. D. BOONE KILL A BAR. 1803.

HILLY: O.K.

FLO: Now on these cases, you have to use Windex and a cloth. Not a paper towel. Not ever. It makes a streak.

She gets a cloth.

Like this.

HILLY: *(beginning to get exasperated)* Anybody can clean things.

FLO: Not Daniel Boone's things, they can't.

HILLY: What about inside the cases?

FLO: You try and steal anything out of these cases and they'll have you in jail, mister.

HILLY: Who said anything about stealin'?

FLO: You've probably been in jail anyway.

HILLY: Do I look like I've been in jail?

FLO: You do. Actually.

HILLY: Well, what if I was?

FLO: What did you do?

HILLY: You know that statue of Daniel Boone in Cherokee Park?

Her face pales as she remembers what happened to that statue.

FLO: That was you?

HILLY: It was.

FLO: And they actually gave you this job after you did that?

HILLY: It was the judge's idea. Somethin' about my debt to society.

Flo throws down her broom, and heads for the door.

FLO: I'm going to get Mr. Wilson down here right now. I will not have a known vandal all by himself in this museum all night, I will not.

He grabs her arm.

HILLY: He already knows what I did. The judge told him all about it.

FLO: Well I don't trust you. You'll mess it up! You'll bring in your spray paint or your whatever it is, you'll pee on it.

HILLY: I will not. What I did to Daniel Boone I did for personal reasons. And I'm not gonna do it again, because . . . because I'm not. *(changing tone)* I'll do this right. You watch. I'll do it so good, they'll think you did it. O.K.?

And suddenly, her attention is drawn away from him.

IN A TEEPEE

Daniel Boone is pushed into the room by a young Indian brave, who ties him to a totem pole, then leaves.

IN THE MUSEUM

FLO: O.K.

IN A TEEPEE

Chief Blackfish enters and walks up to Boone. Then all around him, studying him. Boone is badly beaten up.

BLACKFISH: So this is the famous Daniel Boone.

BOONE: Pleased to meet you, Blackfish. Where are all the others?

BLACKFISH: You speak our language.

BOONE: I speak your language. I walk your land. I kill your bear.

BLACKFISH: Are you scared?

BOONE: Yes, sir.

BLACKFISH: Good.

Chief Blackfish leaves.

IN THE MUSEUM

HILLY: How long you been doin' this?

FLO: Start with the birds.

HILLY: Yes, ma'am.

Flo sits down in the guard chair, and wraps a shawl around her shoulders. Hilly begins to dust the birds.

IN THE TEEPEE

Russell is thrown into the teepee, more or less at Boone's feet.

BOONE: Russell.

RUSSELL: They made you run the gauntlet. Why did you have to run it and not us?

BOONE: All part of the deal I made.

Flo gets up from her chair.

RUSSELL: What else did you promise them? How come we're not dead?

BOONE: I said when spring came, I'd lead the war party back to Boonesborough, and they could capture everybody else too. Sell *all* our scalps to the British if they felt like it.

RUSSELL: What did you do that for?

BOONE: Just tryin' to get 'em to relax, Russell.

RUSSELL: But you're not really gonna do that, are you?

BOONE: Not unless I have to.

Flo takes a piece of jerky out of her pocket, walks over to the teepee and hands it to Russell. Russell takes a bite, then looks at Daniel.

RUSSELL: Where's yours?

BOONE: I ate already.

Russell notices the look Flo is giving Boone.

RUSSELL: I don't believe it. This Indian woman's in love with you.

BOONE: She doesn't look like an Indian somehow. She looks like a white woman.

RUSSELL: She looks damn hostile to me.

BOONE: I've heard of this. Some lost white woman wanderin' around out here.

RUSSELL: Does every damn thing you hear interest you?

BOONE: Don't it you?

RUSSELL: No, it don't.

BOONE: I think this girl knows more about this country than any man we know. Look at how she moves. If we weren't watchin', we wouldn't even know she was here.

RUSSELL: If we weren't watching, we wouldn't know we was here.

Flo turns to leave the teepee.

BOONE: *(To Flo.)* Hey. You don't have to leave. Where are you goin'?

FLO: To get you some blankets.

She leaves.

RUSSELL: What did she say?

BOONE: She'll be back.

RUSSELL: Did you know this girl was in this camp?

BOONE: I reckon I did.

IN THE MUSEUM

Flo walks back to the guard chair and sits down. She pours herself a cup of coffee from a thermos.

FLO: Why'd you do that to Daniel Boone?

HILLY: Because he pisses me off.

FLO: He's the best man who ever lived in Kentucky.

HILLY: See what I mean?

FLO: He came through the Cumberland Gap and found Kentucky. He saved the fort at Boonesborough.

HILLY: And then named it for himself.

FLO: The other settlers named it for him because they'd have all died if he hadn't been there.

HILLY: Come on, Flo. This was a guy went around writin' his name on the trees.

FLO: He wrote his name on the trees because he just killed a bear and he had to stay awake all night watchin' it.

HILLY: Is that what you do when you can't sleep? Carve up your furniture?

FLO: I watch TV.

HILLY: O.K.

FLO: O.K. what? He didn't have a TV.

HILLY: He wanted to be a star.

FLO: He did not. He saved his daughter from the Indians.

HILLY: There's not a man alive who wouldn't go save his daughter from the Indians.

FLO: What Indians?

HILLY: It's not my fault there aren't any Indians to save my daughter from. Daniel Boone chased them all away.

FLO: He did not. He liked Indians.

HILLY: Then where are they, huh? *(He points to his work.)* How's that look?

IN THE TEEPEE

Chief Blackfish re-enters.

BLACKFISH: How many white people are in the fort?

BOONE: Twenty, thirty, maybe.

RUSSELL: The Chief speaks English now?

BOONE: He does if he wants you to understand what he's saying.

BLACKFISH: Do they have water?

RUSSELL: They have water.

BOONE: Not enough. But killin' those people won't stop the rest of 'em you know. There's too many of 'em. Just over the mountain. It's like the mountain is a big dam holdin' them back.

BLACKFISH: So is that why they have sent you, to find a way through the mountain?

BOONE: They *didn't* send me. I'm just . . . tryin' to get out of their way.

BLACKFISH: They don't belong here. This is Shawnee hunting ground.

BOONE: No, I know. But the way white people see it, a place don't belong to somebody unless they bought it. Just keepin' it sacred, like you done, that don't count. So as soon as this revolution is over they're gonna come in here, chase you off this land, divide it up and buy it.

BLACKFISH: From whom?

BOONE: From you if you'll sell it to 'em. The best way to let white people know somethin' is yours is to tell them what you want for it.

BLACKFISH: What would I do with the money?

BOONE: I don't know. Isn't there something you want?

BLACKFISH: I want the white man to get back.

BOONE: Then sell him the land for his guns.

BLACKFISH: *(In disbelief.)* They wouldn't do that.

BOONE: Try it.

IN THE MUSEUM

Flo laughs out loud. Hilly turns around to see what she's laughing at.

FLO: Sorry.

And he turns back to his work.

IN THE TEEPEE

BLACKFISH: I think you could be very useful to us.

BOONE: Could be. Can you untie Russell here, and the rest of the men, or do they have to stay tied up?

RUSSELL: Whose side are you on, here?

BLACKFISH: Do I have your word that they won't attack our women?

BOONE: What do you say, Russell, can you keep yourself in line here?

RUSSELL: They took my gun, didn't they?

BOONE: *(To Blackfish.)* They'll be O.K. for a while.

BLACKFISH: Then we will untie them. But if they escape, we will kill you.

BOONE: That's fair enough.

Blackfish leaves.

RUSSELL: So I can't run off or they'll kill you?

BOONE: You can go whenever you want.

RUSSELL: And they won't kill you?

BOONE: Maybe they will. I don't know.

RUSSELL: Do you just not care if they kill you?

BOONE: It's not the worst thing that could happen.

IN THE MUSEUM

FLO: Where are you from, Hilly?

HILLY: Hart County.

FLO: I know Hart County. Mammoth Cave is just about my favorite place in the whole state.

HILLY: Is that what you're gonna do next? Go get a job cleanin' Mammoth Cave?

FLO: I'm going to Boonesborough, if it's any of your business.

HILLY: Did you used to go to Mammoth Cave with your boyfriend and smooch while they turned the lights out?

FLO: When they turned the lights out, I looked back the way I came and saw the silhouette of Martha Washington on the wall.

HILLY: You really looked at that?

FLO: I think you'd better get back to work.

HILLY: I have to admit, though, I liked that Echo River. I always felt like you could step out of your boat, follow some dark passage with your torch, and come right up on John Hunt Morgan makin' gun powder under a ledge.

Flo doesn't answer immediately. But this is exactly what she wanted to do.

FLO: You went in your own boat?

HILLY: Lot of times. What did you do? Pay to go with a guide? How many times did you do that?

FLO: If you went in your own boat, you *could* get off. How did you get in? Is there another entrance to the cave?

HILLY: Well sure there is. I'll take you there if you want, but I wouldn't count on seein' John Hunt Morgan, if I was you. He's dead.

FLO: So what if he's dead? Everybody I see *here* is dead. Dead people walkin' the streets. Dead people askin' me how I am. If I have to spend my life with dead people, I'd rather be back there, where the dead people did things.

HILLY: I'm not dead. How long you had this idea we was all dead?

FLO: Then you tell me one livin' thing you've done. You think wrappin' Daniel Boone up like a mummy makes you a living human being?

HILLY: Are your folks all dead? Your Mom and Dad? How about your girlfriends? You got anybody living in your building or anything?

She doesn't answer.

HILLY: You've just been goin' around, haven't you, workin' in all the state historical things, lookin' for a way in, haven't you. A way back into history, I mean.

FLO: They do it in the movies.

HILLY: Maybe you should go work in the movies.

Flo wishes she hadn't said any of this now.

FLO: Me?

HILLY: Why not? I'd go to see you. What time do you have?

FLO: Eight-thirty.

HILLY: Is it O.K. if I go call Linda? She's about ready for bed by now.

FLO: It's time for your break anyway.

HILLY: Thanks.

Hilly leaves. Flo opens one of the cases and gets out a gun.

IN THE TEEPEE

RUSSELL: So what's the worst thing?

BOONE: I don't know what you mean.

RUSSELL: You said gettin' killed wasn't the worst thing.

BOONE: No.

RUSSELL: So what is?

BOONE: Oh, I don't know. Gettin' marched back to North Carolina, I guess. Stayin' there my whole life. Bein' buried in my corn field.

RUSSELL: Well, I'm goin' back.

BOONE: But what are you goin' back *for*, Russell. Nothin's gonna happen 'til the spring. And at least bein' here, we're eatin' up the Shawnee's food instead of what little they got left at the fort.

RUSSELL: What about Rebecca? Don't you think she'd like to know you're not dead?

BOONE: What she'd like to know is if I'm not dead, how come I've been gone so long.

RUSSELL: Come on. Go with me. You could leave again as soon as you wanted. Surveyin', scoutin'. Anything. There's always somebody wantin' to hire you.

BOONE: I'm not hirin' out ever again, Russell. Every trail I blaze is gonna mean a thousand people followin' me stompin' it down. Every fire I build's out here's gonna have a homestead around it in five years.

RUSSELL: People tellin' their children, right here is where Daniel Boone made his first camp in this county.

BOONE: But I can't quit leadin' any more than they can quit followin', so right now, it's just a flat out relief to be right here, where I can't go no further.

A moment.

Only thing that would make me happier is if I was tied up.

Boone looks up as Flo enters the teepee. She is very glad to see him, but her affection is laced with some aggravation. She is carrying some blankets and a gun. She gives him the blankets.

RUSSELL: Well, look at that.

FLO: I got your gun back for you.

BOONE: Thanks.

Flo hands Boone the gun. He looks at it carefully.

BOONE: This isn't my gun.

FLO: It has your initials on it.

BOONE: No, I know. Russell here, goes around the whole world carvin' my initials on things.

FLO: Where do you want to go? Do you want me to take you back home?

BOONE: Not right away. I was thinkin' I'd let 'em . . . get the crops in first.

FLO: So what did you do? Get yourself captured so we could go fishin'?

BOONE: Maybe I did. What's runnin'?

FLO: Looks to me like you are.

BOONE: Right into your arms, Flo. I sure am.

She leaves.

RUSSELL: What was that all about?

BOONE: She said she'd lead you out if you want.

RUSSELL: I am not draggin' some Indian woman back to Boonesborough.

BOONE: Well, that's the difference between you and me, Russell. I never could say for certain what I wasn't gonna do.

Blackfish enters with Flo.

BLACKFISH: Shel-ta-we.

BOONE: My father.

BLACKFISH: It is a wise leader that persuades his men to live peacefully with their enemy.

BOONE: And it is a wise chief who treats his captives with respect.

RUSSELL: What's going on? I told you she was trouble.

BLACKFISH: As a token of my friendship, I give you this woman for your wife.

RUSSELL: Your wife. What kind of pagan practice is that?

BOONE: I can't refuse him, Russell, you know that.

RUSSELL: You don't want to.

BOONE: No. That's true. Unless she objects.

BLACKFISH: I have spoken with her. She will abide by my wishes.

IN THE MUSEUM

Hilly comes back into the room, and Flo reappears from behind one of the cases.

FLO: Is Linda your wife?

HILLY: My daughter. You oughta have a child, Flo, before it's too late. You'd like it. Make you forget every damn thing except how to do right by her.

FLO: I'm not married.

HILLY: Well, get married then, if that's all that's stopping you.

FLO: No thanks.

HILLY: You got somethin' against marriage? Daniel Boone was married.

FLO: You lay off me and Daniel Boone.

HILLY: I can't do it, Flo. I can't see a nice girl like you throwin' yourself away on a dead guy.

A beat.

Didn't you ever meet anybody you liked?

FLO: Why are you askin' me all this?

HILLY: I want to know what you want in a man.

FLO: Why?

HILLY: So I can see if I've got it.

FLO: You?

HILLY: Why not? You want me to put on one of those buckskins?

FLO: What I want, is to get through this night and never see you again.

HILLY: Flo. You never know when you're gonna meet the right person. You can't count somebody out just because they're available.

FLO: I am not attracted to you in the slightest. You have no interest in history, and no sense of responsibility to the present.

HILLY: How do you know that?

FLO: You think women are so desperate to find a man that they'll take anybody who's even half-way nice to them.

HILLY: I'd go a lot further than halfway if you'd let me.

FLO: I'm sure you would. But if there was any other woman in this building, you wouldn't look at me at all.

HILLY: Not so. I saw women all day today. And you're the first one I wanted to talk to.

FLO: You're playing with me and I don't like it.

HILLY: Yeah, well, you're ignoring me and I don't like that either.

FLO: I have responded to every single thing you've said.

HILLY: You have not. You think I'm a bum.

FLO: I do not.

HILLY: O.K. A criminal.

FLO: I think you talk too much.

HILLY: It takes a lot of talk to get through to you, Flo. I don't like that name. What's the whole thing, Florence?

FLO: I have to go to the ladies.

HILLY: I'll be here.

IN THE TEEPEE

Russell is preparing to leave. Boone is now dressed like an Indian, and from all evidence, is being treated very well.

BOONE: So what's your idea here?

RUSSELL: Simple. Go back. Let everybody know you're alive. See what's goin' on. Come back and get you.

BOONE: Why don't you just stay put if you get there. Give Rebecca a hand. File my claims, too, if you think of it. You know. Get the fort ready.

RUSSELL: When do you think they'll attack?

BOONE: Not as long as I'm here. But if somethin' should happen to me here . . .

RUSSELL: That's it, see. I don't trust 'em.

BOONE: Russell, we've been here two months and all they've done is traipse us around, showin' us off to their friends. Why don't you wait 'til the braves are all out huntin' next month. Go then.

RUSSELL: 'Cause you'll probably go hunt *with* 'em.

BOONE: Gotta earn my keep somehow.

RUSSELL: I'm leaving. I'll find a coupla good men, maybe Squire would like to come. We'll march right back here and . . .

BOONE: Russell. They'll bring me back themselves as soon as they decide what to trade me for. You're one of the few fighting men we've got. If you get to Boonesborough, promise me you'll . . .

RUSSELL: Shouldn't be more than a month at the most.

BOONE: If you're so concerned for my well-being, then why don't you just stay here with me?

RUSSELL: 'Cause I'm tired of watchin' you and these Indians, if you want the truth of it, fixin' their rifles, gettin' yourself adopted, marryin' this girl. It ain't right.

BOONE: We've seen a lot of things, you and me.

RUSSELL: And we'll see a lot more, once we get you out of this.

BOONE: It isn't me we're worried about.

RUSSELL: I'll be O.K.

BOONE: Just stay off the trail, then. You hear me? And if they catch you, don't fight 'em. Just take your whippin' and come on back here.

RUSSELL: Yes, sir.

BOONE: So I'll see you in a couple of hours.

RUSSELL: No you won't either.

BOONE: Well I hope not. I had enough of arguin' with you to last me at least a month.

But from the look on Boone's face, we know Russell has very little chance here.

IN THE MUSEUM

Hilly is now working on the glass in the cases. Flo looks up as Mr. Wilson, a rather academic, but not unappealing man dressed in a shirt and tie enters, carrying a Polaroid camera. She seems nervous, but very happy to see him. At first, Mr. Wilson cannot see Hilly.

FLO: Mr. Wilson!

MR. WILSON: Oh hi, Flo. I'm sorry to bother you. I meant to take care of this this afternoon, but the Board of Directors met until almost six, and . . .

FLO: What did they say? Are they going to let you write your book on Sycamore Grove?

MR. WILSON: Uh. No. They said maybe next year.

A moment.

Well, who knows. Maybe they meant it.

FLO: But you're ready now . . .

MR. WILSON: Yes. And by next year, who knows what it'll be like. I mean there's only that one sycamore left as it is.

FLO: But you've applied to some other sources, haven't you? Maybe . . .

Hilly appears. And at the mere sight of him, Mr. Wilson's demeanor changes radically. It's as if Flo disappeared.

MR. WILSON: Well, well. Who's this?

Flo feels like she's been dropped out a window.

FLO: This is Hilly, the new man. Hilly, this is Mr. Wilson.

MR. WILSON: Jeff, Jeff. I forgot this was your first night. Hilly, is it?

(Now clearly flirting) I see you haven't done any big damage yet.

HILLY: Florence is watchin' me pretty close.

MR. WILSON: That would certainly be my approach.

Flo has to get out of there.

FLO: Do you need me to do anything before I . . .

MR. WILSON: No, no. I just have to have a photograph of the Boone knife for the Quarterly. But Hilly can help me.

He gets the knife out of the case.

FLO: I'll be back in a minute, then.

SHE leaves as quickly as possible. Suddenly alone with this handsome man, Mr. Wilson is very nervous.

MR. WILSON: *(To Hilly.)* So. Do you mind?

Mr. Wilson hands Hilly the knife, and proceeds to lay out a mat on which to photograph it.

IN THE TEEPEE

Boone is whittling. Flo rushes in.

FLO: How could you let them leave?

BOONE: Did they get him?

FLO: You let them walk right down the trail like they were invisible.

BOONE: Did they get them both?

FLO: No. Just the other one. Russell got away.

BOONE: That's something anyway.

FLO: But I told you I would help! I could've at least gotten them to the river. Goin' by themselves, they made so much noise, I could hear them halfway across the village. They might as well have been singing.

BOONE: They probably *were* singing.

FLO: You have no business bringing these people out here. That other one just got himself killed trying to show you how brave he was.

BOONE: I know that.

FLO: They don't listen. They think they're you.

BOONE: I know.

FLO: Or what's worse, they think because they're *with* you, they're safe. They think you know where you're goin'.

BOONE: I have never said that. Never.

FLO: You don't have to say it. How could Daniel Boone not know where he's going?

BOONE: I have *never* known where I was going. That's the whole point. Settin' off for someplace I've never been. How *can* I know where I'm goin'.

Suddenly, she is overcome with love for him.

FLO: No, I know. And how can they watch you go and not want to go with you.

BOONE: Come here.

Flo goes to him and he opens his arms and holds her for a moment.

BOONE: What's all that drummin' about? Are they gonna roast him?

FLO: They don't care about him. They're waiting for you to come out there to avenge him.

BOONE: So they're gonna roast me.

FLO: There's some of 'em sure would like to. If you can manage to stay put 'til dark, I'll come show you where they put him and we can bury him.

BOONE: That'd be good. Seein' as I already dug the grave, the least I can do is put the man in it.

FLO: When did you do that?

BOONE: Little while ago. Didn't you hear me?

FLO: The Shawnee say you don't touch the ground when you walk.

BOONE: *(Stroking her hair.)* Try not to. It's quieter that way.

IN THE MUSEUM

Mr. Wilson begins taking pictures, Hilly holding the knife with its point piercing the piece of paper. Mr. Wilson is making a valiant attempt to resist the attraction he feels for Hilly.

HILLY: Did Daniel Boone really carve his name on that tree?

MR. WILSON: Oh, please.

HILLY: He didn't?

MR. WILSON: *(Referring to the knife.)* Now lay it down flat. Good. *(Then back to the subject.)* No, he didn't. The date is way off. Daniel Boone was in Missouri in 1803.

HILLY: Possible he didn't know what year it was, I guess.

MR. WILSON: It isn't just that. The tree says, D. BOONE KILL A BAR. Now if Boone used the past tense correctly in letters, why wouldn't he use it on a tree?

HILLY: So somebody else carved it? But why would they do that?

MR. WILSON: So they could sell it, to somebody.

Mr. Wilson waits for a photo to come out of the camera. Hilly looks at the knife a moment, then holds the knife high over his head, like the statue of Boone.

HILLY: Guess who?

MR. WILSON: *(Laughs.)* That's good. *(He snaps a picture.)*

HILLY: What about the hunting shirt? Was that his?

MR. WILSON: Heavens, no. Boone was big. That shirt would be snug on *(He looks at Hilly.)* either one of us.

Hilly puts the knife down. Mr. Wilson waits for the pictures to develop.

HILLY: So what do you have that really belonged to Daniel Boone?

MR. WILSON: That depends on who you talk to.

HILLY: I'm talking to you.

MR. WILSON: Nothing.

HILLY: You're kidding.

MR. WILSON: Boone was captured so many times, the Indians ended up with all his stuff. All we've got, really, is a cast of his skull upstairs in the vault.

HILLY: What, did the Indians tie him to a post and slap some plaster on his head?

MR. WILSON: The impression was taken after his death, I believe.

HILLY: Jesus.

Mr. Wilson laughs a little, in spite of himself.

MR. WILSON: But we do have a number of authentic Boone documents, land claims, things like that. And one ember carrier that, in all probability, came from the Boone household.

HILLY: I had an ember carrier once, but I forgot where I put it.

MR. WILSON: You are wondering why we have all these things on display if we know them to be fake.

HILLY: I am. You're right.

MR. WILSON: It's for the simple reason that even false views of historical personages are, nevertheless, interesting to historians.

Hilly's real feelings begin to emerge now.

HILLY: But people believe this stuff. They come here to see it. Florence for example, thinks every single arrowhead is something Boone found.

MR. WILSON: No she doesn't. Oh, maybe when she first came here she did.

HILLY: But you straightened her out.

MR. WILSON: I did.

IN THE TEEPEE

Boone and Flo come in the teepee from burying the man who tried to escape with Russell.

FLO: Did you know him, that man we just buried?

BOONE: No, I didn't. Why?

FLO: I just wondered if he had any family.

BOONE: Probably does.

FLO: Will you have to find them and tell them something when you get back?

BOONE: Like I'm sorry, you mean? I could, I guess. But I probably won't. For all I know, he might be better off.

FLO: Better off dead?

BOONE: I had a dream about dyin' once.

FLO: You were dying, or you were dead?

BOONE: Dead.

FLO: How was it?

BOONE: It was O.K. I knew a lot of people there. Nobody was after me for anything. *(He looks at her.)* You were there too.

FLO: I was?

BOONE: And heaven was a great big lake, early in the morning. The water was real still and kind of a gray blue. We were all just sittin' there fishin', two, three people to a boat, drinkin' our coffee and watchin' the sun come up.

FLO: It's gonna frost tonight.

BOONE: That'd be okay too.

IN THE MUSEUM

HILLY: What's the trouble?

MR. WILSON: Hilly, was any other staff member in here tonight?

HILLY: No. Why?

MR. WILSON: There's a gun missing from this case, that's all, but I'm sure someone's borrowed it and just forgotten to sign it out. Would you ask Flo to come see me when she comes back? I'm in my office.

HILLY: Sure.

MR. WILSON: Or you could come tell me she's down here and I'll . . .

HILLY: I'll send her up.

MR. WILSON: That's O.K. I'll come back down in a few minutes.

HILLY: We'll be here.

IN THE TEEPEE

Flo and Boone are more relaxed now.

FLO: Where are you going to go when you leave here?

BOONE: I'd like to just keep goin', I guess. See the rest of Kentucky and keep goin', right on into places don't even have names yet.

A Moment.

Name them all after you. Look real good on a map someday. Here's Virginia, here's Carolina, and everything west of here is Flo.

FLO: I'd like to see that too. Whatever's out there. It wouldn't even matter if I liked it. I know I'd like seein' it. Maybe I'll come with you.

BOONE: I'd like that. Probably wouldn't be any way of gettin' back, though. Couldn't keep goin' if we kept turnin' back.

FLO: That's O.K.

BOONE: *(Patting her.)* That's what we'll do then. You and me. As soon as it's warm.

FLO: What about your family?

BOONE: Well, you've got the right idea about family, Flo. It's better to really be gone. Better than sittin' there with 'em wishin' you were gone.

Flo picks up the gun and stands up.

FLO: I'll go get us a smoke.

IN THE MUSEUM

Hilly is working on the cases as Flo comes back in carrying the Boone gun.

HILLY: I'm tryin' this little treatment I use on our tile at home. Seems to be working pretty good.

FLO: Looks good.

HILLY: *(Noticing the gun she carries.)* The boss says there's a gun missing from one of the cases.

FLO: I know. I just found it back there. Somebody probably forgot to sign it out. They do that all the time. What happened to your wife?

HILLY: My wife?

FLO: Yeah. How come your daughter is living with you instead of with her? I mean, I assume you're divorced.

HILLY: She's dead. She was killed. We were nearly all killed.

FLO: Killed? In an accident, you mean?

HILLY: I don't know. Maybe it was, maybe it wasn't.

FLO: I know you for two hours and you're just now telling me your wife is dead?

HILLY: A lot of people are dead, Florence. It's not your recommended way of starting a conversation, telling you everybody I know who's dead.

FLO: Did you cry?

HILLY: Maybe I did. I don't remember. I was too busy tryin' to explain it all to Linda.

FLO: What did you say?

HILLY: Everything I could think of. Her spirit is free. You'll see her again some day. We only put her in a coffin so she won't get wet when it rains. You know. *(A moment.)* Lie. Lie. Lie.

FLO: And did she believe you? Does she still want to talk about it?

HILLY: So, we finally found something more interesting to you than Daniel Boone. My dead wife.

FLO: You didn't kill her, did you?

A moment.

HILLY: I thought about it.

FLO: What does that mean?

HILLY: It made me really mad, Florence. That she would do that to us.

Flo feels she can't ask anything else. But Hilly relents and tells the story.

HILLY: We both saw the truck coming. I told her she didn't have room to pass. She said she did. That's all. *(A pause.)* It was pretty much of a mess. And it was a long time before anybody came along.

FLO: Were you drinking?

HILLY: Would you get off this subject? You have no right asking me any of this. And I have no desire to tell you any of it. You think the dead are still alive. Well, I'm here to tell you they aren't. O.K.? *(A moment.)* "Were we drinking?" What do you think this is, TV?

FLO: I don't know what to ask. Who watches Linda while you're at work?

HILLY: Why don't you ask how you think you're ever going to get work if you keep stealing things from the museum. Even on your last night. For God's sake, Florence. They probably fired you. Is that what happened?

Mr. Wilson enters.

MR. WILSON: There you are, Flo.

FLO: *(Holding up the rifle.)* I found this in the back. Miss Carter sent it out to be polished. It just hadn't been put in the case yet.

Mr. Wilson takes the rifle and hands Flo one of the two pieces of paper in his hands.

MR. WILSON: Can you do me a favor and decipher these lines for me? *(to Hilly)* Flo's our resident expert on Boone's handwriting. Takes the rest of us two hours with a magnifying glass. All she has to do is look at it. *(He points to a word.)* This one.

Flo looks at the piece of paper.

FLO: "Necessary."

MR. WILSON: To what?

FLO: *(Looking again.)* "Necessary to notice political events."

MR. WILSON: *(Handing her another document.)* And this one?

FLO: "I am Well in health, but Deep in Bankruptcy."

HILLY: So Boone was broke?

FLO: He was. But he didn't write that last one. This looks to me like that Corbin woman again.

MR. WILSON: Good. Thanks. That's what I thought.

Mr. Wilson looks at Hilly, then at Flo. Then speaks to Hilly, or rather, dismisses him.

MR. WILSON: Would you excuse us for a moment.

HILLY: Sure. What do you need? A half-hour, ten minutes?

MR. WILSON: Five should do it.

Hilly leaves. Mr. Wilson returns the gun to the case and locks it.

MR. WILSON: I'm going to miss seeing you when I have to work late like this. I had hoped to get a little party together for you, so everybody could say good-bye. But . . .

FLO: You were the only one I ever talked to really.

MR. WILSON: I mean, I really appreciate the care you've taken with everything here. Do you think you could . . .*(He pauses.)* . . . have dinner with me some-time?

FLO: Have dinner with you?

MR. WILSON: I mean, I've wanted to ask you for quite a while now, but I wasn't sure it was a good idea while we were still working together.

FLO: I thought you were living with someone.

MR. WILSON: He left.

FLO: I'm sorry.

MR. WILSON: It was my decision, really. I'm trying to . . . *(He stops.)* I want to meet somebody. A girl. I want to get married. I think.

FLO: You think.

MR. WILSON: And my therapist says if I really want to meet women, then the first thing I have to do is start really seeing the women I already know.

FLO: And you picked me.

MR. WILSON: Yes, I did. I know you like me. We care about the same things.

Flo is suddenly very angry. She tries not to explode.

FLO: And I seem like the kind of person who would . . .

MR. WILSON: I know it might be hard at first, but . . .

FLO: I probably wouldn't even care if we ever had sex. I probably don't even like it. I'd just be so flattered that somebody from upstairs noticed me . . .

MR. WILSON: I'm sorry. This was a mistake.

FLO: Yes, it was.

MR. WILSON: I hope I haven't offended you.

FLO: Why don't you just . . .

MR. WILSON: Go upstairs and drink.

FLO: No. Go home. Why don't you just go home.

MR. WILSON: I don't want to go home.

FLO: He's still there, isn't he.

MR. WILSON: How can I ask him to leave before I know whether I can do this or not?

FLO: I don't know.

MR. WILSON: Flo. Please. I don't know anybody else. Could I just ask you one . . .

FLO: What.

MR. WILSON: I don't know what women want. I have a good income. And I'm a decent, responsible man. I just want to know if that will be enough.

FLO: In short?

MR. WILSON: *(Gets the message.)* Ah.

Hilly returns.

HILLY: All done in here?

MR. WILSON: *(Very upset now.)* Yes, of course. We were just chatting.

Mr. Wilson turns to Flo one last time.

MR. WILSON: I could give you a ride home later if you wanted.

FLO: I have my car. Thanks.

MR. WILSON: All right. Goodnight, then.

Mr. Wilson leaves.

   And Flo's anger gets away from her. She speaks as though Mr. Wilson were still in the room.

FLO: My same car I've parked in the same spot beside your car every day for the last two years.

HILLY: Did he fire you?

FLO: No, he didn't. He asked me out to dinner.

HILLY: He's gay.

FLO: I know that.

HILLY: So.

FLO: So what?

HILLY: So give him a break.

FLO: You mean go out with him?

HILLY: You know what I mean.

FLO: No, I know.

He sees her regret and her isolation, and likes her for them.

HILLY: You're all right, Florence.

FLO: I'm just so mad all the time. Why am I so mad?

HILLY: It's O.K. I used to feel like that myself.

FLO: And what did you do about it?

HILLY: After I quit drinking, you mean? Well, I thought about what was making
   me mad, and one night, I went over to Cherokee Park and . . .

FLO: . . . wrapped Daniel Boone up like a mummy.

HILLY: *(He grins.)* You got it. Made me feel great.

Flo nods, then continues, as though it's part of the same subject.

FLO: Did the truck turn over? Did the truck driver die too?

HILLY: Are you serious?

FLO: I want to know. Was there a fire?

HILLY: All right, Florence. What's it worth to you?

FLO: Nevermind. I'll just sit here and you can go work.

HILLY: No, I'll tell you what. Eat supper with me. Don't go have your supper in
   the lounge or something. Sit here and have supper with me, and I'll tell you the
   whole gory thing.

FLO: I didn't bring anything to eat. I usually just . . .

HILLY: You eat what's left in the refrigerator, don't you.

FLO: I do. Actually. There's always something . . . nobody wants.

HILLY: Then I'll share mine with you. But I have to warn you that Linda made it,
   so I hope you like cream cheese. Is it a deal?

Flo thinks about it a minute.

FLO: Are you hungry now?

IN THE TEEPEE

Blackfish walks in. Boone wakes up.

BLACKFISH: Shel-ta-we.

Boone stands.

IN THE MUSEUM

HILLY: I am, actually. Do we have to do anything before we eat?

FLO: No, just . . . get the food, I guess.

HILLY: *(Checking his pocket for change.)* What kind of soda do you want?

FLO: Rootbeer.

HILLY: You got it.

FLO: Thanks.
Hilly leaves.

IN THE TEEPEE
Chief Blackfish walks into the teepee.
BLACKFISH: Governor Hamilton has offered us twenty ponies, and one hundred pounds sterling for you.
BOONE: Take it.
BLACKFISH: I think they will offer more.
BOONE: Maybe they will.
Flo walks into the teepee to stand beside Blackfish. Blackfish takes Flo's hand, then speaks to Boone.
BLACKFISH: I think you have brought us great good fortune these few months. I think we will keep you a little longer.
Blackfish leaves.
BOONE: What's this good fortune I've brought them? That doesn't sound right.
FLO: No, it isn't. It's finally occurred to the Shawnee, and to the British, that since you're sittin' here, givin' no sign of tryin' to escape, this would be an ideal time to attack Boonesborough.
BOONE: Does that mean we have to go back?
FLO: You know it does.
BOONE: O.K. then. We'll leave as soon as it's dark.
FLO: You'd get there faster without me.
BOONE: Maybe. And maybe I wouldn't get there at all without you keepin' me headed in the right direction.
She picks up her bedroll.
FLO: Who is it you don't want to see?
BOONE: It's *what* I don't want to see, Flo. Like all my friends gettin' killed in this fight.
FLO: If you *don't* go, they'll be killed for sure. What have you been doin', sittin' here hopin' the settlers will give you up for dead and abandon the fort?
BOONE: I guess. Only what they've *been* doin' is sittin' there, tryin' to hold out 'til I get there. (*He kisses her lightly.*) O.K. Now. You'll need somethin' warmer to wear. (*He picks up his jacket.*) Put this on. You go get us somethin' to eat and I'll go steal us a coupla ponies and we'll go.
Flo takes off her shawl, and puts on his jacket, leaving her shawl on the floor of the teepee.
Flo leaves the teepee.

IN THE MUSEUM
Hilly returns with his bag of lunch.
HILLY: Florence? Florence?

He walks back to the teepee, finds it empty. He notices Flo's shawl on the floor. He stoops and picks it up.

   She enters through another door, wearing the Boone jacket.

HILLY: I found your shawl.

Flo covers her alarm. Hilly notices the jacket.

FLO: Thanks.

HILLY: It was in the teepee. Nice jacket.

FLO: Thanks.

HILLY: Well. Let's see what we've got for supper, what do you say.

FLO: Were you hurt at all, in the crash?

HILLY: I was laid up for a few weeks. Yeah. But I didn't have a job then, so it wasn't like I had somewhere to go.

FLO: So your wife was mad at you for not getting a job. Is that what the fight was about?

HILLY: Jesus, Florence. I got laid off. ·

FLO: Why?

HILLY: They don't tell you why they're layin' you off. They just do it.

FLO: What kind of work was it?

HILLY: It's nice to have somebody to talk to, isn't it, Florence.

FLO: It's not my fault I don't know how to talk. Who have I got to talk to?

He hands her a sandwich.

HILLY: Here.

FLO: Thanks.

HILLY: I got Linda started eating these cream cheese and banana sandwiches. You know. Had to be better than hot dogs. Right? What do you do when a kid won't eat? I thought everybody liked to eat. The books tell you don't make them eat, or they'll have eating problems the rest of their lives. But if you don't make them eat, they're not gonna *have* the rest of their lives, are they. I don't know why they write those books.

FLO: *(chewing a bite of the sandwich)* It's very good.

HILLY: Same thing with sleeping. They tell you, "Just let the kid cry." What they don't tell you is what the hell you're supposed to do while the kid is in there crying.

He takes the bread off his sandwich.

FLO: I feel bad eating up your supper.

HILLY: She's getting better about making the sandwiches, though. *(He picks out a big chunk.)* That's almost what you'd call a slice. Isn't it.

And now from offstage, they both hear a voice.

VOICE: Flo! Where are you! I know you're here somewhere.

FLO: Oh, no.

HILLY: Who's that?

FLO: My boyfriend.

HILLY: Your boyfriend? If you've got a boyfriend I want my sandwich back.
She hands him the sandwich.
FLO: I have to get out of here.
HILLY: What do you want me to tell him?
Flo dashes into the teepee. A large man wearing shorts over a sweatsuit, appears, an envelope in his hand.
RICK: Where's Flo? Who are you?
HILLY: Name's Hilly.
RICK: Where's Flo?
HILLY: In the teepee.
Rick charges over to the Teepee.
RICK: The hell she is.
He tears open the front flap of the teepee. Not finding Flo there, he turns back to Hilly.
RICK: All right, wise guy. Where is she?
HILLY: How should I know?
RICK: Flo! You come out here right now or I'll tear this place apart.
HILLY: Can I give her a message?
RICK: I tell my wife I want a divorce, and then I get this letter from Flo saying she's leaving.
HILLY: You're married?
RICK: What did she tell you about me?
HILLY: Did Florence *know* you were married?
RICK: That's what I came here to tell her. After I told my wife about Flo, then I was gonna tell Flo about my wife. I love Flo. She knows I love her. *(A moment.)* Why don't women ever believe what you tell them?
HILLY: Beats me.
RICK: And now she's gone.
HILLY: She's not gone, she's just . . . You looked in the teepee?
And with that, the men leave by different doors calling for Flo.
RICK: Flo?
HILLY: Florence. It's O.K. He's getting a divorce.

IN THE FOREST
Daniel Boone and Flo appear.
BOONE: How long do you think it will be before they know we're gone?
FLO: They know it already.
BOONE: Then why'd they let us go?
FLO: Because they wouldn't have any fun at all burnin' up Boonesborough if you weren't there tryin' to stop 'em.
BOONE: That's true.
FLO: So how come I don't see you shakin' with fear?
BOONE: I shake so fast, nobody's ever seen it.

She laughs and sits down. He opens a canteen and gives her a drink. Then he sits down behind her, and she leans back against him. He begins to stroke her hair. She turns around, as though she's heard something.

FLO: Was that a bear?

BOONE: Brown. I think.

FLO: I'm afraid of bears.

BOONE: You should be.

He puts his arms around her, and kisses the side of her face.

IN THE MUSEUM

Rick returns, more angry than ever.

RICK: She's not here. I searched the whole place.

HILLY: No, I know. What else did she say, in her letter?

RICK: That she didn't want to see me any more. That she was in love with somebody else, and she was going off to be with him.

HILLY: Did she ever say anything like this before?

RICK: Last couple of weeks, all the time. I told her she was crazy.

HILLY: She *is* a little crazy, I think. Nothin' serious, though. I like her.

RICK: Are you and Flo havin' some kind of . . .

HILLY: No sir.

But Rick is enraged. He grabs Hilly by the shirt and pulls him up off the bench.

RICK: You are! She's leavin' me to run off with you.

HILLY: I just met her tonight. I swear it.

RICK: Then how do you know she's crazy?

HILLY: She's in love with Daniel Boone.

RICK: Very funny.

Rick puts Hilly down as Mr. Wilson enters.

MR. WILSON: Flo?

HILLY and RICK: She's not here.

RICK: He knows but he's not telling.

MR. WILSON: She went home?

HILLY: She's with Daniel Boone.

RICK: *(To Mr. Wilson.)* Who *is* this guy?

MR. WILSON: You were our Santa at the Christmas party.

RICK: Rick. Right.

MR. WILSON: Right. *(To Hilly.)* What do you mean, she's with Daniel Boone?

HILLY: I mean, she's found some kind of way of, I don't know, she goes into the
   teepee and she's gone. And she comes back with things, guns and things, wearing old leather jackets and smellin' like a wood fire.

RICK: She always smells like a wood fire.

HILLY: And does she have a fireplace at her house?

RICK: No.

Mr. Wilson goes back to look at the teepee.

HILLY: Well, there sure as hell isn't one in here. Flo heard your voice and high-tailed it to Boonesborough.

MR. WILSON: You looked in the ladies, I guess.

RICK: I did.

MR. WILSON: All right. *(To Rick.)* I'll check the parking lot. You check the up-stairs bathrooms. And you . . . *(To Hilly.)* check the log cabin room and stay there. She likes you.

RICK: And what if we don't find her?

MR. WILSON: I don't know.

HILLY: What do you mean, you don't know? We have to go get her.

AT BOONESBOROUGH

Flo and Boone stand, inside a cabin. Boone's Indian clothes show the effects of the journey.

FLO: Where is everybody?

A young woman enters. It is Boone's daughter, Jemima Boone.

JEMIMA: Dad!

Boone embraces her.

BOONE: Hello, Jemima. Where's your mother?

JEMIMA: They left. They went back to North Carolina. Everybody left. They thought you were dead. *(She looks at Flo.)* We all thought you were dead. What have you been doing all this time?

BOONE: Jemima, this is Flo. I found her out there, just wanderin' around lost and half-starved. The Shawnee killed her man and child.

JEMIMA: I'm sorry.

FLO: Thanks.

BOONE: Did Russell make it back?

JEMIMA: He came back a long time ago. He's telling everybody that you could've escaped when he did, but . . .

Squire Boone, Daniel's brother, enters.

SQUIRE: Daniel. How did you get through?

BOONE: Hello, Squire.

SQUIRE: Our scout just came back sayin' there's four hundred Indians out there armed with British rifles.

BOONE: He's right. I just talked to 'em.

SQUIRE: Talked to 'em? What did they say?

BOONE: Oh, you know. Give us the fort. Things like that. *(A moment.)* They've got this letter to us from Lt. Governor Hamilton. It says if we abandon the fort, and promise not to come back onto Indian land, the Shawnee will hand us over to the British and nobody will get hurt.

SQUIRE: And if we stand and fight?

BOONE: Well, then, I reckon we'll all be killed.

SQUIRE: We'll be lucky if we aren't the only ones left in the fort by sundown, Daniel. You have to tell our people something.

BOONE: Something like what, I'll stay and die if they will?

SQUIRE: That'd be enough, comin' from you.

BOONE: O.K., then. Let's go tell 'em that.

SQUIRE: *(Feeling much safer suddenly.)* How've you been?

Boone claps his arm around Squire and laughs.

BOONE: Not bad. *(Then turning back to Jemima.)* Jemima, get Flo somethin' to eat.

They walk out of the cabin.

IN THE MUSEUM

Mr. Wilson enters a room we haven't seen before, in which stands a log cabin, to find Hilly dressing himself in the frontier clothes that were hanging on the wall.

MR. WILSON: What are you doing?

HILLY: Going to Boonesborough. Did you find Flo's car?

MR. WILSON: It's in the parking lot, all right. But maybe she's taking a walk.

HILLY: She's gone and you know it.

MR. WILSON: Was it something I said?

HILLY: More like everything everybody ever said.

MR. WILSON: Including me. *(Watching Hilly dress.)* You're serious about this.

HILLY: You bet I am. I want her back. And if I have to steal her away from Daniel Boone then that's what I'll do.

MR. WILSON: I'm going with you.

IN BOONESBOROUGH

Boone and Squire stand at the front gate of the fort.

BOONE: Just see if you can keep everybody makin' bullets, while I go out and tell Blackfish the decision.

SQUIRE: I think I should come out with you. All the Indians have to do is kill you, and everybody else will just give up.

BOONE: Squire, the Indians don't want to kill any of us. I'll be all right. Just tell your man in the blockhouse that if he sees me light out for the gate, don't wait for some kinda signal, just open fire.

IN THE MUSEUM

Rick enters. Hilly sits down to put on the frontier boots.

MR. WILSON: You didn't find her either, I guess.

RICK: Nope. I called her house. She's not there. I called her mother's house. She's not there. And I called the police.

HILLY: What did the police say?

RICK: Nothing, I got a machine.

HILLY: The police department has a machine?

Mr. Wilson reaches into the cabinet for a jacket and begins to put it on.

RICK: Yeah, you know, tell us your name and what happened and we'll get back to you. What are you guys doing?

MR. WILSON: *(To Rick.)* Hilly and I can take care of this. Why don't you leave us your number and if we find out something, we'll give you a call.

RICK: O.K. Sure. I have to go over to the garage and change my ball joints anyway. Maybe I'll stop back when I'm done.

Rick leaves.

MR. WILSON: Flo was dating a mechanic?

HILLY: Get dressed if you're coming. And you can leave that attitude here, O.K.?

MR. WILSON: You actually think we can step inside the cabin, wearing these clothes and be in Boonesborough?

HILLY: I just hope she didn't change her mind and go somewhere else.

MR. WILSON: No, that's where she was going, all right. It's in her file upstairs. Reason for ceasing employment: going to Boonesborough.

HILLY: And that didn't seem strange to you?

MR. WILSON: Well, sure, but she wasn't herself lately.

Mr. Wilson opens the case.

MR. WILSON: But I haven't been myself either. The man I've been seeing . . .

HILLY: I don't want to hear about it. Why didn't you just ask her? "Hey, Flo. When you *get* to Boonesborough, what year's it gonna be?"

Hilly reaches into the case and gets knives, guns and powder horns for both of them.

MR. WILSON: You're right. I should've asked.

HILLY: Damn right you should have. She was counting on you, and him, whatever his name is, Rick, to hear what she was saying and stop her. Catch on. That's what she was hoping for, for somebody, somewhere, to catch on. But nobody did.

MR. WILSON: She seemed happy enough.

HILLY: Oh yeah? What *is* happy enough? She hasn't killed herself yet? The way I see it, you were her last hope, 'til I came along.

MR. WILSON: Then why didn't she say so?

HILLY: If you have to *tell* your last hope that they're your last hope, then it's way worse than you thought.

Mr. Wilson grabs a hat and puts it on. And then begins to get dressed.

MR. WILSON: O.K. O.K. What part of Boonesborough do you think we're going to? When they first built it, or all those little wars in 1777, or . . .

HILLY: What's the worst it could be?

MR. WILSON: The Siege.

HILLY: That's probably it, then. Is there anything I ought to know?

MR. WILSON: It's September, 1778. There are about thirty men, maybe twenty boys and a couple of women and some children inside the fort. Their powder supply is very low. For ammunition, they're digging bullets out of the wall and melting them down. They have no bread, and only root vegetables and a little meat. They have a well, they dug that in 1777, but . . .

HILLY: Just the highlights, O.K.?

MR. WILSON: O.K. It's hopeless. *(a moment)* Boone has no chance. None.

HILLY: Good.

Hilly opens the door to the cabin, peers in, then holds it open for Mr. Wilson. Mr. Wilson looks in.

MR. WILSON: What if we can't get back?

HILLY: Florence gets back.

MR. WILSON: Not this time she didn't.

HILLY: Well this time . . . isn't over yet. After you.

Mr. Wilson steps into the cabin, and Hilly follows him.

ACT II

In the darkness, drums and Indian flutes are heard. Seated on a blanket downstage, Blackfish picks up a burning twig from the fire and lights a long pipe. As he passes it to Boone, a circle of dim light comes up on them.

BLACKFISH: In two days, the moon will be full. By that time, you must take your people and leave this fort, my son.

BOONE: *(A moment.)* Yes, I know. That's what you said yesterday.

BLACKFISH: Will you go?

BOONE: Look. To tell you the truth, even if we wanted to go, I don't know if we could get everything packed in two days. You know, there's all the venison we salted down, and all those candles we made . . .

BLACKFISH: You can leave the meat for us.

BOONE: Well, why don't I send some out for your supper tonight. That way you can . . .

BLACKFISH: If it was up to me, of course, I'd let you stay here.

BOONE: Of course you would. And if it was up to me, I'd just head west, but the fact of the matter is, I have to go along with the rest of my people in there and they've decided to stay and fight.

BLACKFISH: *(Very angry.)* But you will all die if you stay here.

BOONE: No, I know. That's what I told them.

BLACKFISH: Tell them what Dragging Canoe has said: "That a dark cloud hangs over this land." That no Indians have lived her for many years because of this cloud. That the bones of the ancient men rise up in the night and kill him who sets his lodge poles in this place.

Boone takes a moment, and then is struck by a great idea.

BOONE: I know. How about . . . *(A pause.)* if you go away instead of us?

BLACKFISH: How about . . . if we both go away.

BOONE: Good. O.K.

BLACKFISH: And the British can have the fort.

BOONE: No. They can't.

BLACKFISH: So we're back to killing you.

BOONE: I guess so.

BLACKFISH: In two days then.

BOONE: Well. How about if we talk about it again tomorrow?

BLACKFISH: I will see you tomorrow, my son. Perhaps after my belly is full of your meat, I will have some better ideas.

BOONE: Maybe you will.

The light goes out on them, they exit, and the light comes up on

BOONESBOROUGH

And the whole stage now suggests frontier Boonesborough, complete with palisade, cook-pots, and all the other trappings of frontier life.

Flo and Jemima are seated near the cabin door, pouring melted lead into molds to make bullets.

Behind them, a young man walks, as though patrolling the palisade, wearing a tall hat and carrying a rifle.

FLO: You pour and I'll hold the mold. Easy now.

JEMIMA: I don't think we're going to . . .

FLO: *(Interrupting.)* Watch what you're doing.

JEMIMA: We're not going to fool the Shawnee having these boys walk around the palisade all day. They know how many of us there are.

FLO: No they don't either. They've got so many white people lying to 'em about so many things, they don't know what to think.

Russell and Squire walk through arguing.

RUSSELL: If we keep pourin' our water on the roof, what are we going to drink?

SQUIRE: Just because Daniel doesn't know how much water's down there, doesn't mean there isn't enough. We're gonna soak the roof now, or watch it burn later, and those are his exact words.

JEMIMA: Daddy's putting all our water on the roof?

SQUIRE: There's a regiment of Virginia militia on their way, Russell. All we have to do is hold the fort 'til they get here.

RUSSELL: And what are they gonna see, huh? A big battle goin' on? No. Everybody slaughtered? No. All they're gonna find is four hundred Indians standin' around scratchin' their heads, wonderin' why all the white men died of thirst.

Squire and Russell exit.

FLO: *(Seeing Jemima's worry.)* There's plenty of water, Jemima. There's a river under this whole part of the country.

JEMIMA: How do you know that? Have you been down there? You think Dad knows everything. You'd do whatever he said.

FLO: Yes, I would. And everybody else better too or won't any of us get out of this.

JEMIMA: We're not going to get out of this. I should've gone home with Mother. We're going to die here.

Russell is seen sneaking a long drink from his canteen.
    Boone comes up to him.

BOONE: There you are.

RUSSELL: I know that.

BOONE: Did you check that powder supply?

RUSSELL: Not more than two days worth, I'd say.

BOONE: That'll have to do, then.

RUSSELL: I could try makin' a run for Fort Logan, if you wanted me to. Maybe they've got some they could spare us.

BOONE: No. We need you more than we need the powder.

RUSSELL: But what if the fight lasts longer than two days?

BOONE: I don't see how it can, Russell. I mean, once we run out of powder, it'll end pretty quick.

Boone grabs the canteen away.

BOONE: What've you got here?

Boone opens it.

RUSSELL: What do you think it is. Whiskey.

BOONE: I knew it.

And to Russell's surprise, Boone takes a swig.

BOONE: Thanks.

Squire enters.

SQUIRE: Blackfish is signaling he's ready to talk, Daniel.

BOONE: O.K. I'm comin'.

Flo sets one mold aside and picks up another one.

JEMIMA: How old was your child?

Flo hesitates, trying to remember the lie she and Boone worked out.

FLO: Four.

JEMIMA: And your husband?

Flo is not a practiced liar.

FLO: Forty- . . . Forty, I think.

JEMIMA: Did the Indians scalp them or knife them or torture them or what?

FLO: No, they just . . . dragged them off I guess. Maybe it wasn't even Indians. They'd just gone down to the river to . . . get water and when they didn't come back, I went looking for them, only all that was left was . . .

JEMIMA: Was what?

FLO: *(Has no idea what to say.)* Their hats.

JEMIMA: And that's where Dad found you?

FLO: I guess my mind must've gone blank or something. Because the next thing I knew, your Dad was giving me a drink of water and asking me who I was.

JEMIMA: Where are the hats now?

Flo cannot for the life of her think of an answer to this. A look of pain comes across her face.

FLO: *(Quoting Hilly.)* You don't have any right asking me any of this. And I have no desire to tell you any of it. "Where are the hats?" What do you think this is, a story I made up?

JEMIMA: I'm sorry.

They hear the sound of drumming.

JEMIMA: *(Seeing her father at some distance.)* Daddy's opening the gate!

FLO: He's showing them he's not afraid.

Russell enters with a pan of bullets.

RUSSELL: He is not. He's daring them to shoot him so he can die first. *(Then picking up some bullets from Flo.)* Are these ready?

JEMIMA: What do he and Daddy talk about when he goes out there?

FLO: They're trying to work out a treaty, I think.

JEMIMA: What kind of a treaty? I thought we all voted to get killed.

RUSSELL: Is this all you done? Lord God. I'll get you some help over here.

Russell exits.

FLO: Thanks.

JEMIMA: Then is Daddy a traitor? Colonel Calloway says . . .

FLO: Don't you believe what anybody says, Jemima. Your father is the bravest man that ever lived in this country.

JEMIMA: He is not. He's afraid of Mother. He's afraid of Colonel Calloway. He's afraid of the British. He's afraid of the whole state of North Carolina. And most of all, he's afraid of honest work.

FLO: Is that what your mother says?

JEMIMA: Well she ought to know.

FLO: I'm sure she worries about him, when he's gone.

JEMIMA: She doesn't even sleep. Not one minute. How would you feel if you had six children and your husband was . . .

Squire enters and interrupts.

SQUIRE: Jemima. Your dad says come out to the gate right now.

JEMIMA: What for?

SQUIRE: The Indians want to see you. Some of them are the same ones that stole you away that time, and they want to see you.

JEMIMA: I won't go.

Flo grabs her by the arm and takes her over to Squire.

FLO: Yes, you will go, young lady. Your father wouldn't ask you to come out there if it was dangerous so . . . there. Now go.

JEMIMA: Squire, please, don't make me go. I don't want to go out there.

And as she continues to protest, Squire leads her away.

    And then, as Flo returns to her work, the cabin door opens slightly.

    And then opens further, and Hilly steps out.

HILLY: *(Whispering.)* Florence. Hey Florence.

Flo turns and sees Hilly.

FLO: Hilly?

He looks both ways, as though he's crossing the most dangerous street in America. And then steps out.

HILLY: Well I'll be damned.

FLO: What are you doing here?

HILLY: I came to get you.

He walks on over to her.

FLO: Why?

HILLY: Why do you think? To take you back.

FLO: I don't want to go back. And even if I did, why would I go back with you?

HILLY: You must've wanted me to come, Florence, or you wouldn't have told me where you were going.

Mr. Wilson pokes his head out of the cabin now.

FLO: Mr. Wilson!

HILLY: And once he knew I was coming, he came along to pick up some stuff for the museum.

Mr. Wilson is holding an ember carrier.

FLO: You can't stay here. I won't let you. *(She sees Mr. Wilson pick up something.)* Put that down.

HILLY: From the looks of things, I'd say Mr. Boone could use two more men. *(To Mr. Wilson.)* Too bad we didn't bring some real guns, huh, Wilson?

FLO: You two go right back in that cabin and go right back to the museum right now.

Boone enters.

BOONE: Flo, we need those bullets as soon as they're done. And you two, *(He points to Hilly and Mr. Wilson.)* we just lost a man from the blockhouse, so one of you get up there and take his place.

FLO: They can't. They just came in from . . .

BOONE: I don't care where they came from. What's your name?

MR. WILSON: Wilson.

BOONE: Get up there in the blockhouse, and see if you can keep from gettin'
shot in the head. And you . . . *(He points to Hilly)* Come with me.

Boone leaves.

MR. WILSON: *(Looking around.)* Let's see. The blockhouse. The blockhouse.

HILLY: *(Points.)* Up there.

Mr. Wilson leaves.

FLO: Please, Hilly. I appreciate you bein' worried about me, but . . .

HILLY: I can't talk right now, Florence. But you look real good, and I'm glad I
found you. So I'll see you later. O.K.?

FLO: I don't want you here.

HILLY: Then it's a good thing you're not in charge. *(calling after Boone)* Daniel
Boone. Wait up.

Hilly rushes off. Flo sits down, weary and very disturbed.
And Rick comes out of the cabin.

RICK: Son of a bitch.

Flo turns around.

FLO: Not you too.

RICK: What did you think, I'd be too scared to come? I'd just stand there and
watch those two jokers come to the rescue? *(She shakes her head.)* I just didn't
want to come with *them*, that's all.

FLO: But you could get killed here.

RICK: I had some stuff I wanted to talk to you about.

FLO: The way my day is going, you're probably married.

RICK: I should've told you right off. But I was afraid you wouldn't keep seein' me.

FLO: Well, you were right there.

RICK: I'm sorry. I just told my wife I want a divorce. Will you marry me, Flo?

FLO: I don't think so. Thanks, though.

RICK: Why not? You said you wanted to have a child. Well I want to have a child
too.

FLO: *Now* you want to get married. *Now* you want to have a child. *Now* you'll say
anything I want, won't you?

RICK: I had no idea you were serious about this.

FLO: I only told you a hundred times.

RICK: And I was supposed to believe that? Believe you wanted to live at Boonesborough? Believe you were in love with Daniel Boone?

FLO: You didn't even think I was crazy for saying it. You didn't even say I should
go see a doctor. You have no idea how hard it was for me to tell you those
things. And all you did was laugh.

RICK: *(Deliberately.)* I won't ever do that again.

FLO: Not to me, you won't. At least Hilly believed me.

RICK: That hayseed. He'd believe anything.
FLO: You still don't believe it. Even standing here inside the fort, you don't believe it.
An arrow whizzes by him, nearly missing his head.
RICK: All right. I believe it. But it's crazy. I think you should see a doctor.
Russell appears.
RUSSELL: *(To Rick.)* You. Don't I know you from . . .
FLO: He's just leaving.
RUSSELL: No he's not, either. Boone wants a party to go out and kill a buffalo,
    and *(Pointing to Rick.)* he's it.
RICK: *(Quietly, to Flo.)* I'm the buffalo?
RUSSELL: *(Very irritated.)* Why the hell is Boone feeding those savages?
FLO: He's just trying to prove to them that we have food.
RUSSELL: So we're supposed to starve in here?
FLO: We are if it keeps them from attacking.
RUSSELL: *(To Rick.)* Get goin' you. One of the boys just spotted a buffalo down
    by the spring. Unless the Indians got it already. And don't get yourself scalped
    out there or you'll be sorry.
Russell leaves.
RICK: I can't kill a buffalo.
She hands him the gun lying on the ground beside her.
FLO: You'll be all right. They're very slow.
RICK: Will you feel better about me if I come back with one?
FLO: No.
RICK: Yes you will, too.
And with that, he tromps off toward the gate.

AT THE FRONT GATE
Boone offers Hilly a bucket of water.
BOONE: Want a drink?
HILLY: Sure. Why not?
BOONE: Spill as much as you can while you're drinkin' it. I want Blackfish's boys
    to get really thirsty just watchin' you.
HILLY: Why haven't they attacked already?
BOONE: Could be a lot of things.
Boone throws the whole bucket of water on the ground.
BOONE: Maybe one of the other Chiefs isn't here yet. Maybe the medicine man
    says it isn't the right time. Maybe Blackfish is waitin' for us to offer him more
    money than the British.
HILLY: And maybe he knows if they start fightin', one of his braves might kill you.
    And then he couldn't capture you any more.
Flo and Squire come up to them. Boone has a growing appreciation of Hilly.

BOONE: Where'd you say you were from?

HILLY: Up north.

BOONE: You want to walk out and sit a spell with us?

HILLY: Sure.

BOONE: Florence is gonna come translate, in case we run into anything complicated.

FLO: *(To Boone.)* There's somethin' you need to know about him. He's . . .

BOONE: He's part Indian, I can tell you that much. *(To Hilly.)* Let's go.

Boone gives Squire his rifle to hold.

FLO: *(To Hilly.)* Is that true?

HILLY: Yes, Ma'am.

Boone puts his arm around Hilly and they leave Squire behind.

BOONE: *(To Hilly.)* So how's it goin' up north?

HILLY: Pretty quiet. Everybody workin' so hard, nobody much feels like they're doin' anything.

BOONE: Work is like that.

HILLY: Feels like all the excitement is somewhere else. You know. Like how're you supposed to amount to anything if you've got all this crap you have to do.

BOONE: Got to do it though, or else you'll wind up like me, always wonderin' where everything went. Didn't I have some land around here somewhere? Anybody seen my wife?

IN THE BLOCKHOUSE

Mr. Wilson is standing guard, pointing his rifle out the hole in the wall. Russell pokes his head up into the blockhouse to talk.

RUSSELL: Boone said there was a new man up here.

Mr. Wilson adopts a new way of speaking, what he imagines to be a frontier dialect.

MR. WILSON: Wilson. Yeah. What's goin' on out front?

RUSSELL: Nothin'. I want to know where you stand, Wilson.

MR. WILSON: Right here, sir. As long as you say.

RUSSELL: Where you stand on Daniel Boone, mister.

MR. WILSON: What do you mean?

RUSSELL: The man hides out with the Indians for the winter, and then shows up here lookin' like a redskin himself. Spends all his time out there talkin' with that savage like he was his old friend. I say let's chain Daniel Boone to the gate and get the hell outta here, every man for himself.

MR. WILSON: What about the women and boys?

RUSSELL: What about 'em?

Mr. Wilson summons his courage and hopes his dialect will hold.

MR. WILSON: They wouldn't stand a chance and you know it. I'm stickin' with Boone. I figure if I'm gonna die, I'd just as soon go with people I know.

RUSSELL: Nobody knows Boone. Nobody ever will. He didn't come back to save this fort, he came back to give it to the British and walk away from it. If we get out of this, the first thing I'm going to do is charge him with high treason.

MR. WILSON: You're just scared, is what you are. Why don't you crawl back into your little rat hole and stay there 'til we get through here.

Russell, filled with disgust and hatred of this newcomer, turns and leaves.

And Mr. Wilson sights down his rifle and repeats his little speech, sounding like every hero he ever heard.

MR. WILSON: You're just scared, is what you are. Why don't you crawl back into your little rat hole and stay there 'til we get through here.

AT THE INDIAN BLANKET

Boone is seated on the blanket opposite Blackfish.

BLACKFISH: So. You've finally decided to surrender.

Boone laughs.

BOONE: We have actually.

From behind him, Hilly gets into the spirit of things.

HILLY: But everybody's so excited to meet you, we're kinda havin' some trouble gettin' 'em to line up right.

Boone has a look of great relief. Like finally, he's got some help.

BOONE: Yeah, you should see them. Me first, no, me first.

HILLY: So while they're workin' that out, in there, we thought we oughta come out here and talk about how you're gonna torture us after we give up.

Boone laughs and motions for Hilly to come sit down beside him.

BLACKFISH: A worthy discussion. Every tenth man I will give to the warriors to do with as they like. The others I will turn over to the British. As for the women, there will be no torture for the women. The women I will keep all for myself.

BOONE: That sounds good. *(He turns to Hilly.)* That sound good to you?

HILLY: Except for Florence.

BOONE: Well of course except for Flo *(He looks back at Flo.)* Flo you must save for me.

HILLY: *(Looking back at Flo.)* No, no. Florence you must save for me.

Boone immediately seizes on this as a delaying tactic.

BOONE: He will not. This woman is mine. If you need a woman, you can have my daughter.

HILLY: I want Florence. I came here to get Florence, and I'm not leaving without her. You'll have to kill me to get that woman and I'm ready to fight you any time you say.

BOONE: *(Enjoying this immensely.)* You little thief. I don't even know you. I never walked any path with you. You just show up here aimin' to take my whole joy in life away from me, in front of my friends.

Hilly stands up.

HILLY: It's not my fault she's all you've got. If you hadn't always been runnin' around tryin' to be the first man to see every tree . . . What are you afraid of anyway, that if you stay put they might find out about you?

Boone stands up.

BOONE: Find out *what* about me, you little . . .

BLACKFISH: We will do no more talking until this matter is settled. You will fight for her.

FLO: No you will not. I am not some prize that . . .

Boone has already stripped off his shirt.

BOONE: Just stand back, Florence.

FLO: Hilly, this is ridiculous. All they need is to see Daniel Boone worn out from beating you up, and they'll start the attack right now.

HILLY: No they won't either. As soon as I whip his ass, they'll know we're every one of us as tough as Daniel Boone, and if that's true, they can never beat us. They'll light out of here as fast as they can.

Flo turns to leave.

FLO: I'm having no part of this. None of this . . . has anything to do with me.

BLACKFISH: Go then. Remain with the women. I will send a messenger when you are needed.

Flo leaves.

Hilly takes off his shirt. And as Boone and Hilly are circling each other, Flo joins Squire, Russell and Mr. Wilson who are watching from the front gate.

AT THE FRONT GATE

Russell stands with Squire and Mr. Wilson.

RUSSELL: What is all that about?

SQUIRE: Looks like another one of Daniel's little tricks to me. Have a little fight. Waste a little more time. Well, what can it hurt. When the Indians see how Daniel humiliates this man they'll know who they're up against anyway.

MR. WILSON: Hey now. Don't count Hilly out, here. He's not as slow as he looks.

The fight begins.

FLO: I can't watch.

MR. WILSON: Come with me to the east palisade, then. There's somethin' funny goin' over there.

Flo and Mr. Wilson exit.

A circle of light forms around Boone and Hilly.

Hilly takes the first swipe. Boone counters well and Hilly goes down. An Indian pitches Boone a large staff. Boone looks at it, pitches it to Hilly. Hilly holds it, looks at it, and pitches it back to the Indian. And the fight begins.

SQUIRE: Uh-oh.

JEMIMA: Daddy.

RUSSELL: What'll we do now?

SQUIRE: Not a thing. One move from us and the whole thing could start right here.

We hear the sounds of cheering, the thumps of the blows. Boone seems winded and out of shape, compared to Hilly. But Boone is sneaky. There are some moments when we think they are just playing with each other, but then Boone begins to take it seriously, and finally, wrestles Hilly to the ground and forces him to give up.

BOONE: Say it, you thief. Flo is mine.

HILLY: I won't. You're dead.

BOONE: You will. The man hasn't been born that can beat me, at this or anything else. Now say it.

Blackfish lets out some kind of warrior cheer. But Hilly will not give in.

HILLY: You've got a wife. If she still wants anything to do with you. What about her? Florence is mine.

Boone looks up, seeing someone arriving in the Indian camp.

BOONE: Well. I'll be . . .

HILLY: What?

BOONE: It looks like the folks old Blackfish has been waitin' for, have arrived.

HILLY: Who are they?

BOONE: The British one is new to me. But the Chief standin' beside him is a real mean character. When he shows up, you know the talk is all over.

Blackfish approaches.

BLACKFISH: I must go and greet my brothers. As for you, my son has beaten you. The woman he calls Flo, and you call Florence, is his. You will leave the village by sundown.

HILLY: I won't.

BLACKFISH: You will.

BOONE: He can't.

HILLY: I won't.

BLACKFISH: Whatever.

Blackfish begins to walk away. Boone stops him.

BOONE: Hilly can't leave the camp because I need him. And Flo can't be mine because I've got a wife. And the way we do things is a man can only have one wife. Now we enjoyed the fight and all, but this thing's not settled yet.

BLACKFISH: Very well. I will take the woman back.

HILLY: No! Now I've told you how this thing has to go.

BLACKFISH: All right. If my son does not want this woman he has won, he can give her to you.

BOONE: Good. That's what I'll do then.

HILLY: All right.

Blackfish starts to move away again. Boone catches him.

BOONE: But I would ask for the son's privilege of having the marriage performed in the lodge of my father.

BLACKFISH: And I would agree to anything to end this conversation.

BOONE: Done.

Blackfish leaves.

Hilly grins at Boone.

HILLY: Done.

BOONE: *(Looking after Blackfish.)* I'm gonna miss him.

AT THE EAST PALISADE

FLO: I'm sorry I got so mad at you, when you asked me out to dinner.

MR. WILSON: Why shouldn't you be mad? I didn't give one thought to what you might be feeling.

FLO: The truth is, I had such a crush on you when I first came to work at the museum. I thought you were the handsomest, the smartest, the most charming man I'd ever seen. And it took me so long to accept that you would never be interested in me, that last night, when all of a sudden, you were interested in me . . .

MR. WILSON: For a minute.

FLO: I could've killed you.

MR. WILSON: No, I know.

FLO: I wanted to knock you down and jump on you. Throw you into the Boone tree and crash my cart into you. Yell horrible things at you, tie you up and swat you with my mop and . . .

MR. WILSON: Go on.

FLO: You're not mad?

MR. WILSON: Of course not. I like you. I want you to be happy. If it would make you happy to hit me with a mop . . .

FLO: *(Laughing with him.)* Stop.

MR. WILSON: Come on. You have to see this.

They duck walk up to the edge of the palisade.

FLO: Where?

MR. WILSON: Over there. See that little mound of dirt at the edge of the forest. So are you serious about this Rick?

FLO: He's very sweet. But if I had known he was married, I would never have started seeing him.

MR. WILSON: Well, of course you wouldn't. So is there anybody else? Now what about Hilly? I mean, I like him. And it's obvious he's crazy about you. And you know what? I think my therapist is crazy. I don't want to get married, I'm fine just the way I am.

FLO: Of course you are.

MR. WILSON: Maybe my therapist wants to get married.

Squire approaches with Boone and Hilly.

MR. WILSON: *(Referring to them.)* There they are. Squire? Daniel? Come see what you make of this. It looks like the Indians are digging a tunnel. I think they're trying to tunnel under the fort.

SQUIRE: I think you're right.

BOONE: Goddamn the British anyway. Whoever heard of an Indian digging a tunnel?

SQUIRE: What should we do?

MR. WILSON: I say we start a tunnel of our own, aimin' to cross theirs, but underneath it, so where the two tunnels meet, their will collapse.

BOONE: You think that would work?

MR. WILSON: I know it would.

SQUIRE: O.K., then. Get some of the boys and get on it.

BOONE: Where's your rifle, Wilson?

MR. WILSON: I had to give it to that Timmy. In the block house.

BOONE: *(Hands his rifle to Mr. Wilson.)* Here. take mine, then. Good work.

Mr. Wilson takes the rifle with a look of absolute awe. Flo is not eager to hear about the outcome of the fight.

BOONE: Now. Flo.

FLO: If it's anything to do with that fight, I don't want to hear about it.

BOONE: You're Hilly's woman. Fair and square. Blackfish says the two of you will spend the night in the lodge of his sons, and in the morning, you'll be man and wife.

FLO: That's what you think.

SHE leaves.

HILLY: Florence . . .

Boone grabs him to keep him from running after her.

BOONE: No sense chasin' the girl. Where's she gonna go?

Hilly isn't so sure of that.

BOONE: She'll come around. You'll see. I'll talk to her. First time I ever saw her that scared though.

HILLY: That's because I'm so mean.

BOONE: Well, what do you say we go back out there and hear what kind of treaty the British have dreamed up.

HILLY: O.K.

They turn and walk offstage.

BOONE: You know, if you haven't got any place special to go after this, why don't you come on back to North Carolina with me.

HILLY: Thanks.

BOONE: So you'll come?

HILLY: Probably not. *(A moment.)* No offense.

BOONE: None taken.

BACK AT THE FRONT GATE

Flo stands at the front gate fuming.

JEMIMA: Did your mind just go blank again?

FLO: Your daddy's tryin' to marry me off.

JEMIMA: That's nice.

FLO: I won't do it.

JEMIMA: But if you don't get married, where will you go after this? Cause you can't come home with us, you know. Mother is there.

FLO: No, I'm not coming home with you.

JEMIMA: Oh, that's right. I forgot. We don't *have* to go *anywhere* after this. We're going to die. *(Greatly relieved, she waves.)* O.K. Good luck.

Jemima exits and Flo looks up and sees Rick enter dragging the carcass of a buffalo.

RICK: So. What do you think? Pretty good, huh? Lotta damn meat, on this thing.

FLO: Uh-huh.

RICK: What's the matter?

FLO: I want you to take me home.

RICK: *(Speaking so no one else will hear.)* Take you back to the museum, you mean? I can't. Not for a while, anyway. I saw a coupla more of these dudes down there at the spring, and I figure I might as well get them too while I'm at it.

FLO: Oh, forget it. I'm beginning to understand why the rest of the women left already.

RICK: Besides, it's perfectly clear to me I'm out of the running here.

FLO: What running? What are you talking about?

RICK: For you, Flo. These guys have got it all over me, any day. Hilly fighting Daniel Boone. Mr. Wilson figuring out about that tunnel. What have I ever done? Kept the garage open so people can get another two years out of their old car?

FLO: What's wrong with that?

RICK: I know, I know. Dad would love it if he saw the thing was still going. The kids like to come over and crawl under the cars. I mean, I guess I'm proud enough. Lot of other guys went under the last ten years.

FLO: That's because they don't know what they're doing.

RICK: Look, Flo. You want a hero. You deserve a hero. Now, I'm a nice enough guy and all, but I'm the first one to say it. Fixin' a guy's transmission isn't exactly a heroic act.

FLO: It is if it's really fixed.

RICK: Thanks.

She looks at him a moment. Then down at the buffalo.

FLO: They owe you the tongue for killing it.

RICK: That's O.K. They can have it.

FLO: No. You eat it. Or dry it, if you want to. Doubled over, a dried buffalo tongue would make a nice pouch for a wrench, or something.

RICK: O.K. Great. I'll do that.

Squire comes up to Rick and Flo.

SQUIRE: Looks like Daniel and Blackfish are about finished out there.

FLO: But the Virginia regiment isn't here yet.

SQUIRE: They're not. We just received word that they turned back.

FLO: They're not coming?

SQUIRE: Nobody's coming. This treaty better be good. God help us.

THE CABIN

Seeing Boone and Hilly returning from the Indian encampment, Jemima, Russell and Mr. Wilson come up to where Squire, Rick and Flo are standing. Rick has still not adopted the use of a frontier dialect.

JEMIMA: They're coming in. Open the gate. Open the gate.

RUSSELL: So what do we think this treaty says? We all agree to become Indians and tear the fort down for 'em?

Rick and Mr. Wilson move slightly apart from the others.

RICK: What's his problem?

MR. WILSON: Who cares? What's that all over your shirt?

RICK: Blood of the buffalo, man.

MR. WILSON: Wait a minute. That's not your shirt. That's *our* shirt. You took that shirt right out of the case.

RICK: And shot your dinner in it, yes, I did.

MR. WILSON: What are we having?

Hilly and Boone come up to the group.

BOONE: O.K. It looks like we got somethin' to talk about anyway.

He hands his handwritten paper to Squire.

MR. WILSON: *(To Rick.)* Do you have any idea what that piece of paper would be worth?

As Flo moves to avoid standing near Hilly, Squire reads from the paper.

SQUIRE: "There will be no battle. There will be peace between the white men and the red men forever." *(He looks up.)* I don't understand.

JEMIMA: Does that mean we can stay here? They'll all go home and we can stay here?

RUSSELL: No, it does not. It means there's somethin' he's not tellin' us.

BOONE: I don't know what it means. Except that Blackfish isn't calling the shots any more.

SQUIRE: Who is?

BOONE: Some Frenchy lieutenant in the British army, and Chief Moluntha.

FLO: What's *he* doing here?

BOONE: No, I know, it's not a good sign. But what they *say* is that they don't want to fight us.

RICK: *(To Mr. Wilson.)* They must've heard we were here.

BOONE: They want to set the Ohio River as a boundary. South of the Ohio would be Indian land. North would be white man's land.

SQUIRE: And if we sign this treaty, they'll go home?

BOONE: And we'll go home. That's right. Alive.

RUSSELL: And what else do we have to sign?

BOONE: An oath of loyalty to King George.

RUSSELL: I knew it.

SQUIRE: You're already a subject of King George just by virtue of bein' born in Virginia, Russell.

RUSSELL: I won't sign. I won't. Virginia is at war with the British.

SQUIRE: We have to sign it. It doesn't matter what it says. That or be slaughtered.

RUSSELL: I told every one of you what *I* thought we ought to do, only now it's too late.

MR. WILSON: *(To Rick.)* I worked for a guy like him once.

BOONE: I figure we should, you know, take a vote on it, get some sleep, and then, if everybody is agreeable, in the morning, eighteen of us will meet eighteen of them under the sycamore at dawn and sign the treaty.

RUSSELL: And then they'll kill us. It's a trick.

BOONE: No, I know it's a trick. But we'll have a pretty good idea by then what they plan to do.

RUSSELL: And just where are we gonna get an idea like that?

BOONE: Flo and Hilly are spendin' the night in their camp.

FLO: We are not. I told you that out there.

BOONE: Blackfish has the lodge all fixed up, Flo. Besides, it's just too good an opportunity to pass up. You'll spend the night spyin' out the situation, and just before dawn, you'll sneak back inside here and tell us what's going on.

FLO: I can tell you right now what's going on, in case you've forgotten. That's a war chant, they're singing.

BOONE: No, I remember. So at least we know they won't start anything 'til morning. That damn song goes on forever.

FLO: And what if this is a trick, too? What if all Blackfish wants is a couple of hostages to bargain with tomorrow.

BOONE: He doesn't. He likes Hilly here. He's just trying to help him out with you. Besides, you know how he likes weddings. *(Flo walks away a little)* So, now. Like Russell says we have to assume that the attack will start right after we sign the treaty. So between now and then, I want every gun oiled, every knife sharpened, and buckets of water placed every five feet along the palisade.

Squire, Boone, Rick, Mr. Wilson and Jemima all leave with Boone, as he continues to talk.

BOONE: Every man's gonna have a bandage or somethin' he can use for a bandage in his pocket or somewhere. And I want a list drawn up of who's reloading whose gun so when we got out there in the morning, everybody's gonna be in position.

Russell has remained behind, standing between Flo and Hilly. Now, he regards Hilly with suspicion.

RUSSELL: You won't really be married, you know.

FLO: *(Genuinely to Russell.)* Thanks.

Russell exits and Hilly looks at Flo. She turns away from him.

HILLY: This lodge business wasn't my idea, Florence, you know that. The only reason I even fought with Boone was to buy us some time. That, and I didn't want him takin' you away without a fight. But . . .

FLO: But since you won, and since we're back here in the wilderness, you'll just act as wild as all the rest of them. *(She grabs her hair.)* "Come on, girl."

HILLY: No, Florence. That's what I was trying to say, if I could finish my sentence please. I didn't win. Boone did.

FLO: What do you mean?

HILLY: I mean, he won the fight. I lost.

FLO: You mean he lied to me?

HILLY: And he wanted some spies in their camp overnight, so he thought up this lodge thing. *(A pause.)* But I'm not going to force you to spend the night with me. If you'd rather just go get a burger or something, let's go.

FLO: No. He's right. Somebody should be out there.

HILLY: So should I go get your stuff?

FLO: I don't have any stuff to get. But if you lay one finger on me out there, I'll kill you.

HILLY: Fair enough. So are you ready now?

FLO: I'm ready.

As the sound of drumming increases, they approach the teepee, and night falls.

AT THE ENTRANCE TO THE TEEPEE

HILLY: The only thing I'm worried about is what happens if we step inside this teepee and wind up back in the museum?

FLO: That would suit you just fine, I bet.

HILLY: How does it work anyway? Me and Wilson didn't have to say any magic words or anything. We didn't do anything except step inside. And you didn't either, I bet. So how did we get here?

An owl hoots in the distance.

FLO: *(Suddenly very tired.)* I don't know, really. The first night I did it, I was just standing there in the museum feeling like there was nobody in the whole world I wanted to see. Nobody I wanted to call. And nobody I wanted to call me.

HILLY: Because you already knew what they were going to say?

FLO: More like we'd had our chance, you know, and we blew it. Like we'd already decided it wasn't going to work, so why go on with it. Like it was just easier to give up. Nobody even blames you for giving up anymore. It's like being in love is something people used to do. When they had more time.

HILLY: So you said, the hell with that. I'm in love with Daniel Boone.

FLO: I did. I didn't even care if it was crazy. Suddenly, I knew exactly what to do, break all my dates, stop seeing people I didn't care about, and just love Daniel Boone. Then I picked up my broom and walked into the teepee to sweep it out, and here I was. I mean, there he was. Standing right in front of me.

HILLY: That's how I felt, too.

FLO: You did?

HILLY: About you. Not here though. Back there. At the museum. I'd known for a long time who I was looking for, and all of a sudden. There you were. As soon as I saw you, I knew I was gonna end up loving you.

FLO: How did you know that?

HILLY: *(A moment.)* You're a believer, Florence. *(A moment.)* A man needs a woman like that.

The sounds of the war chant get louder.

FLO: I hate that sound. I hate it.

HILLY: *(He holds the flap of the teepee open.)* It's O.K. We'll be O.K.

FLO: You go on in. I'm just going to walk around a little out here. See if I can learn anything.

HILLY: Do you want me to come with you?

FLO: I want to know why you're not scared by any of this.

HILLY: I've been in situations a lot tougher than this.

FLO: Back there, you mean.

HILLY: Sure I have. Everything is harder back there.

FLO: It's O.K. Blackfish is watching us. You go on inside. I'll be back in a little bit.

Hilly steps inside the teepee, as Flo walks away.

HILLY: Just be careful.

FLO: Thanks.

Flo walks away and Hilly enters the teepee.

INSIDE THE FORT

Boone is cleaning his rifle and talking with Jemima.

BOONE: I know somethin' is eatin' at you, Jemima. You might as well tell me what it is.

JEMIMA: I think Flo is an Indian. I think she's your Indian wife. *(Her anger rising.)* I think you brought your Indian wife back inside this fort with you, like nobody would even notice. What if mother had still been here?

BOONE: She might be an Indian. I don't know. I don't have any idea who Flo is. She told me she was married to a trapper and she got tired of him always smellin' of dried blood and wet fur and run off.

JEMIMA: Well, she told me the Indians killed her man and her child.

BOONE: No, *I* told you that to keep you from thinking she was my Indian wife.

JEMIMA: *(Furious.)* Is she your Indian wife?

BOONE: Not any more, no. Looks to me like those times are all gone.

JEMIMA: Are you gonna ask me not to tell Mother about this?

BOONE: You're a grown woman now, Jemima. What you tell your mother is between you and her.

Jemima softens considerably toward him.

JEMIMA: Are we going to die tomorrow?

And Boone hugs her, suddenly seeming like an ordinary good dad.

BOONE: No we are not. If we made it this far we'll probably live forever.

Flo approaches. Jemima clings to Boone for a moment.

BOONE: Florence, what are you doin' here?

FLO: I wanted to tell you what I heard.

JEMIMA: I'll be inside, Daddy.

Jemima leaves and Flo watches her go.

FLO: Is she all right?

BOONE: She's just scared, that's all. How's the enemy doing?

FLO: Well, Blackfish wants to go home, but Moluntha and the British feel more like a massacre.

BOONE: O.K. Thanks. You go on back out there now, and I'll see you in the morning.

FLO: I'm . . . uh . . . not going to be here in the morning. I'm going to walk on down the path, I think.

He takes a moment.

BOONE: Gonna miss all the excitement if you leave now.

FLO: I can't shoot worth a damn. You know that.

BOONE: You're runnin' from that man out there. Aren't you.

FLO: What if I am? You've done it enough.

BOONE: Yes I have. So I can tell you right now, it won't work, Flo. Rebecca done the same thing to me, got it into her mind that I was hers. You'll never get away from him, and you wouldn't be happy if you did. Best thing for you to do is give up and grab a hold.

FLO: I can't. I hardly know him.

BOONE: How much do you have to know? He came here to find you, he told me that himself. Then he fought me for you. Not a lot of men would do that. Give him a chance.

Flo doesn't answer.

BOONE: I mean how're you supposed to know *what* you think, standin' around here waitin' to get shot? Maybe if you just went back out there and spent one night with the man, you'd feel different about it.

FLO: Never.

BOONE: People aren't like the country, Flo. You and me, we can walk away from all the fine places we've ever seen 'cause we know there's always gonna be a nicer place further on. But you walk away from a man like this, and chances are, you'll never see his like again.

FLO: It's not just him. It's somethin' about you, too.

BOONE: No, I know. I'm not gonna be much fun here for a while.

FLO: It's not that.

BOONE: Well. Maybe not.

FLO: Don't you want to know what it is?

BOONE: No, I don't think I do.

FLO: See. That's it, exactly.

BOONE: Well, I can't help that. It never *did* matter to me what other people did. Not that I wouldn't have an opinion about it. 'Cause I've known some people done some things I didn't like at all . . . *(A slight pause.)* But I would never try and stop 'em from doin' it, whatever it was. Never. It wouldn't be right.

FLO: Where are you going to go after this?

BOONE: Back home, I guess. It's time I went back to civilization and tried to redeem myself somehow.

FLO: Did you ever write to Rebecca, to tell her you were alive?

BOONE: No, I don't think I did.

FLO: Why not?

BOONE: I don't know. Nothin' out here to write on except the trees. And I'm sure as hell not going to do that. *(a moment)* You go on now. If you're determined to lose this man, you'd better get goin' before he comes lookin' for you.

FLO: Not one for a sentimental farewell, are you, Daniel Boone.

BOONE: Nope.

She just stands there a moment. And then, suddenly, is very angry.

BOONE: I'll see you again sometime.

FLO: No. I don't think you will.

BOONE: Well. Maybe not. *(She turns away.)* You watch yourself, now.

Flo walks away from him and over to the palisade behind the cabin and turns on the lights and she is

BACK IN THE MUSEUM

She takes off her shawl and whatever other articles of frontier clothing she is wearing and hangs them back up where they belong.

She goes into the back room for a minute and comes out with her purse. She gets out a piece of paper and sits down to write a note.

As she is writing, Hilly comes out from the back room and stands and watches for a moment.

HILLY: You must think I am the dumbest man on earth.

She turns around, startled.

HILLY: You didn't think I would know what you were doing? "See you later, Hilly, I'm just gonna go check on the Shawnee."

FLO: I did check on the Shawnee. And then I told Daniel Boone what I saw.

HILLY: Give me a break.

FLO: That's what he said.

HILLY: What Boone said?

FLO: Yes, he did. He likes you. He said I should give you a chance.

HILLY: Well then?

FLO: So. I'm leaving you my phone number.

HE takes the paper from her.

HILLY: You are not. You're telling me *(He reads.)* "thanks for helping out at the fort, but I'm not ready for a relationship right now." What is it, Florence? Am I goin' too fast for you?

FLO: Yes, you are.

HILLY: No, I'm not either. You've been prayin' that somebody with some nerve would come along, and here I am. Now. What else is it? Is it Linda? Are my jeans too tight? What?

FLO: It's not Linda.

HILLY: It's my jeans. I knew it was my jeans. Well that's just too bad. This is exactly what I like in jeans. Every pair I have is just like this.

Suddenly, Rick and Mr. Wilson burst back into the room from the door of the cabin. They are covered in blood and dirt, and look like hell.

RICK: Jesus, God. What happened to you guys? We thought they captured you. Boone made us search the whole camp just to make sure you didn't get scalped.

HILLY: You mean it's all over?

RICK: What a battle. They went out to sign the treaty, and one minute, they were all standin' there, shakin' hands and everything, and the next minute there were guns goin' off, and tomahawks flyin' through the air . . .

MR. WILSON: Nobody even knew who started it.

RICK: And then they all rushed back into the fort and it was two really tough days, I'm here to tell you. Boone got hit, Squire got hit. Jemima got shot in the butt.

MR. WILSON: Kids reloading rifles, and Indians climbing up the walls, and fire arrows landing on the roof, and all the time we're trying to dig this tunnel . . .

RICK: And tryin' to stay awake and not go crazy from all the screamin' and yellin' . . .

MR. WILSON: And then it started to rain.

RICK: The one thing that could save our ass actually happened. Middle of the day, this mother of a storm hits. We thought, great, now we're gonna fuckin' drown here.

MR. WILSON: But when it was over, the Indians were gone.

RICK: Boone said Blackfish would see the rain as some kind of a sign.

MR. WILSON: I don't know. I saw a couple of Indians pretty close up that last day. They weren't really into it.

HILLY: So Boone is all right. That's good.

RICK: Except right as we were leavin', that little jerk Russell got Colonel Calloway to arrest Boone for treason.

HILLY: For treason? That's ridiculous. They'd all have died if it hadn't been for Boone.

RICK: So where were you guys?

HILLY: I wanted to stay. But Florence was tryin' to run away from me again.

Rick and Mr. Wilson begin to take off their frontier clothes.

RICK: I'm glad I'm not gonna have to explain to anybody what happened to these clothes.

MR. WILSON: They're not too bad. I'm very good at this sort of thing. We'll let them dry overnight, then I'll brush them off and put them back in the cases. No one will ever know.

HILLY: What finally happened to Boone? Did he go to jail for treason?

MR. WILSON: *(Now speaking as a historian.)* No. He beat it. But just barely. And then he went to North Carolina to find Rebecca and the children, and it took him almost a year to get back to Kentucky. Where he fought the Indians some more, and they killed some more of his family. Until finally he got chased out of Kentucky because he'd lost all his land, and owed so much money. So he went with two of his sons to Missouri where he lived 'til he died. *(A pause.)* And then he stayed buried a while, until they dug him up and brought him back to Kentucky and buried him again.

HILLY: At least you think it was him.

MR. WILSON: That's right. Well. I'm going home.

RICK: Yeah. Me too.

MR. WILSON: Flo? Are you still leaving us?

FLO: I am.

MR. WILSON: But am I ever going to see you again?

FLO: I don't know.

RICK: Well, *(Indicating Hilly.)* he's gonna keep workin' here, isn't he?

MR. WILSON: He is, if I have anything to say about it.

RICK: So, you can just ask *him.* He'll know where she is.

MR. WILSON: Well good. That's what I'll do.

And Mr. Wilson and Rick walk out together like old army buddies, remembering the old stories.

RICK: So, did you see when that tomahawk landed in Boone's neck?

MR. WILSON: It was amazing. Like all he was worried about was where the next one was comin' from.

RICK: Never saw anything like him. Standing next to Boone, I even had the feeling those two dead guys might pull through.

MR. WILSON: He could've never done it without us, though. Two less men, and who knows what might have happened.

They exit and Flo and Hilly are left alone.

HILLY: So. Where were we?

FLO: Your jeans.

HILLY: O.K. You don't like my jeans. I don't like that long skirt.

FLO: *(Very tired.)* It's not your jeans. It's your whole attitude. You think you ought to have what you want just because you want it.

HILLY: It's not just because I want it. It's because I'm willing to pay for it.

FLO: What do you mean, pay for it? Are you buying me now? What do I cost, Hilly?

HILLY: I don't know, Florence. Maybe everything I've got. Maybe my job. Maybe my whole way of lookin' at things. Maybe you're gonna drive me crazy. Maybe Linda won't like you and I'll lose this thing I have with her. Or maybe she'll like you better than me, and I'll feel like a jerk for bringing you in there. Or maybe it'll be wonderful and I'll love you to the end of the earth and you'll have a heart attack and die. Or you'll run off with somebody else and I'll have the heart attack and die. I don't know what you'll cost me, Florence. And I don't care.

FLO: But what do you know about me?

HILLY: A lot.

FLO: Do you know I get depressed?

HILLY: I figured you did.

FLO: Do you know I don't want to work? That all I really like to do is read? Do you know that I hate my hair and spend a whole lot of time thinking about it? What about my folks? Wouldn't you like to know they're not insane or something?

HILLY: Not unless they're gonna live with us.

FLO: No. They're not.

HILLY: O.K., then. Marry me, Florence. Come and . . . be with me. Be whatever you want. You want to go invent electricity, or pan for gold, whatever it is, I'm in. *(A moment.)* I love you.

FLO: No, I know.

HILLY: So what do you think?

FLO: I think you're the first man I ever knew who actually just . . . heard what I said.

Flo stands there a minute.

HILLY: You're tired, aren't you.

FLO: I am. I think I'm almost asleep.

HILLY: Tired is O.K. Sad is O.K. Running away from me again is not. O.K.?

Flo stands there a moment.

FLO: O.K.

And he opens his arms to her, and slowly she walks into them and he holds her. And after a while, he speaks.

HILLY: It's gonna be great. I promise. I mean, it won't be great every damn day, but overall, it's gonna be great. You'll see. I'm the best man ever lived in Kentucky.

THE END